THE INEQUALITY
EQUALIZER

THE INEQUALITY EQUALIZER

WANT IT, CLAIM IT, OWN IT — AND MAXIMIZE YOUR CAREER SUCCESS

JENA E. ABERNATHY
WITH KELLI CHRISTIANSEN

ANKERWYCKE

Cover design by Elmarie Jara/ABA Publishing.
Interior design by Betsy Kulak/ABA Publishing.

Printed in the United States of America.

20 19 18 17 16   5 4 3 2 1

Library of Congress Cataloging-in-Publication Data

Names: Abernathy, Jena E., author. | Christiansen, Kelli, author.
Title: The inequality equalizer : want it, claim it, own it—and maximize your career success / Jena E. Abernathy, with Kelli Christiansen.
Description: Chicago, Illinois : American Bar Association, [2016] | Includes index.
Identifiers: LCCN 2015045550 (print) | LCCN 2016000597 (ebook) | ISBN 9781634253741 (hardcover : alk. paper) | ISBN 9781634253758 ()
Subjects: LCSH: Career development. | Women—Vocational guidance. | Professional employees. | Success in business.
Classification: LCC HF5381 .A445 2016 (print) | LCC HF5381 (ebook) | DDC 650.1—dc23
LC record available at http://lccn.loc.gov/2015045550

Discounts are available for books ordered in bulk. Special consideration is given to state bars, CLE programs, and other bar-related organizations. Inquire at Book Publishing, ABA Publishing, American Bar Association, 321 N. Clark Street, Chicago, Illinois 60654-7598.

www.ShopABA.org

For Kara, Olivia, and Campbell—my girls

Contents

Introduction

Get Real About Getting Ahead

I was stunned.

And when I looked across the table at Lauren, one of our newer, younger associates, and Webb, their boss, I could see that I wasn't the only one in the room who couldn't believe what they'd just heard. Entry-level newbies just don't talk to senior-level executives like Megan just did. For that matter, senior-level executives don't even talk to one another like that—at least not in the open, not if they value their reputation and career. But Megan seemed to have no idea that she had said anything inappropriate. Nor did she have a clue that her body language was equally out of line.

Like many young, up-and-coming, eager-to-get-ahead business professionals, Megan is articulate, talented, and well educated. During eighteen years of grade school, high school, and college, she had earned her MBA and mastered many skills. She writes well-structured sentences. She understands accounting and is technologically savvy. She's well versed in her field and is a quick study. But Megan's defensive words in response to questions about the source of some numbers and the conclusions in her report, teamed with her angry red face, rolling eyes, and huffing deep breaths, revealed a glaring deficiency in her education—and dangerously undermined her potential. Like many of her contemporaries, Megan was sorely lacking in political savvy and other practical skills she would need to succeed long term.

I interrupted her display of exasperation by asking Lauren and Webb if I might speak to Megan alone. Sensing trouble, Megan gulped. Her facial color transformed from scarlet to ashen white. Her gaze followed her supervisor and colleagues out the door and didn't seem to want to return to look me in the eye.

"Am I in trouble?" she asked, giving me a sheepish and genuinely perplexed look.

I took a brief pause to gather just the right words and to muster just the right tone—habits Megan lacked. "Megan, I'm not angry," I began, "but I do want to help you understand some things, things that will profoundly affect your career—here or anywhere else you might go."

When I said "go," Megan's eyes widened. It was obvious that she was starting to imagine the worst.

Since that wasn't my intended message, I promptly assured her that her job was not in jeopardy—yet. My purpose wasn't to chastise her or give her a scolding; I simply wanted to help her begin to understand that social skills are not silly frills. They are essentials if you want to climb higher than the bottom rungs of the business ladder.

Over the next two hours, Megan and I discussed her goals, her ambitions, her background, her life at the time, and, most importantly, what she would need to learn and do in order to move from where she was to where she wanted to be.

As she left my office, Megan thanked me and asked if we could meet again for more counseling sessions and maybe even work on some of her issues by e-mail. She asked if I would consider serving as her mentor—no holds barred—and if I would help her see what could be considered blind spots so that she could advance.

I was surprised, frankly flattered, and definitely pleased. "Megan," I told her, "I will help you, but know that you might not always agree with and might not follow my advice. Your career is about *your* choices, and I want you to own your decisions. I hope you learn from my successes—as well as from my mistakes; I've made too many and likely have made mistakes I haven't even identified yet. Still, I believe I have some wisdom to share."

I suggested that we utilize e-mail as much as possible during this modern-day mentoring process. In that way, we would be able to think about what we wanted to ask each other and how we wanted to reply. Also, our dialogue would be off the company clock.

And that's how it all began, a mentor–mentee relationship that promised to provide both of us with any number of benefits: professional growth, insight, respect, collegiality, and tips and strategies for gaining confidence, building skills, and getting real about what it takes to build long-term career success.

Megan isn't the only one who could benefit from some no-holds-barred mentoring. Many of today's up-and-coming, eager-to-get-ahead business professionals are articulate, talented, and well educated. They're technologically savvy. They're quick studies. But too many of these bright young professionals can all too often be defensive, inappropriate, poorly mannered, and obtuse. They lack the political savvy and practical skills that will help them succeed in the long term. They need some tough love. They need some common sense. And they need to get real about what it really takes to get ahead—and stay ahead.

That "up-and-coming, eager-to-get-ahead business professional" might well be you—even if it might be difficult or uncomfortable to recognize yourself in the part of that description that flags some faults. But know that all of this comes from a place of love—albeit, of course, a place of tough love.

Here's the thing: Whether "junkyard dogs" or "pedigrees," today's young professionals—people just like you—are in need of mentors who will tell them what it really takes to climb above the bottom rungs of the corporate ladder to achieve their goals. As a former C Suite executive, an executive recruiter, and a career coach, I hope to be that mentor for you. As a no-nonsense Southern woman who knows what it takes to balance that junkyard dog in you (the scrappy, hard-charging, rough-edged go-getter) with your inner pedigree (that polished, poised, advantaged professional), I know what it's like to learn the hard way what it takes to get ahead—and stay ahead. You see, although today most people think I'm a pedigree, I'm actually one of those self-professed junkyard dogs. I've worked hard to fit in to the world of the pedigrees—without compromising my values or leading an inauthentic life.

In the pages that follow, I will share a lifetime of real-world experience and insight, all designed to help today's young professionals get ahead while improving their reputations—and without leaving a wake of professional destruction behind them. I'll share wisdom (a code word for "old," I know, but useful nonetheless) gained not only from my own successes and failures, but from real-world examples of the many people I've mentored over the years, people who have worked their way from the cubicle to the C Suite—that is, the exclusive enclave where the CEO, CFO, COO, and other top-level executives do their thing.

Some of the insight and wisdom in these pages might sound a little harsh. That's because sometimes facing reality is harsh. And, with that, my first bit of advice—a mantra that I want you to repeat to yourself over and over again—is to get real.

Yes, you read that right: Get real.

You might be smart and savvy and full of vim and vigor. But get real: So is just about everyone else you work with.

You might have great ideas that you're sure will propel you to the top of the professional heap. Get real: Plenty of your colleagues have equally great ideas. It's how you present those ideas and how you act on those ideas that matter.

You might have a shiny new MBA from an elite school. But get real: Your scrappy colleague from that state school you never heard of is equally bright—and you both need to learn how to work together as colleagues and, very likely, teammates.

And, just as you have to get real, you have to get over yourself. Let's face it: Although plenty of books and self-help guides and online articles are full of five or seven or ten tips that profess to teach you exactly what it takes to make yourself indispensable at work, the truth is that everyone—including you (even though you *are* fabulous)—is dispensable. In the real world, business is all about "what have you done for me lately?" And if you're not performing, if you're not presenting yourself and your ideas in the best light, if you're promoting yourself and your ideas aggressively instead of assertively, well, then, you can pretty much expect that the next rung on the corporate ladder will be out of reach.

That is, it'll be out of reach until you figure out what it takes to get ahead—and stay ahead.

Millions of young professionals—or perhaps I should say would-be young professionals—are struggling in an economic climate that in late 2015 was improving but remained tough. Unemployment levels are decreasing, but roughly 4 million workers between the ages of 18 and 35 remained unemployed or underemployed as of early 2015.[1] Toward the end of 2015, the numbers had improved only slightly: Among 25- to 34-year-olds, the unemployment rate hovered around 5.5 percent, higher than the national average.[2] Women account for higher percentages of unemployed and underemployed work-

1. Bureau of Labor Statistics. *Employment Status of the Civilian Population by Race, Sex, and Age.* Retrieved March 23, 2015, from http://www.bls.gov/news.release/empsit.t02.htm.
2. Bureau of Labor Statistics. *Labor Force Statistics from the Current Population Survey.* Retrieved August 27, 2015, from http://data.bls.gov/pdq/SurveyOutputServlet.

ers; 67.7 percent of men over the age of twenty are employed compared to 55.4 percent of women.[3]

It would be easy to assume that those workers are somehow lacking in the skills, education, or experience they really need to land that perfect job. That might well be true of at least some of them, but the reality is that many of these would-be workers are perfectly capable individuals who likely might do well in their chosen fields. But in today's highly competitive world, being capable isn't nearly enough.

Sadly, that's not a message that enough young professionals hear. Over the past decade or so, we've taken to telling our young people that each and every one of them is a winner. We tell them that just making an effort—any effort—is enough to win the game, to get the prize. We give them trophies just for showing up.

Seriously?

Again, we need to get real.

In the real world, in the professional world, the only trophy you get for showing up is a paycheck at the end of the week. No one climbs the corporate ladder with minimal effort. And by no means is everyone a winner.

No, in today's world, professionals need to learn the dos and don'ts of business. They need to know what to do—and what *not* to do—in order to move ahead, to strategize their careers, and to climb that corporate ladder all the way to the C Suite. It is in this knowledge that employees can level the playing field, regardless of pedigree or tenure.

We'll talk about just those things in the pages that follow, and we'll start in right away. Right off the bat, in Chapter 1, we'll look at how career-long success depends on balancing your inner junkyard dog with your pedigree. What's a junkyard dog? A junkyard dog is that scrappy, street-savvy, tenacious professional who has worked hard for everything she's got. A pedigree

---

3. Bureau of Labor Statistics. *Employment Status of the Civilian Population by Race, Sex, and Age.*

is that advantaged, well-educated, poised worker who often is lucky enough to work connections in order to leapfrog up the corporate ladder. One isn't necessarily better than the other, and certain situations might call for one over the other, but long-term career success depends on balancing these two inner beasts. As a born-and-bred junkyard dog myself, I know about this firsthand, and I'll share my insight in Chapter 1.

Balancing your junkyard dog and your pedigree has much to do with branding yourself, a topic we'll address in Chapter 2. Does your manager consider you a leader? Do your colleagues think of you as a resource? Early in your career, you might earn a reputation as the go-to person, the one who gets things done. Over time, you need to become the person who gets things done through others. All of this speaks to the ways in which you brand yourself throughout your career. All you have is your reputation, and you need to protect your reputation at all costs. Whether you become known as a junkyard dog or a pedigree is wholly within your control, so long as you do what it takes to build your own professional brand. Part of that requires you to balance your inner junkyard dog with your pedigree. It also requires you to be authentic—because branding yourself means being yourself. In Chapter 2, we'll look at how to brand yourself, what it takes to brand yourself, and why it's important to protect your personal and professional brands.

Just as you think about your professional reputation and your personal brand, you also need to think about your overall career strategy. This is something that a lot of us—and women in particular—never really think about. Too many of us just sort of roll along on our career trajectories, getting promoted here and there, taking a new job now and again, but without really thinking about what we really want, what our long-term career goals are, or what we need to do to achieve those goals. But the reality is that few of us get through our careers—much less land on top—without really wanting it. You can't just hope your way to the C Suite. You have to want it. You have to claim it. And then you have to own it. You can't be a little bit CEO or a little bit COO. You have to know what job you really want—and then you have to go for it. This means you have to be prepared for opportunities when they come along. It also means you can't be afraid of what you want, because "I want it" has nothing to do with gender or pedigree. In Chapter 3, we'll look at why it's important to understand what you want and why you want it—and what you'll do with it when you get it.

Being prepared for opportunities means more than just keeping your eyes open for good things that might cross your path. When you're looking for opportunities, you need to look for those opportunities where you can have an impact and where you can be visible. You need to network, you need to join a task force, you need to sign up for continuing education, you need to join interagency task forces. You need to make the most of opportunities that will help you grow your career. This means that you can't be afraid to take risks. You will be challenged throughout your career. Sometimes you'll succeed. Sometimes you'll fail. If those risks—and even those failures—help you grow as a leader, then the chance was worth taking. Don't allow fear or hard work to dissuade you from taking chances, because when you come out on the other side, it builds your confidence—and you'll know you can take on other opportunities. In Chapter 4, we'll look at why it's important to look for opportunities and to take risks—and how both junkyard dogs and pedigrees can make the most of challenges.

Taking risks and making the most of opportunities will matter little if you can't make the most of them. And that means you have to keep track of every risk you take and every opportunity you leap at. Why? Because the best leaders manage based on results. This means you have to keep score of your accomplishments—and you have to claim them. Make sure to take credit for the work you've done, whether good or bad, whether success or failure. Lead in every direction, learn from every level, and get feedback from those around you, whether above you, alongside you, or below you. Whether junkyard dog or pedigree, it's important to manage for results across the organization. Because it's all about performance—regardless of gender, regardless of pedigree. In Chapter 5, we'll look at why learning how to manage up, down, and sideways is crucial for young professionals who want to get ahead.

Leaders keep score. They manage based on results. And they also know how to make the most of leadership styles that work. Of course, every leader is different. Studies have shown that while men are more likely to adopt a transactional leadership style, women tend to assume a transformational leadership style. This means that women naturally work at building consensus and encouraging teamwork, which can go a long way in getting effective, long-term, sustained results. That doesn't mean that more transactional leadership can't be useful, particularly in the short term, but it does mean that women have a natural tendency to employ an effective leadership style. In Chapter 6, we'll look at the differences between these two leadership styles, when one might be more preferable than the other, and how junkyard dogs and pedigrees alike can make the most of leadership opportunities.

Leadership style is important, as is knowing which style to deploy in which situation. But style has to be based on substance, and that means that you have to understand the business of business. Think about it: Do you understand the numbers that get your business to the bottom line? Do you understand the strategies that position your business in your industry? Or are you so caught up in your day-to-day role that you're not looking at what it takes to run your company's business? It's easy to fall into silos and not think about the business as a whole. But you can't understand the mission if you don't understand the margins. You need to understand what's happening on Wall Street and Main Street. You need to understand market share, service lines, and product offerings. You need to understand the competition. And you need to understand where your organization fits in. Whether junkyard dog or pedigree, you must know what's going on in your industry and in your organization—and what your own effect on the bottom line is. Do your homework. Be prepared. And people will listen. That has nothing to do with gender or pedigree; it has everything to do with knowledge. In Chapter 7, we'll look at the key areas that young professionals need to understand, and I'll explain why knowing the business of business can help pave the way forward.

Moving forward requires today's young professionals to balance a lot of things at once. Understanding the business of business, employing appropriate leadership style, keeping score of successes and failures—all of that is crucial if you want to get ahead. But you can all too easily derail your upward trajectory if you fail to understand business etiquette, cultural competency, and all those little things that reveal to your colleagues—and to your bosses—who you really are and what you're really like. Believe me, I've seen it all: Cleavage during an interview. A flash of gold anklet during an executive-level meeting. Lower-level employees who incessantly drive the conversation during a client dinner while the boss fumes from across the table. Whether junkyard dog or pedigree, everyone can benefit from a little etiquette know-how and some cultural competency. In fact, understanding these issues is crucial for anyone who's aiming for the C Suite. In Chapter 8, we'll tackle some commonsense issues when it comes to culture and etiquette, providing the crucial training in an area that is too easily overlooked.

Another thing that so many professionals—regardless of gender, pedigree, or tenure—overlook is the value of intuition. Intuition is something most of us recognize even though few of us could explain it well. We know something because we just . . . well . . . *know* it. Intuition is that sixth sense that often helps us make decisions and avoid danger. High-level business leaders often have to make quick, intuitive decisions. But "intuitive" doesn't mean "uninformed." We need to know the facts about our business, but we also can develop our intuitive abilities by using them wisely. Part of that requires us to trust ourselves and those around us. Trust is a two-way street, though, and so it's important to know whom to trust and when to trust them. In Chapter 9, we'll look at how young professionals can use trust and intuition to their advantage. We'll also examine how women in particular—both junkyard dogs and pedigrees—can develop skills in this area in order to help them become better decision makers.

Women, men. Pedigrees, junkyard dogs. Throughout our careers, all of us will deal with all sorts of people from all walks of life: men and women, junkyard dogs and pedigrees. We need to learn how to work with everyone. We also need to learn how to network with everyone. Why? Because you never know who might be able to help you advance your career. And you'll never know who you're sitting next to—on an airplane, on the subway, at a conference—unless you talk to that person. You never know if the next person you meet is going to be a friend, a mentor, an advocate, or an employer. Build your sphere of influence and seek out new people. Introduce yourself, and you will be remembered. Do it even if you're shy or reluctant. Because networking—especially for women and especially for junkyard dogs—opens doors in ways nothing else can. In Chapter 10, we'll dig into the whys and hows of networking and building relationships.

Networking is a great way to level the playing field. It is a real equalizer. Because regardless of how much we might like to think that men and women are equal, the truth is that every woman will face a variety of gender issues throughout her career. Once chastised by a male colleague for wearing a pantsuit instead of a skirt to a client meeting, I know about such issues firsthand. But the reality is that most business issues—financial details, corporate strategy, management, and leadership—aren't gender issues. Of course, gender issues are still out there, and today's young professionals need to understand when, where, and why they'll pop up—and how to deal with them. Whether junkyard dog or pedigree—or a little bit of both—today's professionals (and women in particular) need

11

to learn how to handle gender issues with grace. We'll discuss some real-world strategies for doing just that in Chapter 11.

Networking and building relationships is a lifelong activity. In fact, as we move up the corporate ladder, it becomes incumbent upon us to lend a helping hand to those who are coming up behind us. When we're able to share our experiences and give back, we can pull each other up. Today, only 18 of the Fortune 500 CEOs are women. Women account for just 15 percent of C Suite positions.[4] Lending a helping hand means becoming a mentor—and avoiding "Feline Syndrome." Help someone get promoted. Give someone some guidance. Give another woman your business. Be generous with your time, your knowledge, your experience, and your spirit. Remember where you came from and what it was like to work in the trenches. These efforts are inequality equalizers that can help level the playing field. Whether junkyard dog or pedigree, women can—and should—help other women up the corporate ladder. In Chapter 12, we'll look at why doing so is a win–win for everyone.

As you move through your career, following the strategy you've plotted for yourself, it's important to keep networking, to build relationships, to lend a helping hand to those around you. But it's also important to be true to yourself. We all evolve and change during the course of our careers, but it's crucial to keep those parts that are essential to you. Claiming the pedigree in you doesn't mean giving up or completely silencing your junkyard dog—that scrappiness, that resourcefulness, or that assertiveness can still come in handy. By learning to be constructive instead of critical, assertive instead of aggressive, accepting instead of defensive, you can honor yourself and your values while still making the most of the environment in which you work. Find your junkyard dog, keep your junkyard dog in check, and balance it with the pedigree in you. In Chapter 13,

---

4. Aaron Taube. "'Lean In' Isn't Enough: Women's Progress in Leadership Has Stalled," *Business Insider*, September 23, 2014. Retrieved October 11, 2015, from http://www.businessinsider.com/why-women-arent-getting-more-c-suite-jobs-2014-9.

I'll share some commonsense advice for honoring yourself and your values while working your way toward the C Suite.

Being true to yourself requires some balance. In fact, "balance" is a buzzword we hear a lot these days, particularly when it comes to that mythical "work–life balance." Work–life balance is something people have been talking about—if not achieving—for decades. How, in a highly connected, 24/7 world can today's young professionals balance work and family and volunteering and health and all the other issues that come with life? How do women handle Mommy Guilt? These are issues that everyone has to deal with, whether junkyard dog or pedigree, and I have been no exception. I know what it's like to miss key moments in a child's life. I understand what it's like to realize that everyone—*everyone*—is dispensable. Work should be enjoyable. It should be meaningful. But it shouldn't be everything. In Chapter 14, we'll look at what it really means to balance work and life.

Look: Moving up the corporate ladder isn't easy. Earning a chair in the C Suite requires today's professionals to balance work and life, to balance their inner junkyard dogs with their pedigrees, to build relationships and network while balancing gender issues. It requires knowing what you want, going after it, and then owning it. A lot of self-help books, business guides, and advice columns tell readers that just by following their dreams, they'll live happily ever after, rich in happiness and fulfillment, if not in dollars.

Let's get real: It takes a little more than simply following your dreams if you hope to make it to the C Suite. Sometimes, following your dreams and finding your passion means discovering anew something you're good at, something that matters to you, and something that gets you fired up. Today's young professionals need to learn that they can discover passion for their work through any number of routes—if they're open to it. That's because passion is about being the best you can be at *whatever* you do. In the last part of the book, I'll share a few words about what it takes to fuel your career and how you can

13

tap into a variety of passions about your work to find lasting success and fulfillment.

Tough love is good for us. Everyone could use a little tough love now and again. Everyone could use a dose of reality. And everyone would benefit from tactics to help level the playing field, regardless of gender, pedigree, or tenure.

Of course, you might not like some of the things we're going to discuss in these pages. I'll be the first one to admit that some of the insight and advice I'll share will be bitter pills, indeed. But instead of Pollyanna-ing your way through life, why not just face reality? Let's all get over ourselves and get real. Let's admit that we're not all born winners—but we can all become winners if we accept some tough love, use some common sense, and employ some tested, real-world strategies for climbing the corporate ladder all the way to the C Suite.

Balancing Your Junkyard Dog and Your Pedigree

From: "Jena Abernathy" <jabernathy@email.com>

To: "Megan Watson" <mwatson@email.com>

Subject: Mentoring—Junkyard Dogs and Pedigrees

Megan,

I know you're disappointed that Charlotte won the promotion you wanted. You probably know that Charlotte graduated from an Ivy League college, as so many of today's top female business executives have. I know you graduated from a mid-level state-run university—so did I. Unlike Charlotte, you have no special family connections, no Ivy League degree, and no other obvious advantages. That means you have to rely more on hard work, determination, and moxie. You, like me, are a junkyard dog—which is fine, so long as you balance that with your inner pedigree.

—Jena

Early on in my career, I was probably a junkyard dog.

No . . . I know I was.

And I was proud of it. I wore that badge with honor.

I was sassy and assertive. I was a little rough around the edges. I could handle anything. I was like a dog with a bone. A junkyard dog.

Junkyard dogs are those of us who have had to fight our way up the corporate ladder. We're scrappy. We have a lot of common sense, a lot of street savvy. We know how to get things done.

But I was probably too aggressive. I didn't know how to balance being aggressive with being assertive. I did not fully comprehend that being aggressive demonstrated a lack of respect. I was being aggressive, because I wanted to emulate my male counterparts, and I thought I was playing the game.

Let me give you an example. Early on in my career, I interviewed for a VP spot at a national company. The COO, who was conducting the interview, was very brash and in-your-face, firing one question after another at me. At the end of the interview, he said, "What makes you think you can do this job? We have had experts, PhDs, and none has succeeded. No one has been able to do what we need to have done." I looked him in the eye and said the first junkyard dog thing that came to my mind: "I've got the balls to get the job done. Any further questions?"

That probably wasn't my best move ever, but it was, nonetheless, my move—and I did end up getting that job. In fact, I was told I got it over a "frat boy," whom the COO preferred. It was a turning point in my career, one that solidified in my mind the difference between junkyard dog and pedigree.

At that point in my career, I was usually the only woman at the table—a table full of men. I was used to a lot of shoptalk. As I was shifting from manufacturing to the service industry, I was in for a rude awakening about what different cultures are like—and when shoptalk is and is not appropriate.

One day, I was in an executive team meeting, and the person in charge of sales and relationship management gave a presentation during which he asked a question about what losing a major client would mean for our organization.

"What's in our pipeline?" I asked.

"We don't have anything in the pipeline," he said.

"What the fuck?!" I blurted. "How can you be in that position and not have anything in the pipeline?"

The room went silent—after everyone gasped.

I didn't think much of it right then. I was used to an environment where my colleagues and I said what needed to be said—and we didn't waste a lot of time thinking about how or when to say it. So, during this meeting in my new organization in this new industry with my new colleagues (and my new boss), I said some things that I thought were important to say. I was feeling pretty good about myself. Sometimes, "doggone it!" just doesn't convey the same passion or level of frustration.

Shortly after that meeting, I was called into my boss's office. "I've given this a lot of thought," he said, "and I'm going to do you a big favor. I'm sending you to a three-day executive coaching session."

"I'm going to charm school?!?" I thought. I had never experienced such a thing. No one had ever told me I needed coaching. Up until then, my junkyard dog had served me pretty well. I was highly offended. I really wondered whether I should leave, whether this wasn't the right culture for me. None of my male colleagues was being sent to charm school.

"Wow," I thought. *"I must really need a lot of polishing."*

So, I was sent off to charm school. In Minnesota. In January. And I don't have a parka. I definitely felt like I was being punished.

I spent an intensive three days with an executive coach—one on one.

Although I resisted at first, and although I was really angry about the whole thing, I soon realized that the goal wasn't to

17

change who I was. It was to make the good things in me better. It was for me to become more aware.

So, after shoving the chip off my shoulder and accepting my lot, I learned how to better present myself. I learned about understanding issues and when to bring them up. I learned about balancing passion and emotion. I learned not to be defensive. I learned how to listen. I learned how to be constructive instead of critical. I learned that the derailment factors that exist for so many people in their careers are real, and they will follow you everywhere you go if you don't become self-aware.

Becoming self-aware during that three-day executive coaching charm school was a turning point in my professional life. It was likely the best thing that could have happened to me. Because it changed me. It helped me to grow as an employee, and it helped me to become a better leader.

As a junkyard dog, I always had something to prove. I could deliver anything that was asked of me. I could always figure out how to get over, around, or through walls, but I didn't always do it without leaving a path of destruction behind me. I was hard-charging, hard-driving, and demanding. I was a junkyard dog with a chip on my shoulder: If you bite me, I'm gonna bite you back—harder.

Are You a Junkyard Dog or a Pedigree?

Many of today's workers are junkyard dogs: scrappy, tenacious professionals who have had to work hard for everything they've got, often putting themselves through college (typically a state university), studying the behavior of those around them, and delivering results through hard work and common sense. Often, they find themselves scrambling to keep up with pedigrees: well-educated Ivy Leaguers who have lived lives of advantage, complete with the gold-plated networking circles that have helped them skip the lower rungs of the corporate ladder in order to land in positions of power and influence. This imbalance creates an inequality that exists in many corporate settings.

One isn't necessarily better than the other, but career-long success does depend on balancing your junkyard dog with your pedigree. It also depends on learning to live and work well with both types. That's because no matter where your work takes you, you'll be working with a mixture of junkyard dogs and pedigrees. And if your career takes you into Corporate America, chances are you'll be working for a pedigree: By some measures, roughly 35 percent of Fortune 500 CEOs and more than 85 percent of powerful men attended elite schools[1] (this latter statistic is an important measure since men make up about 90 percent of Fortune 500 C Suites[2]).

So, what does a junkyard dog look like? Let me explain that by sharing a little about myself. My family was working class. We followed NASCAR before it became mainstream. We ate TV dinners, and we survived paycheck to paycheck, with dignity and humility. My father wore a suit only when he had to go to a wedding or a funeral. I attended public schools. I worked from the time I was fifteen and paid for all my clothes, my car, and all of the expenses associated with my education. I am, without a doubt, a junkyard dog.

I've worked with many Harvard MBAs, Ivy League graduates, and the best in Corporate America—the pedigrees. Many of these people come from privileged backgrounds. They're born into families that are well off. They attend the best schools. They spend their lives hobnobbing with people in similar circles and circumstances, which allows them to build

19

1. Jonathan Wai. "Frank Bruni Is Wrong About Ivy League Schools," *Quartz*, March 22, 2015. Retrieved March 23, 2015, from http://qz.com/367077/frank-bruni-is-wrong-about-ivy-league-schools.
2. Aaron Taube. "'Lean In' Isn't Enough: Women's Progress in Leadership Has Stalled," *Business Insider*, September 23, 2014. Retrieved March 23, 2015, from http://www.businessinsider.com/why-women-arent-getting-more-c-suite-jobs-2014-9#ixzz3VEzefD3A.

strong networks of people who spend a lot of their time at the top. It would be easy to say that pedigrees have led charmed or easy lives, but, of course, that's not always true. Their backgrounds are certainly different from junkyard dogs, but that doesn't mean that one is better or worse than the other—just different.

Over the years, I have learned that this dog—my inner junkyard dog—can hunt. I've never pretended to be a pedigree. Pedigrees are bred to compete in the show ring, but a junkyard dog is a survivor, an innovator with the tenacity to forge ahead. I don't offer apologies for my lack of a pedigree; in fact, I decided very early in my career to embrace my working-class background and let people consider how far I've come and wonder: *If she's already come this far, how far can she actually go?*

As a junkyard dog, I don't have an advanced degree from an elite institution, which is uncommon for professionals like me, at this point in my career and at this level in my industry. Instead, my advanced degree is from the School of Hard Knocks, and it has served me well. I have always focused on learning from others, understanding my profession, and carefully calculating how I could contribute to or lead a team to focus on the success of the organization.

With the right grooming, training, and instinct, a junkyard dog can attain the skills and status of a pedigree. Confidence breeds success. Pedigrees may have an advantage, at least early on in their careers with their platinum-plated degrees, but anyone can self-destruct or fall off the rails. We all have to accept that self-motivation is the characteristic by which we derive success. No matter a person's background, education, religion, sexual preference, race, ethnicity, or gender, she can be successful in the corporate world if she is willing to take risks, to reinvent herself, to continuously learn from others, and to accept that we are all a work in progress.

OVERCOME THE MIGHTS

The business world doesn't allow anyone—especially a woman—to rest on her laurels. It can be harder for women to climb to the top in business,[3] not least of which because females are often held to a higher standard and are more critically evaluated.

For example, men are far less likely to be held back because of *mights.* The line of thinking is that a female might get married and leave the company in a cloud of dust . . . she might get pregnant . . . she might not make critically important meetings or deadlines because she has to take care of a sick child or orchestrate the carpool . . . she might not make hard-pressing decisions because she has to balance the demands of her family and work . . . she might leave if her husband is offered a better position in another town. She might, she might, she might.

Every successful woman in business has to demonstrate, through her words and actions, that her career is at the top of her priority list, that her career is not her avocation. She has to demonstrate that her career is her vocation, a vocation about which she is most passionate.

These what-might-happen barriers can block young women's paths, and this is especially true for junkyard dogs. Junkyard dogs like me—and probably you—are by no means inferior; we just don't have the advantages some others have from birth. In most cases we probably have to work harder to reach the top, but when we get there—just like the pedigrees or anyone else—we have to prove our worth daily, especially as women.

21

---

3. In fact, the data prove that it, in fact, is harder for women to climb to the top. At Fortune 500 companies in late 2014, women accounted for just 17 percent of board members, 15 percent of C Suite executives, and 5 percent of CEOs. Taube, "'Lean In' Isn't Enough: Women's Progress in Leadership Has Stalled."

Making the Most of Your Inner Junkyard Dog and Your Inner Pedigree

During the course of my career, I've noticed that two types of people get to the top: pedigrees and junkyard dogs. Pedigrees often reach the top because they have "the goods" from prestigious universities—and because they have important family connections. But, it's highly unlikely that any board of directors or any C Suite executive or even any mid-level manager will put up with a poor performer for long, regardless of pedigree.

That means you have to tap into both your inner junkyard dog and your pedigree when confronted with any new challenge, any new opportunity. So, when you come to the table to solve a problem, to work on a project, use your inner junkyard dog—that scrappy, tenacious fighter full of common sense—to figure out how to get it done. Focus on solving the issue, finding the answer, and leveling the playing field.

Make the most of your inner junkyard dog, because having an MBA from an Ivy League school matters not if you can't apply yourself. Know your facts, understand your biases, realize that you are not always right, and pace your delivery. Learn to work through others by creating strong followership. Listen to your intuition; it will be your best guide in life, and especially in your career. Know your strengths, and work to improve your weaknesses. Resolve to execute and deliver results, on point and on time.

But you also have to tap into your inner pedigree—even if you've never set foot on an Ivy League campus.

That means you have to learn how to present yourself, your information, and your ideas in a manner that is both authoritative and ardent without being aggressive. You have to know how to work both the conference room and the back channels, building support among colleagues, clients, and C Suite executives. You need to understand the social norms that manifest in business settings. This is because the higher you climb, the more exposed you become to the expectations of representing the organization and socializing within a business construct.

Junkyard dogs like me can easily develop tendencies to come on too strong, too loud, and too fast. We often find ourselves relying on gut instinct rather than real information. Pedigrees, on the other hand, can find themselves refraining from constructive dialogue because they fear rocking the boat. Often they become risk-averse and can get mired in the status quo or caught up in analysis paralysis.

For those of us who are apt to bulldoze our way through work, we need to keep our inner junkyard dogs in check. For those who are pedigreed, you need to find your junkyard dog.

But you need to balance both in order to be successful.

===

INEQUALITY EQUALIZER

Be yourself at work—so long as you're being your best self. Balance your inner junkyard dog and your inner pedigree so that you can be both scrappy and savvy as well as poised and polished. Level the playing field by playing up the best parts of you.

===

Be Assertive Without Being Aggressive

Your inner junkyard dog often can serve you well—up to a point. Same goes for your inner pedigree. The key is to balance your inner junkyard dog with your inner pedigree while staying true to yourself.

For junkyard dogs, this means finding a way to complement your common sense with lifelong learning. You might not have an Ivy League degree. You might not have an MBA. But you have to educate yourself one way or another—through mentorship, reading, continuing education, coaching, whatever. As a junkyard dog, you have to do whatever it takes to cover all your bases and ensure that you can back up your instincts and know-how with information and knowledge.

INEQUALITY EQUALIZER

Not everyone can afford a world-class education at a renowned private institution—but that doesn't mean you can't pursue lifelong learning. Look to your community college as an affordable option for taking business classes, pursuing certifications, and obtaining professional licenses—all of which can help level the playing field.

It also means you have to balance planning and poise, passion and defensiveness, assertiveness and aggressiveness.

This doesn't mean that pedigrees are off the hook. They, too, need to strike a balance. Often that means finding some middle ground between understanding numbers, data, and statistics and understanding people, processes, and politics. Pedigrees need to understand not only what makes a business work, but what makes it tick.

This all might sound easier said than done. It's one thing to tell someone to strike a balance, that perfect balance between junkyard dog and pedigree, but it's another thing to actually go about doing it in the real world. So let's look at some of the key steps in finding that balance and what you can do to level the playing field.

The first step to equalizing the inequality is to get over yourself. Junkyard dogs need to accept the fact that a lack of pedigree, a lack of an Ivy League degree, a lack of an MBA or PhD doesn't mean they're better or worse than their colleagues who are pedigrees. They're just different. They need to accept the fact that different people come at the same problems from different directions. And instead of getting defensive, they need to calm down, step back, and assess the situation. They need to listen to what their colleagues are saying.

Similarly, pedigrees need to understand that junkyard dogs have something to offer even if they don't have a framed diploma from an esteemed university hanging on their office walls. They need to understand that there's something to be said for common sense and street savvy and gut instinct. And they need to value what their junkyard-dog colleagues can offer.

The second step is to get real. We'll be saying that a lot throughout this book because a good mentor will remind her mentees that sometimes you just have to face reality. When it comes to balancing your inner junkyard dog and your inner pedigree, you have to get real. You have to realize that no one likes dealing with an abrasive loudmouth who hard-charges through every meeting. Nor does anyone like dealing with a smug show-off who tries to impress everyone with big words and grandiose ideas.

It's all about balance. A little bit of some charm-school education never killed anyone. So get over yourself and get real. Recognize the inner junkyard dog in you. Find the pedigree in you. And make the best of both. Because who you are determines your reputation, and your reputation is your brand, which is the subject of our next chapter.

Tough-Love Lessons for Balancing Your Junkyard Dog and Your Pedigree

- Find ways to become more self-aware about your strengths and weaknesses. This might mean going to charm school, finding a career coach, or seeking input from colleagues. Be open-minded about the feedback you receive, and find ways to work on the things that need improving.
- Recognize and accept your inner junkyard dog and your inner pedigree, and understand that one isn't necessarily better than the other. Consider those around you and think about how they learn and express themselves so that you can find new and better ways to communicate and work with them.
- If you're more junkyard dog than pedigree, keep educating yourself about your organization and your industry. If you're more of a pedigree, look for ways to tap into the street-savvy side of yourself and develop your intuition.
- Balance your inner junkyard dog with your inner pedigree. This means that you have to get over yourself and get real about recognizing what you do well and where you could improve yourself.

= 2 =

Branding Yourself: Protect Your Reputation

From: "Jena Abernathy" <jabernathy@email.com>

To: "Megan Watson" <mwatson@email.com>

Subject: Your Brand Is Your Reputation

Megan,

Thanks for connecting with me on LinkedIn, and for asking for feedback on your profile. In addition to formulating your page as you would your professional résumé, think about the photograph you select for your profile. Is the selfie you have up on your page now the image you want to project to current and prospective employers and professional colleagues? Think about it . . .

—Jena

When Justine Sacco tweeted a quip in December 2013 while en route from New York to Africa about the unlikelihood that she might catch AIDS during her travels, little did she know that her feeble attempt at humor would cost her her job—and her reputation.

Until that tweet, Sacco was well on her way to the C Suite, working as the senior director of corporate communications at InterActive Corporation, the organization that owns popular websites like Match.com and Vimeo. You might think that a savvy PR executive would have thought twice about tweeting anything that might have even smacked of insensitivity, but so it goes. Sacco's unfortunate tweet ignited a firestorm, burning her career, her brand, and her reputation to a crisp and exacting a hefty emotional toll. Although she eventually found a new job at a new organization, rebuilding her reputation will take time and perseverance.[1]

Sacco isn't—by far—the only up-and-comer to suffer a fatal shot to her reputation. Homophobic rants on Twitter and elsewhere led to the release of NFL running back Larry Johnson from the Kansas City Chiefs, the organization reportedly furious about his utterances.[2] Scott Bartosiewicz, a contractor for Chrysler, found himself out of a job when a tweet marred by a four-letter expletive went out on the carmaker's account rather than his personal account.[3] And, of course, there's Anthony Weiner, the New York State Representative whose salacious texts and tweets cost him his office. I could go on and on.

---

1. Jon Ronson. "How One Stupid Tweet Blew Up Justine Sacco's Life," *The New York Times Magazine*, February 12, 2015. Retrieved March 25, 2015, from http://www.nytimes.com/2015/02/15/magazine/how-one-stupid-tweet-ruined-justine-saccos-life.html.

2. Judy Battista. "As Johnson's Suspension Ends, So Does His Time with the Chiefs," *The New York Times*, November 9, 2009. Retrieved March 25, 2015, from http://www.nytimes.com/2009/11/10/sports/football/10chiefs.html.

3. Associated Press. "Man Fired Over Obscene Chrysler Tweet Is Sorry," NBC News, March 17, 2011. Retrieved March 25, 2015, from http://www.nbcnews.com/id/42132041/ns/business-autos/t/man-fired-over-obscene-chrysler-tweet-sorry/#.VRMyd0amRPQ.

Corporate executives, professional sports heroes, politicians—social media doesn't play favorites when it comes to brands and reputation. An insensitive tweet, a thoughtless Facebook post, a silly Instagram photo, an offhand comment on LinkedIn . . . anything can be misconstrued, taken out of context, or overhyped. All it takes is one tweet or post to ruin your reputation.

When it comes to business and your career, all you really have is your reputation, and you need to protect your reputation at all costs. All of your accomplishments, all of your successes, every performance measure you've met or blown out of the water—all of that speaks to your professional reputation. You can spend a career building and honing your reputation as a hard-charging, results-driven go-getter, only to have it spoiled in an instant with one stupid, thoughtless, off-hand remark that shoots around the world in a microsecond thanks to social media.

Whether male or female, entry level or tenured, pedigree or junkyard dog, your reputation is all you've got when it comes to your career. In fact, in one sense, building your entire career is very much about building your reputation. How you go about building that reputation—how you brand yourself—says a lot about who you are.

29

Building Your Brand Starts Now

Your reputation follows you wherever you go. Very often, it precedes you. The instant you apply for a job and someone in HR thinks you might be a qualified candidate, your reputation is on the line. Everything that shows up in a Google search, everything that's public on your Facebook page, on your LinkedIn profile, and on your Twitter page is fair game when it comes to deciding whether you're a good fit for an organization. Every photo you've ever posted is out there for someone in HR to discover. Don't kid yourself that no one will be able to find that picture of you wasted at last year's Super Bowl party. It's out there. Forever.

What do all those photos, posts, and tweets say about you?

Social media has amplified the importance of building and protecting your reputation. Of course, social media isn't the be-all and end-all when it comes to branding yourself. Everything you say and do, everything you write, every presentation you make, every contribution you make, every interview you go on—all of that speaks to your image, which informs how people perceive you, which, in turn, speaks to your reputation.

When it comes to your career, know this: You are always on. Whether you're at work or off duty, the reality is that your reputation never gets to take a vacation. This can be a difficult lesson to learn, especially when you're new to the work world.

For instance, I once worked with a young manager who was very talented, very bright, and particularly beautiful with a figure that rivaled that of any cover model. During a break while our company was at a conference, this beautiful young thing took the opportunity to don her bikini for a stroll along the beach with some male colleagues. She looked great: fit and stunning.

As I spied her out of my hotel room window, where I was working during that same break, I wanted to run down and cover her up. I couldn't help but grimace when I thought about what that bikini-clad stroll meant for her reputation. Was she branding herself as a savvy professional who knew how to handle herself at a corporate conference? Or was she branding herself as a good-looking babe who could carry off a bikini?

I mentioned this to her later that day, and let me tell you, she was not thrilled with my insight. I asked her if she wanted to be known as the chick with a hot body. I asked her if she saw any of the executive team wandering around the beach or the pool deck in their swimsuits, a question to which she could only answer "no." But even so, she took offense at the advice I offered her, which was this: It's crucial for you to cultivate your brand. And your image and your brand go hand in hand. You are still working, even during "free time" when you're attending a conference on your company's dime. When it comes to work, you are always on.

In this global, 24/7 Information Age, there is no escaping publicity. Thanks to social media, the publicity machine is always on. Not only is every tweet and post out there for the world to see, but anything you ever say that gets quoted in the media, any article or white paper you write, every presentation you've done that ever got uploaded to YouTube or SlideShare, all of that is searchable. Everything your name is attached to is something someone in a position to hire or fire you can find. Your name is your reputation.

Your name, your image, and your work history combine to form your reputation. Whether you call it image or brand or reputation, it's all tied together. Whatever you say, write, and do speaks to the person you are.

Building your professional brand and balancing that with your personal life can be tricky. When I was starting out in my career, it never occurred to me to think about my name. I never got past Jena with one "n" for the correct pronunciation. I never thought about searching the Web to see if others had my same name and if I would be associated with someone I only shared the same name with, which is why you might consider adding your middle initial for your business name. I never realized how much a name meant or how important it was to protect my name. It didn't occur to me to think about any article I might be quoted in, anything that could live on for generations. I didn't realize my political donations, for instance, would one day be searchable and reflect on my character and how potential employers might view me.

Everyone is going to have their opinions, their views about you. They're going to have their own stories about you, some exaggerated, some factual, some you might not even remember if you grew up in the 1970s. Most young people never think about this. I know I didn't when I was starting out.

But these are all things that matter. Once you start a career, that career is mobile, and so your brand is mobile, too. Your brand goes with you everywhere you go. You need to be able to protect it. You have to think about everything your name is attached to.

Your brand is with you when you're interviewing, whenever you meet someone, when you're at a company function. You want to stand out because you're an excellent employee. Your job isn't to be the funniest guy in the room or the prettiest girl in the room. It's to be the best employee you can be no matter where you are.

Not that you want to be a fuddy-duddy elitist who isn't one of the team. It's just that you want to be known as someone who takes her career seriously—and that's what you want to stand out for. Not because you're the one who organizes the after-work drinks party every Thursday night.

If you want to level the playing field, it's crucial to build a career that's separate from everyone else. You have to make sure that no one ever questions why you were promoted above them, and this is difficult to do if you get bunched up into a clique that always goes out for drinks after work or if everyone sees you as the one who takes the company softball team more seriously than the company's bottom line.

Remember that the office is where you go to do your work. It is your professional laboratory. It's where you build strong, credible professional relationships. It can be hard to separate professional relationships from personal relationships. Doing so requires that you pick your friends carefully, not in the least because today's friend might be tomorrow's boss. Out of the office, social sessions can often lead to conversations that revolve around the workplace and people. You must steer clear of the gossip mill and the association of being one of the tribe if your goal is to move up in the organization.

Be Known for the Right Stuff

I was never a bikini-wearing kind of gal. Not that if I were I would have worn one in the presence of my bosses, male or female. Even if I could have mustered the gumption to wear a bikini in public, I would never have projected an image among my colleagues as the girl in the bikini. I didn't ever want anyone to have a snapshot of me—real or imagined—in a bikini during a work function. The notion of someone having taken a selfie with me in a bikini and then posting it on Facebook is horrifying.

To the contrary, I was always very careful about cultivating my image. At one point in my career, when I moved into a role leading HR at a national company, I received a sign-on bonus. I took a portion of that bonus, found out where the businesswomen in town shopped, and made an appointment with the personal shopper at one of the favored boutiques in the community. I invested in a good, basic, professional wardrobe, including some Madeleine Albright–like pins, which have since become a personal trademark.

I knew instinctively and intuitively that I wanted to be— needed to be—viewed as a professional, as someone with a careerist mindset. I was working hard to build a career, and to build a name for myself, and I knew I had to make sure that no matter what I decided to do, I had to recognize that anything I said or did would be out there for the world to see forever.

You might think that what you do today won't matter tomorrow. But things change. As your career grows, you may find yourself one day wishing that selfie of you red-faced drunk during your best friend's wedding wasn't the one you chose to use for your Twitter profile or posted as your cover image on Facebook.

You are your own brand. It's really hard at twenty-something to think about that. It's difficult to consider the differences among famous and infamous and notorious. You don't want to be infamous or notorious. The kind of celebrity asso-

33

ciated with reality shows on television isn't exactly what you should be shooting for.

If you want to build your brand, you have to set out to be known for your accomplishments. This can be a bigger challenge for women than it is for men, simply because of the way society views women and because of our inherit tendency to shy away from any form of boasting.

I'm not the first to point out that women are treated differently in the workplace. (And I won't be the last.) As of 2015, for example, women employed full-time were still making only 78 cents to the dollar compared to what men earn.[4] The reasons for this are myriad (though rarely are any of them justifiable): Women often leave the workplace to raise children, women often don't jump at opportunities like their male colleagues do, women typically don't negotiate as hard as men do. But one of the sad truths that most people don't want to talk about is the fact that, all too often, instead of touting their accomplishments, women often seek validation through their appearance. I have seen this time and time again, and I'm not alone. Studies have shown that, frequently, "the personal power of a woman is conveyed by her appearance."[5]

Women and appearance is an issue that, consciously or not, affects the perception of performance and therefore professional brand. This is true across industries, from healthcare to STEM fields to law to academia. In fact, the issue is so prevalent that at least one organization raised a red flag when it became known that female professors were being evaluated in superficial ways that their male colleagues were not. In an article in *Inside Higher Ed*, Colleen Flaherty reported that Adam Scales, vice dean at Rutgers University School of Law at Camden, was alarmed enough about the situation to issue an

---

4. Catherine Hill, PhD. "The Simple Truth About the Gender Pay Gap," *AAUW Economic Justice*, Spring 2015. Retrieved March 26, 2015, from http://www.aauw.org/research/the-simple-truth-about-the-gender-pay-gap.
5. Ellen L. K. Toronto (Ed.). *Psychoanalytic Reflections on a Gender-Free Case: Into the Void*. New York: Routledge, 2005, p. 190.

e-mail that went viral. "Throughout my academic career," he wrote, "I've displayed an array of sartorial styles. For years, I veered sharply between 'Impoverished Graduate Student' and 'British Diplomat.' Of course, one would never know any of this by reading my student evaluations. That's because I'm a man."[6]

Scales recognized that, for any number of reasons, women are required to be more cognizant of their appearance—and what their appearance says about them—than men. It's just the way it is. And it's not going to change anytime soon, regardless of how many memos are issued admonishing students or staff or colleagues to not judge a woman by her looks.

Oddly enough, I've encountered women of all ages and at all points in their careers who somehow have failed to receive the message that appearance matters. I've interviewed women whose cleavage was so distracting I could barely think straight. I've interviewed women wearing flashy gold anklets, women with insanely long, heavily lacquered fingernails, and women in the shortest skirts they could wear in public without getting arrested.

But appearance goes beyond clothes and makeup. I've seen countless women use hearts to dot the "i"s in their names. I've seen too many women append smiley faces to their signatures. I've seen innumerable women sign their name in pink or purple ink. I have witnessed many women clean crumbs off the table after a meeting or volunteer to go pick up coffee and lunch for everyone. This diminishes your value and casts you in a stereotypical role that creates an unconscious perception of you that is not what you are striving for if you want to advance. When you do things like this, you are driving the wedge even deeper into the inequality gap, unconsciously or not.

---

6. Colleen Flaherty. "Brains, Not Clothes," *Inside Higher Ed*, January 29, 2015. Retrieved March 26, 2015, from https://www.insidehighered.com/news/2015/01/29/rutgers-camden-law-dean-asks-students-stop-talking-about-women-professors-attire.

Never once in my whole life have I seen a man add a heart or a smiley face or a flower—or a flourish of any kind—to his loopy, curly, pink-ink signature. I have never witnessed flowers or a candy dish in a man's office. Those things do not work at work, regardless of gender.

INEQUALITY EQUALIZER

Be careful to avoid taking on stereotypical female or male roles. Women should avoid becoming den mothers, and men should avoid expecting their female colleagues to be their den mothers. The easiest way to rid the workplace of gender bias is by not engaging in gender bias. Don't play into the stereotypes associated with males or females—and don't expect your colleagues to fulfill typical gender roles, either.

Appearance matters, whether we like to admit it or not. In fact, it's such an issue that Loyola Law School–Los Angeles recently reminded its students that cleavage and stilettos were not part of appropriate work attire.[7] The memo, issued to externs working in legal settings, went on to note that, "Your reputation in the legal community starts now!"

This advice and memos like these have generated a lot of feedback from women and men alike, much of it flagging gender bias and noting that men aren't called out for their attire and appearance. That anger may be justified, but so what? The truth of the matter is that, like it or not, women are more

---

7. Staci Zaretsky. "Law School Sends Memo About Inappropriate Student Cleavage, Hooker Heels," *Above the Law*, March 19, 2014. Retrieved March 26, 2015, from http://abovethelaw.com/2014/03/law-school-sends-memo-about-inappropriate-student-cleavage-hooker-heels.

frequently assessed, judged, and evaluated, at least in part, on their appearance.

Get over it.

And get real.

If you want one day to be counted among the executive team, that means no cleavage. No stilettos. No flashy gold anklets. No inch-long acrylic fingernails with glitter and rhinestones. No hearts. No visible tattoos. No smiley faces. There are rules for men, too, although they tend not to be as harsh as they are for women. That said, for men we might say no trendy slim suits with nerdy bowties, no going sockless, no khakis with frayed hems, no clothing of any kind that has anything to do with the NBA, NFL, NHL, or MLB.

None of that is anything you want to be known for.

What you want to be known for is someone who not only plays the part well but also dresses the part to a T. Remember the old adage "dress for the position you want, not for the one you have"? Well, it's still true, even if it sounds old fashioned. If you want to make it to the C Suite in Corporate America, you have to dress the part. You have to find your uniform, your armor. I have found that my "power suit" actually conveys more confidence and makes me feel empowered, especially when I'm getting ready to go into an important meeting. Early in my career, I adopted the uniform (a dark suit), and even on Casual Fridays, I wore a blazer to be consistent. In today's world, dressing professional may not be as "buttoned-up," but dressing like a professional is still expected—a given, even—for those wanting to move into key leadership roles. While a hoodie may work for some in the technology arena, it does not work for anyone aspiring for the next level in business, law, or medicine, for example.

Perhaps it is physiological, but for me it was reality: Dressing the part really did give me the confidence as a junkyard dog to compete effectively in the workplace. Dressing for success is an equalizer, and it's an easy tool to use. Professional attire can have different interpretations in various industries. Fashion,

37

technology, PR/marketing firms, and start-ups may have a very different look on a daily basis than financial, legal, or corporate entities. However, if you are with a start-up and on the team that's pitching a deal to an investor, you need to power-up because impressions are formed in the first thirty seconds. So while the patterned tights and a smoky eye may have looked great on Saturday night, you will cast the wrong impression right from the get-go if you wear that to work. And who wants to spend the next few hours trying to overcome perceptions when you're supposed to be closing a deal?

DEALING WITH IMPOSTOR SYNDROME

In 1978, Pauline Rose Clance and Suzanne Imes wrote a paper about "the impostor phenomenon," which they described as a term "used to designate an internal experience of intellectual phonies, which appears to be particularly prevalent and intense among a select sample of high achieving women." Having studied more than 150 "highly successful women," the researchers found that "despite their earned degrees, scholastic honors, high achievement on standardized tests, praise and professional recognition from colleagues and respected authorities, these women do not experience an internal sense of success."[8]

In the nearly four decades since this paper was published, the notion of what today is more commonly referred to as Impostor Syndrome has resonated with countless women (and men, of course, though it's more prominent among women). Standouts such as Sheryl Sandberg, author of *Lean In*; Academy-award winning actress Kate Winslet; Liz Bingham, managing partner of Ernst & Young; and Nobel laureate Maya Angelou have admitted to feel-

8. Pauline Rose Clance and Suzanne Imes. "The Imposter Phenomenon in High Achieving Women: Dynamics and Therapeutic Intervention," *Psychotherapy Theory, Research, and Practice*, Volume 15, Number 3 (Fall 1978). Retrieved March 30, 2015, from http://www.paulineroseclance.com/pdf/ip_high_achieving_women.pdf.

ing like failures despite their achievements.[9] By some estimates, anywhere between 40 and 70 percent of people have experienced feelings of failure despite their success. In my experience, most people feel like this at one point or another during the course of their careers.

And you know what? That's okay. In fact, it's normal.

Whether junkyard dog or pedigree, chances are you'll experience feelings like this at least once in your life. In corporate settings, junkyard dogs might feel like they're not one of the gang, especially those who have come up as working class. It can be easy for junkyard dogs to feel like they aren't worthy, like they don't measure up in the conference room amidst a sea of Ivy League MBAs. Pedigrees, too, might at times feel like impostors, carefully guarding the perception that they are bright intellectuals who are always up on the latest trends and who understand the latest corporate buzzwords, even if they're not as attuned as they'd like people to believe.

The truth is that sometimes you have to fake it till you make it (although never to the extent that you're simply bullshitting your way through).

That means that, when it comes to overcoming perceptions of inadequacy (whether your own self-perceptions or others' perceptions of you), it's important to keep educating yourself about your company, your division, your industry, your competition, and so on. It's essential to do your homework, preparing well for every meeting, learning as much as possible about the topics being discussed and about the people attending the meeting. It's also important to keep track of your successes (we'll talk more about keeping score in Chapter 5) and to accept the praise and accolades that come your way. And, no matter whether you're a junkyard dog or a pedigree, it's crucial to not underestimate yourself.

39

---

9. Margie Warrell. "Afraid of Being 'Found Out?' How to Overcome Impostor Syndrome," *Forbes*, April 3, 2014. Retrieved March 30, 2015, from http://www.forbes.com/sites/margiewarrell/2014/04/03/impostor-syndrome.

Everyone feels like a fraud at one time or another. But no one should allow that feeling to become so embedded that they allow "fraud" or "impostor" to become part of their brand. As long as you're doing everything you can to protect your reputation, you can rest easy in the knowledge that your success is deserved.

Put on Your Game Face

During one of the many team-building exercises I've partici-pated in over the years, everyone was asked to draw a self-portrait. If you closed one eye and squinted at mine, my self-portrait kind of looked something like an Andy Warhol image. When it came time to reveal my drawing, the facilitator was puzzled.

"What's that?" she asked.

"It's my mask," I answered. To a room full of stares, I explained. "I wear a mask every day."

It can be difficult, especially for younger employees, to real-ize that, every time you walk into the office, you're playing a role. Part of your role as an aspiring professional requires you to put on your game face. For me, and for many people like me, that game face is really a mask.

This flies in the face of much of today's feel-good personal-growth advice, the kind of advice that calls for authenticity at every moment and in every facet of your life. This line of thinking argues that the road to true happiness, the path that will lead to success at work and home, requires you to "be yourself" at all times in every aspect of your life with everyone you encounter.

Whatever that means.

Here's the thing: I don't think you can be truly authentic in the workplace. Sometimes you have to do whatever it takes to get where you want to go. Oftentimes that means you have to constrain the real person inside you. You don't always get to fully be yourself. Instead, you learn to play up your work-related strengths and play down the aspects of your personality that don't work in a corporate setting.

Many of the best employees find ways to compartmentalize themselves in order to make it to the next level. No one can be the same person in every situation. No one is exactly the same person at work that she is with her best girlfriends.

Now, I grant you that this can be exhausting, and studies are divided as to the effects this duality has on people. In a study conducted by the University of Texas in Houston and the University of Greenwich in London, researchers found that "authenticity at work is not at all correlated to the well-being and job satisfaction" and that authenticity had no bearing on happiness at work or at home.[10] In contrast, a Harvard Business School study found that when employees were encouraged to express themselves and their true personalities, they performed better than employees who stuck to a strict corporate code.[11]

Regardless of whether authenticity is good for you or bad for you, it can be a challenge to be one person at work and one person at home. Cable, Gino, and Staats note that, "Given that organizations are made up of people, and many people spend the majority of their waking hours at work, the human drive for authenticity creates a basic tension for organizations."[12]

I'll be the first to admit that this tension can be stressful. But think about it. When you're at work, you can't act like you do when you're out with your best friends. Much of work is an act. (And, in fact, I encourage budding professionals to

41

---

10. Oliver C. Robinson, Frederick G. Lopez, and Katherine Ramos. *Should You Bother 'Being Yourself' at Work? Relationships Between Social Context, Authenticity, and Well-Being.* Retrieved March 27, 2015, from http://www.reflect-beratung. de/DE/_pdf/Relationships_Socialcontextauthenticitywellbeing.pdf.

11. Dan Cable, Francesca Gino, and Brad Staats. *Breaking Them In or Revealing Their Best? Reframing Socialization Around Newcomer Self Expression* (Working Paper), September 2012. Retrieved March 27, 2015, from http://citeseerx.ist.psu.edu/ viewdoc/download?doi=10.1.1.359.4436&rep=rep1&type=pdf.

12. *Ibid.*

take acting and improv classes to learn how to play different roles.) You put on your costume—which is your crisp business suit—and you play the role. That costume is like a suit of armor, allowing you to gear-up and prepare for battle. You've got to put on the suit. You've got to armor-up. You've got to put on the mask. You've got to put on your game face. You have to act like you belong.

This might not be what you're completely comfortable wearing to work every day, but it is what it is. Of course, this doesn't mean you have to go against your values. Never do that. But know that you won't always be able to be truly authentic in every situation because business often requires you to do some things that might not sit well with you.

For instance, whenever I've had to fire someone, I had to put on the mask. Believe me, it is no fun to fire someone, even if the person is obviously not the right fit for the job. But I had to play the part that was expected of me. I couldn't show empathy, no matter how sorry I might have felt for someone who, say, had to support a family and was losing his or her job. But the role I signed on for required me to be firm, and sometimes that has meant I've had to wear a mask to make it through the task.

I have had to wear the mask at other times, too, such as when being scolded or chastised by a boss. At times like that, I was grateful for the mask. Mentally donning my mask helped me get through a tough situation, serving as a reminder to control my emotions. Because you can never let them see you cry. Bite your lip, ask to be excused, or put on your mask—in tough situations, you have to get real. The mask is an equalizer that keeps you from displaying the kind of inappropriate emotion that skews the playing field.

Wearing a mask and putting on your game face is never about sacrificing your values. It is about recognizing the fact that sometimes you have to do things you don't like or don't agree with. Get over it. Learning that business is business and not taking it personally will help you to focus and channel your emotions.

This can be especially difficult for a generation that was raised at a time when everyone is considered a winner, when you got a trophy for first place, second place, fourteenth place, twentieth place, whatever. When you got an award just for showing up. Unfortunately, many of this generation all too often feel entitled. They want to start at the top, and if they can't start there, they too often expect a raise and a promotion simply for doing what is expected of them. According to Dan Schwabel, founder of WorkplaceTrends.com, "Millennials want more of a transparent and authentic workplace."[13]

Millennials and Gen Yers want to be who they are. That might be all well and good, but all too often, these younger employees don't fully understand that they also have a role to play and that they are working for a different generation with different expectations. I see this a lot in younger employees who want to protect their time off. This is probably a good thing, as too many of us leave too many vacation days on the table, which is unhealthy. On the flip side, though, I see this manifest itself in younger employees who take time off even when they're needed by their teams to meet deadlines. I recently worked with a twenty-something woman who, in the face of a looming deadline, informed her team that she would be taking Friday off because one of her girlfriends was coming into town. She didn't ask if that was okay with her team. She simply assumed she could—and would—take that time off. And so she did.

Well, that's fine if the team makes its deadline, if the team gets all of its work done and done well. But to this particular employee, taking the time off was more important than the work that needed to be done.

That sends a message. Could her team work around her scheduling demands? Certainly. But that kind of behavior gets

13. Liz Faiella. "Can Millennials and Baby Boomers Work Together?" *New Hampshire Public Radio*, November 22, 2013. Retrieved March 27, 2015, from http://nhpr.org/post/can-millennials-and-baby-boomers-work-together.

noted and filed away. Forever. And you get only so many hall passes during the course of your career. Do you want your team members to think of you as a team player who does whatever it takes to get the job done? Or do you want your team members to think of you as the one who doesn't pitch in when it's crunch time?

I tell those starting out in their careers to arrive early or, at the very least, right on time. Do not be in the herd stampeding out the door at five o'clock every evening. Make it a point to be seen by the "powers that be" after hours. The key is to craft an image of someone committed to their job and someone who exceeds expectations.

I see differences here not only between generations but also between pedigrees and junkyard dogs. To some extent, it can seem like some pedigrees have been born with a collection of hall passes. People covet having pedigrees on their team. They love having someone from Harvard or Yale or Dartmouth on their team. As a result, that love often manifests itself in the form of carte blanche, allowing pedigrees to get away with much more than their junkyard dog colleagues can get away with. Pedigrees can often float along in the glow of accomplishment, regardless of how much they contribute or how meaningful their contributions. Junkyard dogs don't have that luxury.

Whether junkyard dog or pedigree, putting on your game face at work can be difficult. But it has its benefits. It reminds you to act professionally, keeping your behavior and emotions in check. It can help guard you against intense situations, allowing you to approach issues more objectively and to treat colleagues more evenhandedly. It reminds you to act rationally.

As such, the game face—whether you think of it as a mask, a costume, or a suit of armor—actually helps level the playing field for junkyard dogs and pedigrees and for men and women. The game face is an inequality equalizer. Why? Because it keeps us from unleashing the pit bull within us. It keeps us from acting with hubris or arrogance. It keeps us from coming across as bitches or acting like jerks.

Our game faces aren't used as tools to pretend we're someone else or to create an alternate personality. Rather, they're used to present our best face so that we can showcase our strengths while minimizing our weaknesses. We want our best face to be our brand.

AVOID COMMON BRANDING MISTAKES

Showcasing strengths while minimizing weaknesses while continually educating yourself about your company, your industry, and your competition while keeping score of your successes while protecting your reputation . . . well, that can be a lot to handle. It can feel like a lot of pressure. And sometimes it isn't easy.

With that, it can be easy to make some mistakes along the way. In fact, we all make mistakes along the way. The key is to learn from those mistakes . . . and, of course, to do what you can to avoid making them in the first place. Here are some common pitfalls to avoid when it comes to building your brand and protecting your reputation.

- **Don't Fail to Promote Your Own Brand.** Think carefully and seriously about how you want to be perceived, and work hard to secure that perception. This includes how you dress, how you talk (what you say and how you say it), your body language, your behavior, your work habits, and so on. Make sure you get noticed in the right ways for doing the right things.
- **Don't Be Afraid to Become More Self-Aware.** It can be helpful—and illuminating—to learn how people truly perceive you. Take a self-awareness course, an improv class, or an acting class, which can provide opportunities to be evaluated by your classmates and peers. Also, think about how your background, your education, and your upbringing reveals itself and affects your brand. Adjust

your behavior as necessary, highlighting those aspects that positively affect the way others perceive you.

- **Don't Forget to Define Success on Your Own Terms.** When you're thinking about your career, think about how you will measure success. Will it be measured by awards you've won? By your title? By the size of your office? By the quality and quantity of clients and revenue you've brought to your firm? You have to define what success means to you, and then you have to own it. (We'll talk about that more in Chapter 3 when we discuss strategizing your career.)
- **Don't Fail to Get Noticed.** As you rise through the corporate ranks, it's important to make sure not only that you're doing excellent work but also that you're being noticed. It's important to make sure that the powers that be are aware of your work and know who you are. This means you have to get as much exposure as possible at corporate headquarters and among the executive team. So much of your success will depend on access. Make sure you're doing whatever you can to gain access to the people who have the power to pull you up the corporate ladder with them.
- **Surround Yourself with Successful People.** Build relationships with others outside your company from whom you can learn and garner advice. My mother always said, "Show me who your friends are, and that will show me who you are." Take this advice to the bank, because surrounding yourself with successful business associates will maximize your network and knowledge base.

Branding, reputation, image: Although it's easy to believe all those trite notions that you can't control what people think about you and that what people think about you doesn't really matter, the truth is that, at least when it comes to your career, it absolutely matters what people think about you. (In fact, it might well be the only thing that matters: Perception is reality.) But you can manage those perceptions by taking control of your brand and doing whatever you can to protect your reputation, and that includes avoiding some common mistakes that can mar your image.

Consider Your Future Reputation

When you're starting out in your career, whether it's your first job out of college or grad school or whether it's even your third or fourth, it can be a challenge to think about the future. You're busy concentrating on doing your best in the job you have now—and maybe looking ahead at your next position—and so looking twenty, thirty, or even forty years down the road can be a bit of a challenge.

But that kind of thinking is crucial, especially when it comes to building your brand, protecting your reputation, and managing your career. If you want to end your career as an executive in the C Suite, you need to think not only about the positions you hold on the way to the corner office but also how you are perceived in those positions. Does your manager consider you a leader? Do your colleagues think of you as a resource? Do your team members know you to be reliable? Are you considered an innovative forward-thinker? Is your reputation one as a go-to person who works well under pressure? Do your peers think of you as the consummate delegator who knows how to get things done—and done well—through her staff?

Or do your colleagues see you as a wishy-washy nine-to-fiver who follows orders but doesn't do much to lead? Do your managers see you as the office gossip? Does your team consider you an abrasive junkyard dog with a chip on her shoulder? Or do they see you as an arrogant pedigree who thinks she's better than everyone else?

Whether you become known as a junkyard dog or a pedigree, a leader or a follower, a team player or a solo flier is wholly within your control, so long as you do what it takes to build your own professional brand. Part of that requires you to balance your inner junkyard dog with your pedigree. It requires you to be true to your values—because branding yourself means being yourself. It also requires you to strategize your career, which we'll discuss next, in Chapter 3.

Tough-Love Lessons for Branding Yourself and Protecting Your Reputation

- When it comes to your career, your most important tool to move up the corporate ladder is your good reputation, and you need to protect your reputation at all costs. All of your accomplishments, all of your successes, every performance measure you've met or exceeded—all of that speaks to your professional reputation. Whether junkyard dog or pedigree, you have to do all it takes to build your brand on your own terms and protect your reputation.
- You're never not building your brand, whether you're aware of it or not. Everything you do in school, every interview you go on, every interaction with your boss and your colleagues, every conference you attend—all of that provides an opportunity to build your reputation as a polished, poised professional who knows her stuff. You're never not on when it comes to your career.
- Know what your role is, and know how you will define success. Understand that when it comes to playing that role, you have to suit up and put on your mask. That doesn't mean compromising your values or being someone else, but it will mean balancing your role as a professional with the other roles in your life (e.g., parent, sibling, volunteer). Sometimes you have to put a mask on. Sometimes you'll feel like a fraud. But, to paraphrase the great Eleanor Roosevelt, no one can make you feel like an impostor without your consent.
- It's crucial to understand yourself and to understand how others perceive you. The truth is that what other people think of you absolutely does matter when it comes to your career. Whether junkyard dog or pedigree, it's vital to think about how you want to be perceived now and in the future, and to build your brand accordingly.

Strategizing Your Career: Want It, Claim It, Own It

From: "Jena Abernathy" <jabernathy@email.com>

To: "Megan Watson" <mwatson@email.com>

Subject: Strategizing—A Dream Is Not a Goal

Megan,

When it comes to getting the career you want, forget about sitting by the fireside with your iPad or mobile device waiting for the good life to be forced on you. You have to go after it by showing initiative and by having a goal that you're willing to work for in order to make it a reality. That's a true goal. Merely wanting is not getting; it takes planning and effort to get the things in life that are the most important to you.

—Jena

A recent study of sixty large companies by McKinsey, the global management consulting firm, showed that 53 percent of employees in those leading organizations were women. Of those, 40 percent were in management. Only 19 percent were in the C Suite.[1]

The numbers may vary slightly from one study to the next, but the bottom line is the same: As women, we're getting there. But we're not there yet.

When we talk about success in business, it starts with one simple thing: You have to want it. When I ask women why they aren't in the C Suite—despite the fact that so many are very talented and very gifted—a lot of them tell me they just didn't want it. They didn't want to leave their companies for new positions in new organizations. They didn't want to relocate for new jobs. They didn't want to disrupt the balance in their lives. They made choices that are right for them. And that's okay—if that's what they really want.

But if you want to make it into the C Suite, you can't be a little bit CEO or a little bit COO. No guts, no glory. If you're in it, you're in it, and you've got to do whatever it takes to make it happen.

Let's note, too, right off the bat here, that wanting it is not a gender factor. It has nothing to do with being a woman or being a man in the workplace. It's about having a fire in the belly. It's about knowing what you want—and not being afraid to admit it, not just to yourself, but out loud and to everyone who will listen.

But you have to know what you want before you can say it out loud. And wanting it is the first step when it comes to strategizing your career.

---

1. Joanna Barsh and Lareina Yee. *Unlocking the Full Potential of Women at Work.* New York: McKinsey & Co. Retrieved September 9, 2014, from http://online.wsj.com/public/resources/documents/womenreportnew.pdf.

Wishing Is Not a Career Strategy

No one ever just wished their way into a boardroom or the C Suite or even into mid-level management. No one ever kept their career goals to themselves and then magically found themselves on the highest rung of the corporate ladder wondering how in the world they got there.

No, you have to know what job you really want—and then you have to go for it.

That's not always easy. Sometimes, and especially for young professionals, it's difficult to focus ten or twenty years into the future when you're scrambling to get your foot in the door and to make an impression in your entry-level job or even your second job. It's easy to get wrapped up in day-to-day tasks and expectations, which makes it easy to take your eye off the long view.

When it comes to your career, though, that long view has to be on your ultimate goal, whether it's to be CEO or COO or CFO—or any other position in the C Suite. Of course, your entire career trajectory will be comprised of other, smaller goals between your entry-level job and your position as an executive, but you have to want it at each step. If you want to make it to the C Suite, you have to make that your goal. It can't just be a dream that you wish for. Like, "Gosh, it would be nice if someday I could be CEO." That's not going to work at all. Getting to the C Suite has to be a goal that you work toward. That sounds more like "I will be CEO of a Fortune 500 company by the time I'm forty-five."

Let's talk a little bit about goals and dreams. Goals and dreams are far from being the same thing. A dream is something you wish a fairy godmother or guardian angel would make come true without any serious effort on your own part. I have a problem with such notions—and with fairy tales in particular. Too many teach modes of behavior that are detrimental to children—and especially detrimental to girls.

When you look closely at the story of Cinderella, for example, it's not too hard to see that it's about a girl throwing herself a pity party while she works like a slave to please people whom any fool can see will never be happy no matter what she does. But sweet Cinderella does nothing about her situation: She just scrubs those floors and daydreams about some other, better life. Luck, however, saves the day in the form of a fairy godmother who, depending on the version you read, either magically produces an exotic gown and glass slippers out of thin air or takes an old dress, usually one of Cinderella's stepmother's, and transforms it into haute couture. Our heroine then heads to the ball and waits for a good-looking guy with lots of money and a shoe fetish to ask her to dance. He appears on cue, but she runs away, ashamed he'll learn of her humble circumstances when the clock strikes midnight. When he tracks her down and asks her to marry him, she jumps at the offer and allegedly lives happily ever after.

Seriously?

Dreams like that get you nothing but disillusioned and depressed. Just wanting something doesn't make it happen. It's far better to set some real goals for yourself and then chart a course for reaching those goals.

So let's get real about setting career goals. It's important to set real, tangible goals with timetables and deadlines. Here's the key about this step: When strategizing your career, you have to go for title, because title is what keeps you moving on and up. You have to think about your career track and what it looks like. You have to think about where you are now, where you want to be, and how you're going to get there. You have to keep an eye on the big picture and keep your eye on where you want to go.

I recently worked with a twenty-eight-year-old woman who was looking to push her career to the next level. She's a marketing associate now, but she has her eye on the C Suite. So what does that mean? How does a twenty-eight-year-old get to the C Suite before it's time to retire? Does she simply do all her work like she's supposed to and hope for five-star reviews from her boss?

Not exactly.

Yes, she has to do all her work—and then some. Yes, she has to get great reviews—every year. But she also has to volunteer for task forces so she can get cross-departmental experience. She has to get herself to corporate headquarters so she can see and be seen by the powers that be. And, she has to accept the fact that she'll need to move up or out every three to five years during the course of her career. That might mean she has to move around from organization to organization in order to get the title and salary she wants. It might mean she has to relocate herself and her family in order to keep moving up.

If the C Suite is your target, you need to aim for a manager title as soon as possible. Build relationships and connections throughout your organization and within your industry. Learn as much as you can, not only about your own organization but also about the competition and your industry. And let everyone know that you're looking to learn as much as you can about the organization because you're aiming for something higher.

55

INEQUALITY EQUALIZER

Go for title. Don't get mired in an administrative or assistant position for more than twelve to eighteen months. Seek promotion as quickly as possible—even if that means you have to jump ship to a new organization.

As your career progresses, there might be times when you will need to take lateral moves to learn more about an organization or an industry. And that's okay. Some of today's leading women executives have taken lateral moves and profited from them, including Mary Barra, CEO of General Motors, and Shellye Archambeau, CEO of MetricStream, who left IBM when it became clear that the career ladder there wasn't providing her with the experience she needed to make it to the C Suite.[2] In fact, it's important to realize that few of us have career trajectories that follow a straight upward line. Many of us find ourselves taking lateral moves or moving from larger to smaller organizations in order to get the experience or title we need that will help us to perform well and ultimately reach the C Suite.

When strategizing your career, you have to think about your career track and what it looks like. Where are you now? Where do you want to end up? Think about the position you want to retire from. Is it an anonymous mid-level manager lost among dozens of other mid-level managers? Or is it an executive position that puts you in the corner office helping to set the vision, make decisions, and achieve the goals of your organization? Is it as a leader in your field? Is it launching and leading your own company? Is it sitting on boards influencing other organizations because you made it to the C Suite and now you are a sought-after, experienced executive who can help set the stage for other women? What do you want out of your career?

Strategizing your career means that you have to set goals. You have to want to reach those goals, and then you have to claim them.

Claim Your Goals

In order to claim your goals, you really have to know what you want. You have to know with certitude when a job is for you.

---

2. Robin Madell. "Turn Your Lateral Move into a Career Catapult," *The Glass Hammer*, September 6, 2012. Retrieved September 10, 2014, from http://www.theglasshammer.com/news/2012/09/06/turn-your-lateral-move-into-a-career-catapult.

I worked with a woman who had been a partner at a consulting company, where she was running the largest business unit. During her performance review, the CEO at the time asked her about her career plans. To which she answered, "I plan to be the next CEO." To which he responded, "I'm not sure that will happen." And then he asked her why she thought she should be the next CEO.

She went on to talk about all she had done, about all the accolades she had won, and all she had achieved. All of that was well and good, she was told, but the outgoing CEO also told her that an external search would be undertaken, and that because she didn't have an MBA—she wasn't pedigreed, as it were—it would be a disadvantage for her, regardless of the fact that she was a CPA and had consistently performed beyond expectations, delivering results not achieved by her male predecessors.

Undeterred, this scrappy junkyard dog asked the CEO to recommend several of the best MBA programs that would give her a leg up. She went back to school, taking classes on weekends while still doing exemplary work every day for her organization. She got her MBA. The company went through an eighteen-month window knowing the CEO was going to retire, and they initiated the search process. When she made it to the final interview with the company's board of directors, she presented them with a white paper outlining her vision for the direction of the company and what it would look like under her leadership. She explained how she would position the firm against the competition, what new products would be released, and what the company would look like under three years of her leadership.

It was a brilliant move.

The decision was unanimous: She became the next CEO.

She claimed it.

Strategizing your career means you have to identify what you want, and then you have to claim it. But how do you claim

57

it—beyond just saying that you're claiming it? That's a little trickier.

Let's look at our consultant-turned-CEO. She knew what she wanted, she figured out what it would take to get there, she envisioned what it would look like when she got there, and she went after it.

But that vision was more than just a dream of what her future would look like. Instead, that vision was a blueprint, a plan to get from point A to point B. She learned what it would take to become CEO, and she fulfilled those requirements. And, as we have seen, she took it even further, outlining a plan not only for her career, but also for the company she planned to lead. She set goals for herself and for her organization, and she wasn't dissuaded by goals that, to some, might have seemed outlandish.

Be Fearless in Your Goal Setting

Our consultant-turned-CEO knew what she wanted, and she claimed it. She wasn't afraid of what she wanted, and she wasn't afraid to admit it. She was fearless in her goal setting. And you should be, too.

Whether junkyard dog or pedigree, you want to look for opportunities where you can make an impact and where you can be visible. You want to set goals that might seem outlandish at first blush but upon further reflection are totally achievable. Goals can be audacious, but they also have to be specific.

Understand that reaching your goals won't happen overnight, and that's okay—so long as every step you take pushes you closer to your ultimate goal and gets you one step closer to the leadership role you desire.

So, let's return to our twenty-eight-year-old marketing associate. Let's say she wants to be a vice president by the time she's forty and in the C Suite by the time she's forty-five. To do so, she needs to advance every three to five years. She needs to get experience across the organization, in finance, in sales and marketing, in customer service, and in operations. She needs to volunteer to serve on task forces and committees. She needs to get in on award opportunities, new initiatives, and new clients. To make this happen, she needs to set goals for herself. And she needs to be fearless about setting those goals.

What does all of this mean? It means that not only do you have to set long-term goals but that you also have to set interim goals. Aim to be promoted every three to five years. If your organization is so large that moving across departments is next to impossible because there are too many silos, don't be afraid to move to a smaller organization or business unit that will provide you with the experience (and title) you need to achieve your next goal. If your organization is so small that you find yourself getting pegged as a jill-of-all-trades, think about shifting to a larger organization where you can specialize and become known as an expert in your field.

Being fearless in your goal setting also means you have to be fearless in doing whatever it takes to achieve those goals. Don't be afraid to move around, especially if you're not meeting your three- and five-year goals with your current organization. Go to a smaller company if you find your timeline off base. If you feel like you're getting off track at the big company you work for, move over to a smaller place where you can get that next title.

Large companies often have definitive steps and roles that you have to go through in order to be promoted: associate ➡ consultant ➡ senior consultant ➡ manager ➡ director ➡ partner ➡ managing partner ➡ senior partner ➡ vice president ➡ executive. This works for some people, but know that a defined hierarchy in a large organization might hold you back. It's easy for good people to get left out in this kind of organizational structure. It can be politically motivated. A lot of times, the person at the top doesn't want to lose you and so tries to keep you where you are, in that same position with that same title, working for her just as you always have.

The bottom line here is that if your organization or your boss is holding you back, it's time to move on. If your boss won't let you move up, it's time to move on. You can't be afraid to do what it takes to reach your goals. If you are in an environment where your boss is a jerk, definitely find a way to move on. But do not leave your job without having another job lined up, and do not jump from the frying pan into the fire. Really investigate the next opportunity and make sure it fits with your overall plan.

This can be a challenge for women in particular. Too often, we as women are raised to please those around us. We're taught to not make waves. We're taught that it's not ladylike to be too obvious about what we want and that it's not polite to do what's best for ourselves.

That's crazy.

But, sadly, it's also reality.

We all—men, women, pedigrees, junkyard dogs—need to realize and accept the fact that as women, we have plenty to offer Corporate America. The statistics might not show this right now (women currently hold only 4.8 percent of *Fortune 500* CEO positions), but the truth is that there are plenty of women who aren't afraid to set big career goals and to go after them with gusto. Women like Meg Whitman of HP, Indra K. Nooyi of PepsiCo, and Virginia Rometty of IBM didn't get to the C Suite because they set small, simple goals.[3] No, they set big goals for themselves. They knew what they wanted and they went after their goals, kicking ass the whole way.

---

3. Knowledge Center. *Women CEOs of the Fortune 500*. New York: Catalyst, April 2015. Retrieved September 12, 2014, from http://www.catalyst.org/knowledge/women-ceos-fortune-1000.

Claim the Job You Know Should Be Yours

Just as our consultant-turned-CEO did, if you want to reach your career goals, you have to go after them and make them your own. You have to claim it. Strategizing your career means that you have to want it, you have to own it, and you have to claim it. You have to go after the job you want, because no one is going to hand it to you just because you're such a good employee.

How exactly do you go about doing that? First, of course, you have to know what you want. I suggest to many younger employees to write down your goals with a three- to five-year plan. Create visuals that you can post on your iPad or mobile that serve as reminders of what you are seeking out of your career. Set your passwords with inspirational notations that serve as daily reminders of the "eye on the prize" for you. I have, for instance, used passwords like "director2016" or "VP2016," which remind me of important goals every time I log on to my computer.

No matter how you articulate your goals, you can't be afraid to declare what you want, and you can't be embarrassed about going after those goals with gusto. Whether junkyard dog or pedigree, you need to make your career your own. Only you can claim the job—and the life—you really want.

How do you go about claiming the job you want? You have to keep track of your accomplishments. You have to keep score of your successes and failures. And you have to be prepared for every opportunity. We'll talk more about keeping score and making the most of opportunities later on in the book, but let's just take a few minutes to discuss these issues in light of claiming the job you want.

Claiming the job you know should be yours requires that you be prepared to toot your own horn, as it were. You have to be prepared when asking for a promotion, providing your boss with details and data about your accomplishments. This means you should keep track of everything you do, both quantitatively and qualitatively. Do a self-evaluation on yourself and your work. This might mean crafting a kind of unofficial 360-degree review that you ask colleagues at every level to weigh in on. Ask for specific feedback using open-ended questions, and do not get defensive if the feedback reveals negatives or weaknesses. (Remember, this is for you to process and use to your advantage to improve your chances for success.) You might also ask peers in your local Toastmasters group to assess your strengths and weaknesses. (I highlight Toastmasters because learning how to communicate effectively and how to be comfortable with public speaking is a key ingredient for success.) It might also mean talking with groups you volunteer for to get an idea of how they view your leadership skills. The point is to gather all the data and feedback you can and share that information with your boss, noting your strengths and accomplishments (while not highlighting your weaknesses). Whatever you do, don't sell yourself short.

Receiving feedback can be difficult. One way to think of it is to consider it a gift. Rarely do we really get honest feedback, and when we do, we should be prepared to make the most of it. Synthesizing this information will help you to formulate the right presentation to your boss about your strengths and how you are seeking to continuously improve in your role and as a leader.

The most important metric many bosses look for is how you have been able to contribute to the mission and to the bottom line. Frame it accordingly. Think of yourself as your own business unit: How would you rate your performance? How much money have you saved the organization? How many new clients have you brought in? What improvements, ideas, or suggestions have been implemented that you were directly involved in overseeing or supporting? How much revenue did your ideas, suggestions, or team bring directly to the bottom line? What key process indicators for your department can you point to?

When presenting this information to your boss, you have to think in terms of metrics and financials. No whining, no complaining, no justifying—just the facts on how you consistently deliver.

This can be especially difficult for women, because, again, we are programmed from a young age to be modest and humble. We're told that bragging isn't ladylike. We're told that nobody likes someone who boasts all the time.

If we want to level the playing field, it is time to get over that once and for all. In today's highly competitive workplace, you have to do a little bragging if you want to make it to the C Suite. That doesn't mean you have to be a diva or a jerk about it. You can claim credit for your ideas and your accomplishments without being demanding or coming across as entitled. Assess your work objectively and without emotion. Share that self-review with management so it can be incorporated into your annual review. In fact, I've seen it happen many times that management simply uses the employee-provided write-up as the review itself, so grateful are they that the legwork is already done.

The truth is that you can't trust or even expect that your boss is keeping tabs on everything you do or everything you're involved in. So it's crucial that you keep track of your accomplishments. Note your successes and your failures, and for the latter, spin it so that even if an initiative bombed your boss knows that you took a risk, were innovative, and learned from the opportunity. Claiming it means that you own equally your successes and your failures.

Why do you want to keep track of your failures? Because it shows that you're not afraid to take risks. I once had a boss who issued a "Turtle Award," which he gave to people who failed. It signified that these "winners" weren't afraid to stick their neck out. They were rewarded for trying, even if those efforts ended poorly or, at least, not as hoped for.

A lot of corporate cultures don't reward failure, but if you can spin a miss as a hit from which you learned something that can be applied for the next effort, it shows management that you can benefit from experience—good or bad. And that signifies that you are developing as a leader because you know how to take responsibility for outcomes.

CLAIM YOUR JUST REWARDS

One of the most difficult aspects of accepting all of the success you have achieved is negotiating for the salary to go along with that success. Salary negotiations can be one of the most difficult conversations we have with our bosses, regardless of pedigree, gender, or tenure, but studies have shown that women all too frequently fail to ask for salaries that are rightfully theirs.

Before you enter this conversation, do your research to assess your market value and the going rate of your position in your field. Some job boards will post salary ranges for key positions, and some companies even post compensation ranges on their own websites. Various industries conduct annual studies to see where salaries fall, and you can use those studies to assess what your salary should be based on your achievements.

Typically, most companies try to target the midpoint of a given compensation range, but if you're a stellar performer, don't be afraid to ask for more. If you're negotiating for a new job, don't take the first offer. You should always negotiate. Companies will let you know when they are presenting you with their final offer. Be reasonable, but hold firm. This is why it is critical to know your value.

Too, think about when to approach your boss about the compensation conversation. Have the dialogue at the end of the day when your boss is more relaxed and interruptions are less likely to occur. Never threaten to leave the organization if you don't get the income boost you want or say, "If I don't get this raise, I might have to start looking somewhere else."

Whatever happens, never apologize for asking for more money. If you know your value and have done your research, you should feel completely confident in asking for a raise. Role play the dialogue ahead of time with a trusted friend if you're nervous. And, whatever happens, don't get emotional or angry during the conversation. Put your mask on. Your boss may defer the dialogue and say that he needs to confer with the Human Resources Department. Give him a week and then find the right moment to inquire about the status. And remember that this is not personal, it's business.

Take Full Responsibility for Outcomes

We all know that you win some, you lose some. Sometimes your efforts pay off and turn out exactly as you'd hoped. Sometimes your efforts fall flat. Either way, you have to own those experiences. Because experiences—good or bad—all become part of your career history. And because your history does much to shape your future, you want to be sure that you take responsibility for outcomes.

65

Whether working on an individual initiative, a team project, or a departmental goal, it's important to make sure not only that you're keeping track of your contributions and your accomplishments but that you're also taking responsibility for wins and losses. It's easy to claim responsibility when things go well. But employees with real potential—those who demonstrate that they have real leadership abilities—also know how to own their failures.

Owning failure isn't easy. It's usually pretty uncomfortable, and it can be especially frustrating if you have to take responsibility for a failure that might or might not have been your doing in whole or in part. Consider Mary Barra of GM, who inherited an ugly problem when it became known shortly after she took the helm as CEO that the carmaker had been involved in a massive, decade-long internal cover-up regarding faulty ignition switches. It seemed as though the minute Barra was named CEO of the century-old company she was mired in one crisis after another. It would have been easy for her to blame others for the problems GM was facing. She very easily could have blamed the mess on her predecessor, on corporate culture, or even the automotive industry itself. But she didn't. Instead, Barra took responsibility for the disaster, testifying in front of Congress and vowing to get to the bottom of the situation. As distasteful as it was, Barra took responsibility for the outcome. She owned it.

Although pundits and gurus assailed Barra and GM for the massive failure, Barra took on the situation as her own, firing staff who were complicit in the perpetuation of the faulty ignition switches, defending GM's attorneys, and taking the heat from Congress. Doing so didn't mean that she was a failure or that her efforts as CEO were subpar. Rather, her actions proved her a leader willing to take responsibility for outcomes of the company she heads. Not everyone agreed with the way she handled the situation, but she held herself accountable. She owned it.

Whether junkyard dog or pedigree, you have to own your work. For junkyard dogs who tend to be too defensive, taking responsibility for poor outcomes can be especially difficult. You have to be able to accept failure as a part of life and not treat it as a personal weakness or as a reflection of your non-pedigreed status. For pedigrees who might be used to easy success, accepting failure can be especially difficult, so it's important not to look at a failed initiative as indicative of some kind of overarching incompetency. One failed project doesn't mean you are a failure, whether junkyard dog or pedigree.

Instead of dwelling in failure, it's important to take responsibility, learn from it, and move on. Find a way to apply those lessons learned to the next initiative. Same goes, of course, for successes—but here it's important not to assume that what worked with one project or one team or one department will necessarily work with the next. Take responsibility for outcomes, learn from them, and apply them to future efforts. It's all about how you look at it.

Tough-Love Lessons for Strategizing Your Career

- Whether junkyard dog or pedigree, no one is going to hand you a perfect life in which all of your dreams come true with little or no effort. Save your dreams for sleeping. Instead, craft specific goals that will allow you to reach your career objectives.
- Only 15 percent of C Suite positions are held by women. So, if you want to make it to the C Suite, you have to want it—really want it. And you can't be afraid to admit it—to yourself or to anyone else.
- Wanting and wishing aren't enough—and neither is a career strategy. Junkyard dogs and pedigrees alike need to envision their career trajectories, focus on the long view, and set interim goals to achieve their professional objectives.
- If you want it, claim it. Once you've determined what your career objective is, do whatever it takes to achieve it. Keep moving up or moving on—or you'll find yourself stuck and your goals waylaid.
- You have to own your own career. Don't let anyone else take credit for your work, and don't assume that anyone else is keeping track of your accomplishments. Keep score of your successes and failures, learn from them, and demonstrate your ability as a leader. Ask for the reward because you deserve the payday.

67

= 4 =

Making the Most of Opportunities and Risks

From: "Jena Abernathy" <jabernathy@email.com>

To: "Megan Watson" <mwatson@email.com>

Subject: Opportunity Costs

Megan,

Congratulations on being appointed to the Product X Task Force. This is a great opportunity for you to meet colleagues throughout the organization, learn more about the company, and gain some valuable skills. As you continue your work on the task force, it's important to know that passion and hard work aren't enough. It's crucial that you put forth your better-than-best effort and take ownership of your work, whether success or failure. It's up to you to make the most of this opportunity. Good luck!

—Jena

What's to be gained by taking a chance and putting forth effort? What could you lose if you don't take a chance?

Those are two fundamental questions to consider when weighing opportunities and risks. You have to weigh the benefits as well as the costs, looking at the pros and cons of what could happen if you do go after an opportunity and what could happen if you choose not to.

The truth is that, sometimes, opportunities and risks look an awful lot alike. You could, for instance, have the chance to ascend, say, Machu Picchu, the World Heritage site in Peru that sits some two thousand feet above the turbulent Urubamba River. Reaching the top of this landmark Incan ruin would afford you astounding views into one of the greatest empires in history as well as views of the area and the peoples who live there today. What are the risks? You might not make it. You could fall off the mountain. You might have to retreat. The opportunities include challenging yourself to see how far you really can go, achieving a goal that you've set, testing your limits and your potential, and following through on something that is important to you.

In the workplace, an opportunity might come in the form of a particularly challenging team assignment, it might come in the form of a transfer to a new location, or it might come in the shape of a promotion to a new position in a new division leading a new group of people. Whether you see these as opportunities or risks often depends on your mindset and your goals.

Oftentimes, you have to define your own opportunities. That might mean volunteering for projects (especially for visible projects). And when I talk about volunteering for projects, I'm not talking about volunteering to organize the company picnic or lead the company's softball team (although if you do it right, even those could be opportunities, so long as you don't fall into the trap of becoming the company's social director). I am talking about working on an important project that has a direct relationship to your organization's bottom line. I'm talking about volunteering for visible projects that showcase your strengths, that allow you to grow, or that expose you to new aspects of your organization.

Whether you're just starting out in your career or whether you're well into it, it's important to take on new opportunities. Joining a task force, working on a cross-departmental project, taking on a group presentation to a new client . . . things like that give you a chance to find out what you like and what you're good at. Taking on such projects tests your will and your fortitude, especially those projects that are likely to stretch beyond the usual forty- or fifty-hour workweek.

The key is to take on projects that you know you can complete. You need to feel confident that you can deliver. You don't want to be the one who volunteers and then doesn't carry her own weight. Whatever you take on, you have to follow through. You have to push yourself to do it, even if it means you might have to sacrifice your personal time as your work-week extends to seventy or eighty hours for a certain period of time. The last thing you want, especially early on in your career, is to sign up for an extra project and then be the one who always leaves early or never shows up. You don't want to be the one who makes a lot of promises but never delivers. You don't want to be that person.

WHEN TO SAY "NO"

Opportunity and risk go hand in hand, and saying "yes" to opportunity means you're taking on some risk. Saying "no" also can be risky, even when it's the right thing to do.

Sometimes you don't have the luxury of volunteering for extra work. Your boss volunteers you instead, saddling you with a project or a presentation that you have little time for. Some of these projects might not be to your liking, or they might not provide you with the kind of visibility that will put you in line for a promotion. Sometimes you just know that there's no way you can take on another project and give it your all.

So what do you do when you know the right thing is to say "no"?

The key here is to decline politely without actually saying "no." One way to do this is to say something like, "This sounds like a great project, and I'd be happy to help. I'm working on Project X, Y, and Z right now, and so I could take this on early next month. Would that work for you?" or something like, "I'd love to work on this. Do you see this as a priority over Project A, which is due at the end of the week?" Responses like this let your boss know that you're both enthusiastic and willing, while at the same time prompting him to consider your workload and how much time you could reasonably dedicate to the project and still get the job done.

Of course, sometimes it's not your boss that you have to say no to but your teammates. I worked with one woman, for instance, who found that a task force she was on was meeting late every night of the week. Although she was happy to work on the project, she did have a life outside work as well—a life that needed tending to if she was to keep her sanity. Her colleagues, however, didn't like to hear "no" when they asked, yet again, whether she could put in some extra hours.

Her solution? She finally ended up signing up for scuba-diving lessons, which started at 7 p.m. two nights a week. This was the only way she could actually leave the office—because she had another commitment. Her team members wouldn't accept that she simply wanted to leave the office at a reasonable hour to go home. But they would accept that she had another commitment.

Saying "no" can be uncomfortable, but it's often necessary. Only you know how much you can really handle. While you don't want to be afraid to push yourself, it's important to know when to say enough is enough—just so long as you say it in a way that keeps your good reputation intact.

When it comes to making the most of opportunities, know that passion and hard work aren't enough. You have to deliver. So, when you're considering which opportunities to jump at, consider how those opportunities will allow you to build your brand and which opportunities may lead you to be tapped for other, even more important spots.

Remember that there's no point in taking chances if you don't deliver. Think about how you are assessed as talent. You want everyone in your organization to see you as a "HIPO" (i.e., a high-potential employee). You want to make sure that your name is out there in a good way. If you don't follow through, you'll soon be marked as someone who might volunteer for too many things and never deliver. In no time, your offers to volunteer will be declined and your reputation will be tarnished.

Opportunities are everywhere, whether subtle or obvious. No matter what opportunities you choose to go for, the key is to make sure that they will help you build your reputation. Regardless of tenure, pedigree, or gender, it's important to take the right opportunities, overcome the fear of failure associated with risks, and weigh what really matters to you.

73

Take the Right Opportunities

Which opportunities you take and which you don't likely will depend on the culture of your organization. If you're working for a hard-charging company in which everyone is focused on all business all the time, you'll want to find opportunities that allow you to excel in business-related areas. That might mean cross-departmental team projects, task forces, or committees. The trick, especially early in your career, is making sure you don't get labeled as the social organizer or the group secretary or the minute-taker: You want to stand out for your accomplishments.

When you're looking for opportunities, look for places where you can have an impact and where you can be visible. Seek out opportunities that will challenge you so that you can make the most of opportunities that will help you grow your career. Opportunities that give you exposure to other departments, to different colleagues, and to a variety of managers can serve as a way not only to broaden your horizons (which will help you learn what you like and dislike as well as what you're good at and not so good at), but also to get some face time.

So often, opportunities are a matter of planting seeds and watching them grow. For instance, a healthcare company I worked for was going for the coveted Malcolm Baldrige National Quality Award. Pursuing this award was many years in the making, and I felt strongly that we weren't on the right track to win it. So I told my CEO during a company dinner one night, "If you ever need me to take a more active role in Baldrige, I would be happy to do that."

About a week later, he asked me what I thought about a few candidates he was considering to lead the initiative. I asked, "Do you think that they're the right people to lead this from an executive perspective?" He said he thought they could do the work. I said, "Well, think about that. And, if you ever need anything, I will step up to the plate."

See here that I just kept planting the seed. I never fully leaned in and directly asked for the assignment. If I had said, "Let me be the person to lead Baldrige," he would have turned me down flat. He didn't yet see me as the right person for that job, and he thought I already had too much on my plate. But soon enough he realized that he could count on me to deliver, and he told me to run with it. And so I did, pulling together the right team. And we won the award.

It's important here, as mentioned above, that when you take on any additional assignments like this, you are prepared to give it your all. You can't kind of join a task force. If you volunteer for a cross-departmental committee, you have to dedicate yourself to putting forth your best effort—in fact, you have to be ready to put forth better than your best, and you have to get along with the team members. Because it's crucial here to make the most of these opportunities: Don't twist an opportunity into a risk by turning in a subpar performance. This is true for junkyard dogs and pedigrees alike.

Remember that, in today's highly competitive climate, everyone is looking for ways to stand out. Unfortunately, this means that, all too often, your colleagues are keeping score on you. If they consider you a junkyard dog and question your credentials, they may well be just waiting for you to make a mistake, which, in their minds, might be expected. If they consider you a pedigree, they also might be waiting for you to make a mistake, eager to catch the perfect little Ivy Leaguer in a snafu. The only way to equalize the inequality that exists here is to turn in a performance that absolutely wows your task force colleagues, your managers, your clients, and everyone else involved in the work at hand. Extra assignments can definitely be the right opportunities—if you do them right. I have witnessed many careers flourish because of stellar performances on these types of teams.

In addition to taking on extra assignments, I encourage employees at any level of their careers to relocate if necessary. This can be a daunting proposition for many people, especially for those with family or other close ties to their communities. But relocating can often be a high-reward opportunity, even if it also appears to be a high-risk prospect as well. This is particularly true if a promotion is involved and especially if the move allows you to work at your company's headquarters. The same goes for positions that require a lot of travel, particularly international travel.

INEQUALITY EQUALIZER

Build a solid network of contacts at your organization's corporate headquarters and stay connected with the power brokers. Corporate headquarters is the epicenter of decision making in most organizations, and staying engaged and on the radar helps level the playing field.

The benefits of relocating and traveling are myriad. For instance, moving to corporate headquarters gives you the kind of exposure that can be challenging for those working in large organizations with branch offices spread across the country if not the world. Working at corporate headquarters puts you face to face with C Suite executives and other key stakeholders who are in a position to tap those employees they believe have the most potential. If you're not at corporate headquarters, chances are you're not being seen by those on the top rungs of the corporate ladder. When you are there, though, you are more visible and have more opportunities to be recognized as a star performer. This can put you in better stead to be positioned for promotion more quickly than colleagues who spend their careers in branch offices. If you are in the field, assume an operational role with line responsibility and P&L oversight. Success there will help create a visible opportunity for you.

Relocating to a new office, new city, or even a new country provides other benefits as well. For example, you'll meet new people and learn how to work in a new culture, whether a new corporate culture, a new set of customs, or even a new language. Provided that you embrace this as a learning opportunity, relocating can help you learn to be more flexible and adaptable. It can help you learn how to communicate with a new group of people. It can help you learn how to better adjust to changing conditions. And it can provide new networking opportunities that will help you build a larger client base.

Relocating can be intimidating, but it also can be one of those opportunities that yields countless benefits. Chloe Mason Gray, founder of LeanIn 2.0, notes that "working abroad can be a great option, especially if you are at the start of your career" and that doing so "turned out to be the best decision I've ever made."[1]

---

1. Chloe Mason Gray. "The Smart Career Move You Haven't Considered: Working Abroad," *The Muse*, September 30, 2013. Retrieved April 9, 2015, from https://www.themuse.com/advice/the-smart-career-move-you-havent-considered-working-abroad?ref=search.

Of course, just as there are benefits, there are risks involved with relocating. You might have to sell your house. You might have to uproot your family. You might move only to find out that the job isn't a fit.

Relocating isn't always easy. I once moved my family to Houston so I could accept a new position at corporate head-quarters, only to make just about everyone miserable. Even our dogs hated it. They hated the new grass in our new lawn at our new house and refused to go outside and do what they were supposed to do. I literally faced a pile of crap on the drive-way every day on my way in and out the door. Even so, the move was still worth it. Not only did the dogs eventually figure things out, but within six months I moved into an expanded role in which I was able to broaden my experience and gain new skills. Furthermore, I was seen as a driven, loyal employee who was willing to do what it took to get ahead.

When it comes to relocating, you have to consider things like this, weighing the pros and cons as they relate to your particular situation. But whatever that list looks like, it's important that you not let fear rule your decision-making process.

Overcome the Fear of Taking Risks

You will be challenged throughout your career. Sometimes you'll succeed. Sometimes you'll fail. If taking those risks—and experiencing related successes and even failures—helps you grow as a leader, then the chance was worth taking. Don't allow fear to dissuade you from taking chances, because when you come out on the other side, you'll very likely find that your confidence has grown—and you'll know you can take on other opportunities.

The truth is that taking risks—or making the most of opportunities, depending on which way you look at it—is good for you. And I'm not the only one who believes that. Researchers at INSEAD, one of the world's leading graduate business schools, note that, "[e]xposing yourself to risk and failure can help push you up the career ladder. Just make sure someone's watching."[2]

When it comes to opportunities and risk, not only is it important to give each effort your all, but it's also important to take credit for your work. We talked about this a bit in Chapter 3 when we discussed the importance of owning it, and we'll talk more about the importance of keeping score, too, in Chapter 5. But for now, let's take some time to discuss why accepting accountability for your work—whether a success or a failure—is crucial.

High performers—whether male or female, junkyard dog or pedigree—make a habit of taking opportunities, doing whatever they can to ensure that those opportunities don't turn into risks. But sometimes, despite all best efforts, things don't work out as planned. Sometimes there's a high-risk, high-reward component to an opportunity that can make even the brightest star fall flat. Sometimes mistakes happen and the result is failure.

Or, at least, the result is the perception of failure.

The key is to turn those "failures" around and treat them as learning experiences. This is what many of today's top executives do. "By accepting mistakes, executives can show they have a willingness to try new things. They are able to emphasize lessons learned and implement steps to prevent the mishap happening again. In this way they are able to turn mistakes into a positive, and show superiors what they are capable of."[3]

Think about it. Some of the greatest business leaders in history are known for making some of the biggest business blunders in history. Donald Trump, for example, who famously has gone bankrupt several times, has led some spectacular business failures, including Trump Airlines, Trump Casinos, Trump

---

2. Jane Williams. "Make Mistakes Part of Your Career Success," *INSEAD Knowledge*, February 3, 2015. Retrieved April 9, 2015, from http://knowledge.insead.edu/leadership-management/make-mistakes-part-of-your-career-success-3823.
3. *Ibid.*

Mortgage, Trump Vodka, and even Trump: The Game.[4] The short-lived merger in 2000 of AOL and Time–Warner was widely considered a disastrous venture for chairman and CEO Jerry Levin—and for the company's shareholders. CEO Roberto Goizueta was forced to drink crow just seventy-nine days into the calamitous launch of New Coke in 1985, when Coca-Cola took one of the biggest risks in the history of the consumer goods industry—and failed miserably. And, in perhaps one of the biggest mistakes in corporate history, Steve Jobs gave up the helm at Apple in 1977—and didn't again sit in the CEO's chair for another twenty years.

Each of these business leaders would be forgotten, buried under the weight of their mistakes, had they not accepted responsibility for their failures, learned from their experiences, and moved on. By doing so, they paved the way for future success. Regardless of where you are in your career, you can do the same. If you're on a project and it goes south, you can still say that you learned something from it, that you developed a new skill as a result of the experience, or that you were able to devise a new solution that could fix related problems in the future. No opportunity is really a true failure as long as you can spin it so that it's clear you got something out of it. What really matters is what you learn from it—what you would do when faced with a similar opportunity in the future and how you would do things differently.

In everyone's career, there are times when you are presented with situations that you have to determine how to handle. Some situations that seem like opportunities might reveal themselves later to be risks. How you deal with that is what's important.

I've had to do this plenty of times. In one of my first jobs in human resources, for example, I was hired to work at a small, publicly traded bank that was largely controlled by a

79

4. Megan Gibson. "Top 10 Donald Trump Failures—Trump: The Game," *Time Magazine*, April 29, 2011. Retrieved April 10, 2015, from http://content.time.com/time/specials/packages/article/0,28804,2068227_2068229_2068132,00.html.

single family. The bank chairman was the father, and the bank president was the son. I headed up human resources, and the family was very supportive of me. One day, the bank chairman invited me to a party at his house, where he would be hosting the governor of the state. I was so thrilled to be invited to this party that when the chairman asked me to come a little early, I didn't give it a second thought. I knew this would be a great opportunity for me to network with some really interesting and powerful people.

When I got there, the chairman handed me an apron, telling me that I had such a great personality that he wanted me to hand out hors d'oeuvres to his guests.

I could have at that moment turned around, walked out the door, and been completely offended. But that would have been a mistake. Instead, I chose to thank him for the opportunity. I told him I would rather not wear the apron, but that I would be happy to hand out hors d'oeuvres. When the chairman's son, the bank president, saw me passing out hors d'oeuvres, he asked me what I was doing. I told him that his father thought I was there to serve, and that I didn't mind doing so—for a little while. And so, after I passed out a few hors d'oeuvres, I mingled with the other guests.

For me, this was a huge lesson. I made a point the next day to send the bank chairman a thank-you note, telling him how much I appreciated opportunity to attend the party. I didn't mention a word about the hors d'oeuvres.

From that point forward, I received numerous invitations to the chairman's house because I proved I could hold my own in a setting like that—and never again was I asked to serve food to the other guests. I turned what could have been a disaster into an opportunity.

Now, it probably doesn't take a genius to realize that this was one of those situations that junkyard dogs find themselves in. No pedigree would ever be asked by his boss or the host of a party to don an apron and start serving food to the guests. But it can happen to junkyard dogs—and, as my example shows, it does happen.

A lot of people would have gotten angry over a situation like that. My junkyard dog status may have played a part in the request, but I saw it as more of a generational thing than anything else. The father didn't view me as an equal because of my age, and he probably never would have viewed me as an equal, because of age, gender, or status (or perhaps all three). But instead of treating the request as one to be a servant, I was able to turn the situation around and act as the hostess—and there's a big difference there. It was a great life lesson, and how I handled that situation put me in good stead with the bank chairman, the bank president, and the entire organization. And that's what really mattered in the end.

Weigh What Really Matters

When it comes to taking chances—or avoiding risks—the bottom line really is the experience you get from it. All too often, it's easy to pass on an opportunity because you think the costs are too great. Relocating for a new job, for example, might mean you have to sell your house, take a loss on it, and then have to pay for a cross-country move to a city that has a higher cost of living, all while uprooting yourself and your family for a new position that isn't guaranteed to work out. That's a daunting prospect, and one that a lot of people would avoid.

But what's the cost of not taking that opportunity? In many ways, you'll never know. It's the classic "what if" scenario. Not relocating for a new job means that you won't get to build your career in a new organization. You won't get to connect with new colleagues. You won't get to work on new projects with new team members. You might even be passing up a promotion. Too, you won't get to experience living in a new city and exploring what a new region has to offer.

Whether pro or con, both come with associated opportunity costs. Some of those costs are tangible. Some are intangible. In the end, only you can determine how much you're willing to pay for what you might gain by jumping on an opportunity. Remember, though, that sometimes not buying into an opportunity can cost more than taking a chance.

This is true for opportunities both small and large. Relocating is a huge opportunity, and it comes with sizeable associated opportunity costs. But I see employees at all levels of their careers forgo even small opportunities because they just don't see the benefits. For instance, a lot of junkyard dogs tend to discount the benefits associated with memberships in professional associations, social clubs, and even fitness centers. They see the dollar signs without seeing the payoffs. They see a few hundred dollars or even a few thousand dollars going toward a membership that they might not take advantage of or might not get anything out of. But what they fail to see are the benefits associated with memberships.

Of course, the key is to be selective in making the most of opportunities like this. Spending a few hundred dollars a year on membership to a professional organization that grants you access to conferences, seminars, webinars, and other learning and networking opportunities in your field is almost always well worth the price, not just in experience and education but in contacts and affiliations. You never know whom you might meet at one of these functions. You might connect with a person who one day might be a colleague—or even a new boss. You might connect with potential clients. You might connect with an important mentor. The long-term benefits of these connections are priceless.

Similarly, consider social or community organizations you might join, whether civic clubs or country clubs that might require membership fees or volunteer groups that might require your time and energy. These organizations offer opportunities for personal growth outside of work, growth that may well help you in your professional life, too. What skills might you develop, for example, by volunteering to serve on your local park board, arts council, or library board? What connections might you make if you donate your time and energy to an organization that provides pro bono professional services for members of your community? Chances are that whatever you spend in money, time, or resources, the benefits will outweigh the costs. (And, of course, there are payoffs beyond connections and education. Numerous studies have shown that volunteerism promotes feelings of improved health, wealth, and happiness.)[5]

Another opportunity often overlooked by junkyard dogs is joining social clubs and country clubs. Although everyone seems to know intuitively that business happens on golf courses and tennis courts, junkyard dogs often decline to take advantage of such opportunities, scared off by the high fees and by the notion that they typically need to be sponsored or recommended for membership. Younger employees with limited incomes also tend to forgo this channel, usually for financial reasons, even though many clubs, associations, and other organizations have reduced rates and low initiation rates for those under age forty. But nixing this idea out of hand can cost more than membership fees would cost out of pocket. What local officials and business leaders might you meet by joining your local country club? Who might those connections lead you to? How many potential colleagues or clients might you meet on the tennis court? How many deals might you close on the golf course? The world of country clubs and other social clubs is well known to pedigrees. Most of them grow up in this world if not right next door. Junkyard dogs would do well to consider the long-term benefits of joining this world, meeting the people who inhabit this world, and playing a few rounds of golf with them.

83

5. Mark Horoszowski. "5 Surprising Benefits of Volunteering," *Forbes*, March 19, 2015. Retrieved April 10, 2015, from http://www.forbes.com/sites/nextavenue/2015/03/19/5-surprising-benefits-of-volunteering.

In a similar vein, think, too, even about where you work out every day. Are you spending twenty bucks a month at a cheap gym in the suburbs where you run on a treadmill alone after work every night? Or are you spending a couple hundred dollars a month to work out first thing every morning at a downtown fitness center alongside a bunch of C Suite executives who get their workouts in before their workdays begin? If you belong to the former group of exercisers rather than the latter, you might well be saving some money, but what opportunities are you missing out on? What connections aren't you making? What conversations aren't you having? What could be the return on your investment and the payoff for the right connections?

=====

INEQUALITY EQUALIZER

If you want to play with the pros, you have to pay to play. Position yourself alongside pedigrees by becoming a part of their world, through social clubs, country clubs, executive fitness centers, and other organizations where they live and play.

=====

When it comes to opportunities, sometimes you have to create them for yourself, and, always, those opportunities come with costs—costs associated with action and costs associated with inaction. Only you can determine which costs matter most to you. But when weighing those costs, know that money should never be the only consideration, or even the most important consideration.

In fact, studies have shown that when it comes to considering opportunity costs, among the most important factors to weigh are how happy the opportunity will make you in the long term and what you will learn from the opportunity over time. As Ron Ashkenas writes in *Harvard Business Review*, "career success is not about reducing risks. Rather it's about maximizing your happiness in a way that also allows you to find surprises and push yourself into new territory. To do that you may need to maximize your risks."[6]

When it comes to our careers, many of us tend to shy away from opportunities. Whether it's because we perceive them as risks, whether we're afraid of failing, or whether we believe the associated costs are too high, the end result is often the same: We fail to make the most of opportunities that could deliver important long-term benefits, usually because we're afraid of the potential short-term costs. But the truth is that rarely do our worst fears ever come to pass. We might shy away from an opportunity to, for instance, lead an important client presentation because we're afraid our team members won't deliver on their research or because we'd rather die than have to speak in public—but in reality, most teams almost always deliver and public speaking rarely results in death.

It's easy to talk yourself out of taking a chance. It costs too much to move. Membership fees are prohibitive. Volunteering takes up too much time. But those are barriers we erect ourselves, blocking our own paths to success, usually because we're afraid of failure. But the payoff of any opportunity can rarely be measured in dollars. Rather, the benefits come from what lessons we learn, what we experience, what skills we gain, whom we meet, and what connections we make. Even if an opportunity goes south, it provides an opportunity to learn from mistakes.

It's up to you to make the most of opportunities, even if you have to make those opportunities happen on your own. The key is to give it your all, learn from the experience, and make sure to take credit for your work. Keeping score is crucial when it comes to managing your career, which is what we'll discuss next, in Chapter 5.

---

6. Ron Ashkenas. "Embracing Risk in Career Decisions," *Harvard Business Review*, June 18, 2012. Retrieved April 10, 2015, from https://hbr.org/2012/06/embracing-risk-in-career-decis.

Tough-Love Lessons for Making the Most of Opportunities

- High performers understand the benefits of taking chances, even when they seem more like risks than opportunities. They take chances because doing so provides them better visibility, a chance to meet people across the organization, and further opportunity to build their reputations as hard working, credible, and bright.

- Whether male or female, junkyard dog or pedigree, and regardless of where you are on the corporate ladder, you often have to make your own opportunities. This means either volunteering outright if the situation calls for it or planting the seeds if a more subtle approach is required in order to persuade the powers that be that you're the right person for the assignment.

- Top employees understand that growth opportunities are rarely about money. The payoff comes in experience, in new skills, in contacts, in title, and in exposure. When considering an opportunity, you still need to negotiate a fair salary, but also weigh in the payoff in the next three years if you deliver, looking at how it will help you in your next move and how it helps position you in the long run.

5

Managing Up, Down, and Sideways

From: "Jena Abernathy" <jabernathy@email.com>

To: "Megan Watson" <mwatson@email.com>

Subject: Managing in All Directions

Megan,

As we near the annual performance review period, it's important to share with your manager the key details about your accomplishments and lessons learned. It's also important to think about your relationships with others in the organization as well. How well are you managing relationships up, down, and sideways, with managers, subordinates, and colleagues? All of those relationships matter, and how you manage them says a lot about you. How well are you managing your relationships—and your career? It's something to think about.

—Jena

Whether good leaders and good managers are born or made will long remain a point of contention for business gurus, academics, and pundits. For aspiring professionals who have their eye on the C Suite, it's crucial to be both a good leader and a good follower (you can't have one without the other) as you climb the corporate ladder. Because the truth is that, no matter where you are in your career trajectory, chances are you're both a leader and a follower depending on whatever role you're playing for a given assignment or a given position. That means you have to manage in all directions.

Whether junkyard dog or pedigree, male or female, entry-level employee or tenured professional, it's important to manage for results across the organization. It's also important to nurture strong working relationships, as those relationships will create your sphere of influence, which will have much to do with your professional growth. But while relationships matter, in the end, the best leaders manage based on results—and they manage in all directions: up, down, and sideways.

Managing up, down, and sideways isn't always easy. It can be all too easy to focus on pleasing your manager and making your accomplishments known to her, all while forgetting to manage relationships with peers, colleagues, assistants, and subordinates and across departments and divisions. But this is one of those skills that everyone in every organization should master if they want to build the kind of reputations that propel them closer to the corner office. This means that you have to lead in every direction, learn from every level, and get feedback from those around you, whether above you, alongside you, or below you. All this will help you manage your career.

Lead in Every Direction

When you think about leading in every direction, it's important to consider who is in your sphere of influence. This refers to those individuals who work around you, with you, above you, and below you. It includes your manager and everyone he reports to. It includes your direct reports, support staff, colleagues, and team members, as well as industry peers, competitors, clients, and customers. It's important to recognize where you sit in this sphere of influence, how you interact with those who are in those circles, and how the individuals within your sphere of influence perceive you.

In every job I've ever had, I've taken the time to draw my sphere of influence. I'm no artist, so this was just me sketching out who I found in the various circles of my professional life— the people at all levels within the company I was working for, the people outside the company that I worked with on a regular basis (like clients, customers, and even competitors), and the people in related industries and organizations (like professional associations). Together, all these people make up my sphere of influence. It's always interesting to see who's in that sphere and to think about the relationships I have with those people, regardless of where I am or where they are on the corporate ladder.

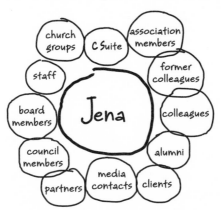

You, too, should think about the working relationships you have with people up and down the corporate ladder. Although most people typically think about managing up and working the relationships they have with their manager, their vice president, their executive directors, and members of the C Suite, it's also important to think about what kind of relationships you have with others throughout your organization and across your industry. How would those in your sphere of influence rate your performance?

Leading in all directions can be inherently easier for pedigrees than for junkyard dogs. Because pedigrees often already have peers at their level and above, it can be easy for them to manage up and sideways, largely because those relationships are already in place. Managing down can be easy for them, too, often because their presumptive status and experience inspire awe and followership in underlings who are easily enamored with their pedigree status.

Junkyard dogs usually have to work harder at building relationships that allow them to lead in all directions. Especially for J-Dogs who come at leadership with a chip on their shoulder, or for those who suffer from Impostor Syndrome, leading in all directions can be challenging. They might feel they don't have the inherent capabilities, experience, or cache to be perceived as leaders. They might push too hard, becoming abrasive in their quest to be considered leadership-quality material, especially when managing up. Managing sideways and down, on the other hand, is often easier for junkyard dogs, who might well find it easier to relate to people at those levels of the organization, regardless of tenure.

Whether junkyard dog or pedigree, however, managing in all directions is one skill that's absolutely crucial to work on, especially if you want to get ahead. In fact, experts note that "constantly managing up, down and sideways will accelerate your success and ensure that you'll always have people that want to work with, and potentially for, you."[1]

So how do you actually go about managing up, down, and sideways? It starts with communicating with everyone at all levels in the organization. As simple as it sounds, communica-

---

1. Sang Lee. "Managing Up, Down and Sideways," *Under30CEO*, October 20, 2012. Retrieved April 22, 2015, from http://under30ceo.com/managing-up-down -and-sideways.

tion is the key. And the easiest way to learn how to lead in all directions is to ask people what they need. It's as simple as that.

Have direct conversations with your staff. Ask those in your sphere of influence what they need in order to do their jobs better—and even what they think you can do better yourself. Ask them what they want. Ask for their opinions as to what would make the company more efficient and more profitable. Talk to them.

For example, when managing up, it's crucial to have conversations with your managers. In fact, studies have shown that communicating with your boss is key when it comes to meeting his needs. Researchers note that,

> It is important to understand what your boss needs from you and just as important for her/him to understand what you need as well. When approaching this relationship, employees can ask questions to confidently know how to best communicate with a supervisor, learn how the manager wishes to be contacted, and in which types of circumstances the supervisor needs to be involved. Staff members who are most effective seek out information regarding their supervisors' goals and problems and pressures.[2]

The same goes for managing sideways and down. Ask how, when, and how frequently colleagues, clients, customers, and support staff prefer to be communicated with. Find out what kind of information they need to do their jobs better. You'd be surprised at how far having these conversations can go when managing in all directions. Not only will people feel grateful that you even asked for their opinion, but they'll provide you

---

2. Molly E. Ward and Jill Zambito. "Managing in All Directions: Up, Down, and Sideways," *The Bulletin*, Volume 81, Issue 6, November 2013. Retrieved April 22, 2015, from https://www.acui.org/publications/bulletin/article.aspx?issue=41800&id=23413.

with valuable information that will help them—and you—do their jobs better.

Of course, finding out how people want to be communicated with and what they need to do their jobs better is only half the battle. You need to synthesize the information you gather from such conversations and meet needs where you can. When managing, your team will want to know that you have their back. They'll want to know that you'll provide them with the tools and the time to get things done and get them done right. By communicating with them, you'll find out what they need in terms of time and resources, and they'll find out from you what your expectations are.

Communicating across, throughout, and outside the organization is something I always do. I take the time to connect with everyone who is in my sphere of influence. I ask them what resources they need and how they like to be contacted. In doing so, I'm able to work with them to set rules of engagement that guide us as we work toward our goals.

For instance, it's no surprise that most employees hate to work on the weekends. With myriad mobile devices and 24/7 connectivity, this is getting harder and harder: We're always in touch with everyone we work with, whether colleagues or clients. In communicating with one of my teams, we set rules of engagement that dictated that no e-mails were to be sent over the weekend unless the issue was extremely urgent. We agreed that no one would send e-mails between Friday night and Sunday night so that employees didn't end up spending their entire weekends fielding routine requests via e-mail. That's because when e-mails are coming constantly, especially after hours or over the weekend, everybody moves into action because they think it's really important. In reality, most things can wait until Monday morning. By communicating with my team and establishing rules of engagement, I was able to let them know what I expected of them and that I had their back—both of which are crucial components of being a good leader.

LEAD BY CREATING FOLLOWERS

Being a leader means you have to guide people in achieving goals and meeting performance measures. You have to assess your staff and put each person in the right position so that the team can succeed. You also have to hold accountable the people who work for you. Managing requires a shift in thinking because you've gone from being an individual contributor focused on her own work and her own results to a leader who is responsible for the work done by a team. That means you have to assemble the best team possible.

Sometimes as a new manager, you're handed a team with whom you have to work. Sometimes you get to assemble your own team from new hires. Either way, you have to make sure you hire the right person for the job and assign the right tasks to the right employees. Your focus needs to be not on who you like the best but on who will do the best work. Remember that you shouldn't be looking to hire someone in your own image or someone you'd like to hang out with after work. You need to hire for results and manage for results.

You can't be an effective manager without leading—or without fostering followership. Followership is akin to leadership, but it's different in important ways. Whereas leadership is about doing the right things in the right ways at the right time in order to achieve goals and hit targets, followership is about taking direction well, being an effective part of the team, carrying out vision, and meeting established performance measures. As a leader, part of your job is to create followers who will work with you, support you, and help you meet your goals.

We can't have leaders without followers. Indeed, "The fact is that in organizations everybody is both a leader and a follower depending on the circumstances."[3] Although followers get much less attention than leaders, the truth is that no organization could

---

3. John S. McCallum. "Followership: The Other Side of Leadership," *Ivey Business Journal*, September/October 2013. Retrieved April 27, 2015, from http://iveybusinessjournal.com/publication/followership-the-other-side-of-leadership.

exist without both. We need people who are ready, willing, and able to work in the trenches, to execute orders, to put plans into action. How do you get those people? By communicating with them. By listening to them. By showing them you believe in them and that you trust them. By following through on the promises you make. By clearly stating your expectations. By assessing them fairly. By providing them with the resources, tools, and time necessary so they can do their jobs.

Although some might argue that good leaders naturally attract loyal followers, the truth is that creating followership requires you to be a good leader—to work at being a good leader. Good leaders communicate well and often with their teams, doing what it takes to manage in all directions.

Learn from Every Level

Many people believe that true leaders have some sort of inherent magical quality that allows them to manage well. But the truth is that most of us have to work really hard to be good leaders and we have to spend a lot of time learning the ropes. Whether junkyard dog or pedigree, leaders need to learn from every level—from the mail room to the boardroom—and then they need to keep on learning from everyone in the organization, regardless of position, status, or tenure.

Business is full of great leaders who have done just that. Tim Cook of Apple, for example, has earned a reputation as someone who listens to the opinions and advice of the people who work with him.[4] Honda Motor Company has been known to assemble innovation groups "from sales, engineering and development, and from different business units across North

4. Paul Morello. "11 Leadership Lessons We Can Learn from Tim Cook," *Lifehack*, n.d. Retrieved April 27, 2015, from http://www.lifehack.org/articles/productivity/11-leadership-lessons-can-learn-from-tim-cook.html.

America" in order to foster a culture of creativity. Similarly, General Electric involves "consumers and business clients in new-product discussions as well."[5] Leaders in these organizations, and companies like them, understand the importance of learning from people at every level, regardless of where they sit on the corporate ladder.

Learning from every level means you have to be open-minded to learning at every stage of your career. At the beginning of your career, it's crucial to make a point to study all you can about the organization you work for and the industry you're in. It's also important to develop an understanding of business and finance in general. Employees who emerged from school with undergraduate degrees in business or MBAs have a leg up in this department. To equalize the playing field in business, you have to read, you have to take classes, you have to attend industry-related seminars, you have to study, and you have to be open to learning—from every level and from a variety of sources.

95

INEQUALITY EQUALIZER

Junkyard dogs can keep up with pedigrees by educating themselves, reading the publications they read, and following the leaders they follow.

Aspiring employees at every level should be reading *The Wall Street Journal, The New York Times, USA Today, Harvard Business Review, Forbes,* and other leading business publications. Make a point to read the best-selling books that are

5. JC Spender and Bruce Strong. "Who Has Innovative Ideas? Employees," *The Wall Street Journal,* August 23, 2010. Retrieved April 27, 2015, from http://www.wsj.com/articles/SB10001424052748704100604575146083310500518.

coming out from today's business leaders (even if you just read the executive summary, at least understand the latest concepts that your boss or your boss's boss might be quoting). Subscribe to the top publications in your industry. Follow the blogs published by the professional associations you belong to. And don't forget to read your own company's website. Follow your organization on Twitter. Subscribe to your company's RSS feed and its newsletters. Read your company's annual reports. Whether you're reading all this material in print or online doesn't matter—but you do need to read beyond headlines and tweets and posts. The object isn't to be able to repeat headlines to your colleagues, it's to learn everything you can about your company and your industry.

READ AT EVERY LEVEL

When you move into a new position or to a new firm, it can be a challenge to juggle all the demands that come with that, especially when you're at the start of your career. You're trying to figure out your new boss, your new colleagues, your new company (and, perhaps trickiest of all, the new photocopier), and all the expectations that come along with that. It can be easy to get caught up in day-to-day demands, but it's important to keep educating yourself not only about your own company, but also about your industry and about business in general.

I advise new employees and new managers to spend their first ninety days reading some business classics and educating themselves on the art and science of management so that they can better maximize their own skills as well as the abilities of their teams. Here are some of the classics I recommend:

- *The Art of War* by Sun Tzu
- *Barbarians at the Gate* by Bryan Burrough and John Helyar
- *Crucial Conversations* by Kerry Patterson and Joseph Grenny

- *Den of Thieves* by James B. Stewart
- *The Essential Drucker* by Peter Drucker
- *Good to Great* by Jim Collins
- *In Search of Excellence* by Tom Peters and Frank Waterman
- *Liar's Poker* by Michael Lewis
- *The One Minute Manager* by Kenneth Blanchard and Stephen Johnson
- *The Predator's Ball* by Connie Bruck
- *The Seven Habits of Highly Effective People* by Stephen Covey
- *The Tipping Point* by Malcolm Gladwell

Of course, there are literally thousands of great business books out there, many of which have become classics in the field. This list represents just the tiniest portion. What's important, especially for younger employees, is to read those books that your managers read as they came up the corporate ladder. Find the business classics from the 1980s, 1990s, and early 2000s, and study them. Ask your manager what books he would recommend. This can be especially helpful for Millennials and Gen Zers trying to bridge the generational gap with their Baby Boomer and Gen X bosses. You'll very likely find that those books will provide some great insight into how your manager thinks, how he leads, and what he expects from his employees.

97

Learning from every level goes beyond educating yourself by reading, taking classes, or attending industry-related conferences, all of which is important. It also means you learn from your experiences. Every experience provides you with valuable information about your organization and your industry as well as about your peers and, if you're paying attention, about yourself. That's another reason why volunteering for key assignments such as cross-departmental teams is such a great opportunity: Working with others from various departments in your organization gives you a chance to learn about what's going on in other divisions, introduces you to key employees across the company, and provides you with insight into how various functions affect the bottom line. Working on team assignments also provides you with the opportunity to develop your skills as a leader and as a follower, depending on whatever role you're filling on the task.

After each assignment, assess what went well and what went wrong. Think carefully about where you excelled and where you fell flat. Where did you make the most important contribution? How did your contributions affect the overall outcome? In what ways did you lead well? What new skills did you learn?

Remember that managing in all directions means that you have to keep score. Remember, too, that no one else is going to do that for you. Your manager has a good sense of whether you're meeting your goals and performance measures, but he's not keeping track of every little achievement or every minor failure that provided you with some lessons learned. You have to do that. It's your job to make yourself look good.

I grew up thinking my job was to make my boss look good. I had a conversation with a male colleague at one point who told me that, in fact, my job was to make myself look good. But it's really both. There has to be some balance there: You have to make yourself and your boss look good. That, too, takes some learning.

As a rising star, your glow shines onto your boss, who likely is more than happy to take credit for hiring that crackerjack new staffer (that's you!). Everything you read, every assignment you take, every goal you pursue should help you propel your own career while making your boss look good. That's a key part of managing your career in all directions. Learning how to do this requires you to assess what your boss needs, what his management style is, and how you can help him meet his goals. It also requires some self-assessment, taking stock of where you can be indispensable, learning how to anticipate what your boss and your organization needs most, and what will help make them (and you) successful.

Learning in all directions means you have to study your company, your industry, your boss, and even yourself. You have to work continuously at your craft every single day. There's never a point at which you can stop developing yourself, no moment at which you've acquired all the skills you'll ever need, no point at which you should stop learning. You'll always need to keep learning.

Get Feedback from Those Around You

Just as you can learn from every level and lead in every direction, you should take the time to get feedback from everyone around you—your colleagues, your clients, your industry peers, and so on. Of course, you should be getting regular performance reviews—and those should be helpful to assess how you're doing—but getting feedback goes beyond ranking your performance from "exceeds expectations" to "needs improvement." What you really need is feedback from everyone in your sphere of influence.

Getting feedback from the people in your sphere of influence might well be likened to the popular 360-degree review. The 360-degree feedback tool popularized in the 1990s by the likes of General Electric (and which actually has been around since World War II) generally seeks qualitative and quantitative feedback from supervisors, peers, subordinates, and customers in such areas as leadership skills, strengths, and weaknesses. By the early 2000s, the 360-degree review, sometimes called "multirater feedback," was being used in about 90 percent of Fortune 500 companies.[6] Although some professionals and

---

6. Terri Linman. *360-Degree Feedback: Weighing the Pros and Cons*, n.d. Retrieved April 22, 2015, from http://edweb.sdsu.edu/people/arossett/pie/Interventions/360_1.htm.

academics question the efficacy of the 360-degree review, it's popularity can't be denied: "Multirater feedback has been translated into over sixteen languages; over five million managers and key staff members have received feedback regarding their leadership skills and behaviors through this method of feedback."[7]

Multirater feedback from all directions is important because leading in every direction is important. Of course it's important to impress the boss, but it's equally important to work well with peers and colleagues, clients and customers, and subordinates and support staff. That means you have to establish yourself as a leader who can work with everyone in the organization, regardless of tenure or status. It means you have the ability to create followership—nurturing relationships and getting results from people who want to work with you—execute your vision, and follow your lead. It means you can build successful, respectful alliances, working among various divisions and departments and building bridges across silos. It means you can build professional, working relationships with disparate groups and a variety of employees, even if you don't like them very much.

Getting feedback from every direction is a great learning tool. It allows you to learn how others perceive you, it allows you to see what your strengths and weaknesses are, and it helps you keep score of your accomplishments, all of which is crucial to managing your career. Whether you use some sort of multirater feedback form or other assessment tool, or whether you seek feedback in a more informal way, it can be helpful to ask colleagues, customers, and direct reports for insight into your performance.

Whether done formally or informally, asking for feedback shouldn't be undertaken lightly. Remember that you're essen-

---

7. Alice Katherine Corbin. *360-Degree Feedback*. May 10, 2012. Retrieved April 22, 2015, from http://papers.ssrn.com/sol3/Delivery.cfm/SSRN_ID2288194_code2082821.pdf?abstractid=2288194&mirid=2.

tially asking those in your sphere of influence for a favor, one that will benefit you but likely will take up a fair amount of time for the one doing the favor. Remember, too, that in asking for feedback, you might well learn that those in your sphere of influence view you in ways that could seem unfavorable. You might learn things about yourself that are uncomfortable. You'll gain some insight not only into your skills and proficiencies, but also into your weaknesses and deficiencies. This can be a hard pill to swallow. The best employees swallow that pill whole, digest it, and learn from it.

I am not saying it isn't painful—it is. In fact the first time I participated in this program, I went through all the five stages of grief. This was right before my "charm school trip," and I was in denial: They obviously gave me someone else's results! This cannot be me! Then I was angry. (Okay, I was pissed—to say it mildly.) Then I tried bargaining, and then I was depressed because I thought certain people did not like me, which I learned is a huge issue for me. Finally I accepted the feedback and realized I could work on all of it. And over the years, I did improve, and, most importantly, my leadership abilities improved as well.

101

INEQUALITY EQUALIZER

Regardless of tenure, gender, or pedigree, everyone can use a mentor who will give them honest feedback and helpful advice. Consider who in your sphere of influence might serve as a mentor, whether formally or informally, and set about developing that relationship.

The key in getting feedback is to use that insight as a learning tool that will help you develop professionally. Take note of your strengths and weaknesses and learn from them. Use the feedback to help you keep score. Use it to help you discover new ways to become a better leader and a better follower. Think of feedback as yet one more tool that will help you manage your career.

Remember here that it's important to get feedback that focuses on results, not so much on anecdotes or impressions. Your relationships matter, as does what people think of you, but the bottom line is really all about performance—regardless of gender, regardless of pedigree, regardless of where you are on the corporate ladder. So, just as the best managers manage based on results, so should you manage your career on results.

Manage Your Career

It's never too early to manage your career. In fact, it's crucial to strategize for every stage of your career, thinking carefully about where you want to be at certain points in your life.

It can be difficult to think so far into the future, but I encourage even entry-level employees to think about the job they want to retire from. Ask yourself how you'll get to that position from where you are now. What skills will you need to acquire (and perfect) in order to get there? As you climb higher and higher along the corporate ladder, more and more skills will be required of you. You need to continue to hone those skills, getting better and better at everything you do.

I advise young employees to think carefully about the first couple of jobs they'll have. When you're starting out, don't take a job just to take a job. It can be tempting, especially in difficult economic times, to take the first job that comes your way. Junkyard dogs can be especially prone to this temptation, often because they have to pay for student loans and because they aren't fielding the offers that come to many of the pedigrees who graduated from Ivy League schools. Sometimes they feel like they don't have the power of an Ivy League degree behind them to secure the best positions at the best companies. As a junkyard dog myself, I can understand the allure of a steady paycheck. It can be easy to tell yourself that it's just a job and that you can switch jobs at any point. But oftentimes one job suddenly leads to another and then to the next one after that, and soon enough you find yourself on a career track you didn't expect to be on. And when that happens, it can be difficult to jump off that track and get back to where you really wanted to go.

So, instead of just taking any job, think about not only what tasks will be involved in the position. Go for a title rather than just trying to get a foot in the door. Look at what kind of opportunities for growth there are and whether there is a career track that will help get you where you want to go. Unless you're getting a foot in the door at a Fortune 100 company where you can network with all the right people and schmooze your way up the corporate ladder, it's important to go for title, even if it's at a smaller organization.

That might seem counterintuitive. A lot of people think they should go for any job as long as it's at a leading organization, even if it means taking a job as a second assistant to a mid-level manager in a branch office in the boondocks. The problem with this thinking is that positions like this rarely have any room for advancement, and if they do, it's often on a track that isn't going to get you to the C Suite. If you have your heart set on becoming an executive in a leading corporation, you don't want to get on the track where the highest position you can attain is as the CFO's executive assistant. You want to be the CFO.

So, go for title. Titles will vary from company to company and from industry to industry, so you'll have to study what the key titles are in your field. Take the time to study the duties and responsibilities required for the positions you want to have during the course of your career. And, then, focus on getting the position with the right title for every point in your career. Even if that means starting out your career as a corporate associate attorney or an associate account executive or assistant human

103

resources specialist at a small business, that title will put you on track to attain the positions you ultimately want, whether in your current organization or somewhere else. If you need to obtain a job as soon as possible after graduating, and you do not have the right opportunity, consider temping at a corporate headquarters to get your foot in the door and to become known, or try to intern at a company prior to graduation.

As you aim for particular positions with the right titles, think also about the milestones your career should include. How should your career progress? What must you accomplish in each position in order to keep moving up? How long should you stay in each position? At what age should you be for each position?

When managing your career, think about where you want to be at certain points in your life. Knowing that "[i]n 2010, the average age of incoming CEOs at S&P 500 companies was 52.9, down from 54.7 in 2006,"[8] consider what that means for your own career path. If you want to be in the C Suite by the time you're in your early fifties, where do you need to be in your twenties, thirties, and forties?

You have to think about these things if you want to make it to the corner office. As I often tell people, hope is not a career strategy. You can't hope your way to the C Suite. You can't hope that your career will be everything you want it to be. You have to work for it. You have to make it happen. And in order to do that, you have to plan for it, managing your career through all the stages of your professional life.

As you can see, a lot goes into managing your career. You have to manage in all directions—up, down, and sideways— building professional relationships with everyone in your sphere of influence. You have to manage for results. You have to get feedback from those around you, and you have to learn

---

8. Spencer E. Ante and Joann S. Lublin. "Young CEOs: Are They Up to the Job?" *The Wall Street Journal*, February 7, 2012. Retrieved April 30, 2015, from http://www.wsj.com/articles/SB10001424052970203315804577207131063501196.

from the insight you glean from that feedback. In fact, you have to learn from people at every level, in every organization you work for, during the course of your entire career. Learning doesn't end when you make it to the C Suite. CEOs from organizations like Amazon, Google, Starbucks, and 3M know that some of the best ideas come from employees, and they make a point of learning from the people they work with, regardless of level or tenure.

Managing in all directions can be a balancing act. It requires you to be a good follower as well as a good leader. It requires you to study, to keep score, and to keep learning. In doing so, you'll learn much about yourself and your own leadership style, which is the subject of our next chapter.

Tough-Love Lessons for Managing Up, Down, and Sideways

- Regardless of tenure or position, junkyard dog or pedigree, male or female, every employee needs to manage up, down, and sideways, working with the colleagues, clients, direct reports, and managers in your sphere of influence.
- Throughout your career, you have to make your boss look good, anticipating his needs, understanding his leadership style, and carrying out his vision, all while keeping score of your own accomplishments and managing for results.
- Leading in every direction cannot be done well without good communication. Top employees make a point of asking what their teams and their managers need in order to do their jobs well, follow through with promises, and do what it takes to deliver results.
- Use a 360-degree or other multirater tool wisely. Accept and learn from the insight you receive from others, and be careful about how you provide feedback to your boss and key stakeholders. Always assume it is an open process and that nothing is secret.
- No one is ever done learning—at least not those who want to retire from the C Suite after a long and successful career. Regardless of experience, gender, or status, the best employees learn from every level of the organization, seeking insight from colleagues and clients, studying their industry, learning everything they can about business and finance, and assessing their own performance.

6

Making the Most of Leadership Opportunities

From: "Jena Abernathy" <jabernathy@email.com>

To: "Megan Watson" <mwatson@email.com>

Subject: Leadership Opportunities

Megan,

Congratulations on getting the team leader spot for the cross-divisional year-end project. This is a great opportunity for you to continue managing up, down, and sideways and to create followership. It's also a great time to think about your leadership style: Are you a transformational leader or a transactional leader? There are merits to both, and it's important to learn how to maximize your leadership style when you take on opportunities like this.

—Jena

In every company, in every department, and in every position you'll ever have, you'll need to perfect various leadership skills, whether you're in an entry-level position or in senior management. It doesn't matter whether you're a junkyard dog or a pedigree, male or female. How you manage as a leader (and lead as a manager) might well vary depending on the situation, the team you're working with, and the assignment or goals you're working to accomplish. Chances are that your leadership style will change and evolve from one situation to the next and as your career progresses. In the end, however, your success as a leader comes down to your own tenacity to complete every project and to succeed at reaching every goal. At question is how you'll go about doing that.

Leadership styles are in many ways as varied as leaders themselves. Affiliative, autocratic, bureaucratic, charismatic, coaching, commanding, cross-cultural, democratic, facilitative, innovative, laissez-faire, pace-setting, participative, servant, situational, visionary . . . terms for various leadership styles are practically innumerable. But in my experience, there are really only two basic styles: transformational and transactional.

Transformational leaders tend to look at the big picture. They're focused on the future. They're not skating toward the puck—they're skating to where the puck is going to go. Transformational leaders learn as much as they can about the industry they're in, and they work hard at determining where their organizations need to go in order to be industry leaders. They ensure that everyone in the organization is aligned with the mission and the vision and that their teams are adept at carrying out that vision and fulfilling that mission. Transformational leaders tend to be good at anticipating, at building morale, at encouraging collaboration, and at motivating employees.

Transactional leaders tend to focus on today, making sure that everyone is on task and doing what they're supposed to be doing. Transactional leaders are typically focused on the bottom line, rewarding their employees for achieving goals (and, often, punishing them for failing to meet goals). They frequently use incentives and promotions to motivate employees, and they work carefully within the cultural norms and expectations of their organizations. Transactional leaders are usually adept at tackling small issues quickly and handling them well, getting them out of the way so they can focus on larger goals.

Is one style better than the other? Not necessarily. Both have their strengths and weaknesses. The key is to recognize which type of leadership each situation calls for, which type of leadership your managers employ, and which type of leadership style you tend toward. It's essential to learn how to be flexible so that you can follow whichever type of leader you're working for at any given moment. Also important is to be able to recognize when one style might be preferable to the other, as well as how junkyard dogs and pedigrees alike can make the most of leadership opportunities.

Recognize Leadership Styles

When so many business gurus call various leadership styles by so many different names, it can be difficult to characterize leadership in any particular way that sticks. And even if you pick some terms that stick, it still can be difficult to recognize different leadership styles in the real world. Rarely does one person exhibit the singular traits of one type of leadership style in all situations. Rather, we all tend to find ways to get the job done, not necessarily thinking about which type of leadership style we need to engage in order to make things happen. We just do it.

That said, it is important to be able to recognize leadership styles, especially when it comes to the type of leadership style your manager typically employs, as well as which type of leadership style you tend toward yourself. Why is that important? Because in order to be a good follower, it helps if you can understand your leader. And if you can recognize the style your manager tends toward, you can better adapt yourself to being the kind of follower who can work well with that type of leader.

We talked a little bit above about some of the general differences between transformational leaders and transactional leaders. Countless studies have researched the issue of leadership, many of them focused on the differences between these two leadership styles. One definition argues that, for example, "transactional leadership is based on exchange; for example, in business, this is often financial rewards for productivity, whereas transformational leadership is a process of inspiring people to achieve shared goals through recognizing individuals' needs, stimulating creative thinking, and aligning values between individuals and groups."[1]

Whether these two leadership styles are in contrast to one another or are, rather, complementary to one another is something we'll leave to the pundits, academics, and researchers to debate. What's important isn't so much whether one is better than the other, but that you be able to recognize which style your manager is prone to. It's not always easy to figure out which type of leadership style your manager tends toward, but we can get an idea of which style he prefers by identifying some key characteristics.

Transformational leaders tend to be good communicators with strong interpersonal skills. They usually are both influential and inspirational. They also tend to be proactive risk takers who are open to new ideas. Although characteristics vary from one individual to the next, of course, and although researchers and leadership gurus all have their own take on the subject, transformational leaders tend to have a positive outlook and an open mind, and they have the ability to engender similar attributes in followers. Some studies argue that transforma-

---

1. Fred O. Walumbwa and Tara Wernsing. "From Transactional and Transformational Leadership to Authentic Leadership," in Michael G. Rumsey, *The Oxford Handbook of Leadership* (Oxford Library of Psychology). Oxford, England, and New York: Oxford University Press, 2013. Chapter 22, p. 393.

tional leaders demonstrate particular "patterns of behavior" that mark their leadership styles:

> First, transformational leadership employs the charisma of leaders in order to gain the respect and trust of stakeholders and to instill pride in the latter. In addition, charisma underlines the provision of a common vision and sense of mission necessary for the transformation. The second characteristic is inspiration through which leaders employ symbols to redirect followers' efforts; they express in a simplistic manner the fundamental purpose of the transformation process, and clearly communicate the accompanying higher expectations. The third characteristic is intellectual stimulation. Leaders intellectually stimulate employees by emphasizing rationality and creativity in problem-solving situations. Finally, transformational leadership offers individualized consideration: leaders treat employees individually offering them personal attention and, whenever necessary, they provide coaching and advice to those employees.[2]

Just as transformational leaders vary from one to another, so do transactional leaders. Similarly, though, some common characteristics are usually shared by transactional leaders. For instance, they tend to be practical and bottom-line oriented. They tend to be rule followers who prefer the status quo and who don't like change. Transactional leaders often consider themselves as keepers of the organization, meaning that they want to ensure that corporate culture is respected, that expectations are clearly set, and that instructions are promptly followed. They tend to recognize and reward performance that

111

2. Didier Cossin and Jose Caballero. *Transformational Leadership: Background Literature Review*. Lausanne, Switzerland: IMD, June 2013, p. 5. Retrieved May 6, 2015, from http://www.imd.org/uupload/IMD.WebSite/BoardCenter/Web/213/ Literature percent20Review_Transformational percent20Leadership.pdf.

exceeds expectations and punish performance that fails to meet expectations.

You might recognize all, some, or none of these traits in the people you report to, whether your manager, your team leader, or the C Suite executives who lead your organization. You might even recognize all of these characteristics in one person from one day to the next. Few of us can be categorized so neatly that we fit the same description every day under every circumstance and with every individual who works with or for us. That doesn't necessarily mean we're changeable and inconsistent leaders; it just means we're doing whatever it takes to get the job done. Depending on the situation, we might be innovative risk-takers one day and status quo-seeking bottom-line thinkers the next. Some people call this changing style "situational leadership theory," which argues that "effective leadership requires a rational understanding of the situation and an appropriate response, rather than a charismatic leader with a large group of dedicated followers."[3] What's important, however, is that you are able to recognize the leadership style your boss tends toward—even if he's a rule-following taskmaster one day when he's almost always an inspirational coach who lets you accomplish your goals in your own way.

This isn't always easy. In fact, one of the toughest things for new employees to learn (and perhaps one that too many forget as their careers progress) is that you work for your boss. Seems simple enough, right? But too many people think they're working for themselves, focused on their own goals and their own performance and what they're going to get out of their jobs. But the reality is that your boss very much holds the keys to your career, no matter where you are on the corporate ladder. It's crucial that you understand where he's coming from. In

---

3. Jim Allen McCleskey. "Situational, Transformational, and Transactional Leadership and Leadership Development," *Journal of Business Studies Quarterly*, 2014, Volume 5, Number 4, pp. 117–130. Retrieved May 11, 2015, from http://jbsq.org/wp-content/uploads/2014/06/June_2014_9.pdf.

fact, doing so—and doing it well—can be one of those things that sets you apart from the competition and levels the playing field.

———

INEQUALITY EQUALIZER

Study your manager's leadership style and find ways to adapt to it. Whether junkyard dog or pedigree, male or female, doing so will set you apart as an adept team player with keen insight who gets the job done.

———

Recognize Which Leadership Styles Fit Which Situations

As noted above, different people tend to employ different leadership styles for different situations, even if they frequently tend more toward one style or approach than another. Good leaders learn how to adapt their leadership style to the people who work for them, tweaking their approach as necessary based on their own work habits and levels of maturity—that is, leadership styles often vary depending on follower styles as well as on various situations, tasks, and goals. In fact, this kind of flexibility is crucial when it comes to growing a business: Some reports estimate that as much as 30 percent of a company's bottom-line profitability can be attributed to a manager's leadership style.[4] So let's consider a few examples so that we can

---

4. Robyn Benincasa. "6 Leadership Styles, and When You Should Use Them," *Fast-Company*, May 29, 2012. Retrieved May 11, 2015, from http://www.fastcompany.com/1838481/6-leadership-styles-and-when-you-should-use-them.

better learn how to recognize which leadership styles fit which situations.

Imagine you're part of a team tasked with issuing a quarterly financial report for your department, which will become part of the organization's overall annual report to stakeholders. The report has a hard deadline, and it must include key elements such as qualitative and quantitative financial information, details about controls and procedures, and related exhibits. Accuracy and timeliness are crucial when it comes to getting the report done. For an assignment like this, transactional leadership will be instrumental, and you might well see your manager doling out specific assignments to individual team members and establishing a precise schedule to which everyone must adhere in order to get the job done, perfectly and on time.

In another example, imagine you've been tasked to work with two or three colleagues to develop a list of potential new clients in new areas for your organization in order to expand sales opportunities for a key product line. Your manager has asked you to brainstorm some ideas, conduct some research, and talk with existing clients in order to develop new leads. She's asked you and your colleagues to prepare a presentation that addresses these new opportunities and explains how they will grow the business. After discussing the assignment with you, she's asked how long you think you'll need to get the job done and what resources you'll need to get it done in a timely manner.

Here we see an example of transformational leadership. A situation like this is more focused on vision and creativity and has a looser schedule. It's more qualitative than quantitative, and the manager is willing to let the team do whatever it takes to get the job done. Rather than assigning specific tasks and setting firm deadlines, the manager allows the team to establish those boundaries themselves.

Different leadership styles for different situations and for different teams. Recognizing these different approaches can help you adjust your own style to the situation at hand. And, learning how to handle each role will help you not only define your own leadership role, but also determine where your strengths and interests lie. You might find you respond well to clearly defined tasks and firm deadlines. Or, you might find that you prefer less structure.

Of course, where some people see less structure as an opportunity to spread their wings, some people see just enough rope to hang themselves. It all depends on the person. For instance, at one point in my career, I was tasked with leading a team that had been charged with restructuring the entire company. This called for some serious transformational leadership—setting a vision and getting the team on board so they would be willing to follow the plan to achieve our goals. It also required some serious creativity and risk taking.

In setting out to restructure the company, I first considered other organizations that had done this—and had done it well. I came up with the NFL, where, every year, each team essentially restructures itself with the draft, with training camps, and with trades throughout the season. I decided to adopt that model for my own company.

115

In order to restructure our organization, we decided to start at the top, picking the leadership team that would run the entire company. Then the executive team picked their leaders. Once we had those leaders in place, we pulled them all together and devised a whole process whereby these leaders would pick new players for their teams through playbooks that we had created which contained backgrounds, histories, and résumés of all our candidates. These team leaders knew everything about the potential players, and they got so many points to use for the costs associated with hiring those players (e.g., relocation, salary, bonus). They each had a budget to work with, and they could trade players amongst themselves. Everyone could always see who was still available.

The night before we launched this unorthodox and unprecedented process, I told my team that there could be only one of two outcomes: either it would fail and I would be fired, or it would succeed and I would be promoted. I knew there was nothing in between these two options. This new process we were using to restructure our organization was a huge risk. I knew that if I got any pushback or if I didn't get full buy-in from the executive team that I would be fired.

Thankfully, it worked! Restructured with new leaders and new players, the company went on to achieve record earnings over the next couple years.

I recognized with the assignment that some transformational leadership was required, especially for something that was both such a huge opportunity and such a huge risk. I didn't see any other option, and I had to take it, even though I knew that success or failure could make or break my career. But because I understood what kind of leadership the situation called for, I was prepared to guide my team toward a successful outcome. And, of course, I recognized the situation as a great opportunity to prove myself as a leader.

Recognize Leadership Opportunities

When we think of leadership, we often think about how managers lead—that is, how our bosses lead. But the truth is that leaders can—and should—live in every corner of the organization. They exist at every level. Leaders aren't necessarily managers (although managers need to be good leaders). Rather, leaders are those who take the reins on any given assignment or in any situation. As such, there are leadership opportunities in most organizations for every employee, male or female, junkyard dog or pedigree.

No matter where you are in your career, it's important to recognize leadership opportunities when they present themselves. We talked about opportunities and risks in Chapter 4, but it bears repeating that no one gets ahead without taking a risk now and again. Whether you view something as an opportunity or risk depends much on your mindset, but whatever you call it, it's important to learn how to recognize leadership opportunities (and to make them, not just take them).

Whenever you're assigned to work with a team on a given task, whenever you're called on to make a presentation, whenever you're asked to shepherd a new employee, you have an opportunity to be a leader. Even in being a good follower, you can demonstrate to colleagues your leadership ability, particularly if you can help them see what it takes to fulfill your boss's vision—and lead the way in doing so.

Leadership opportunities usually don't fall into your office with a thud. Instead, they tend to creep in slowly. For instance, in learning how your boss operates, you can start to demonstrate some leadership acumen. If your boss likes data, then bring him data. Think about not only what he says he needs, but what else might help him get his job done. Anticipate his needs, and in doing so, you're demonstrating that you're a good follower who also very likely has what it takes to be a good leader who can be flexible enough to tap into his more transactional style by being the kind of transformational leader who looks ahead.

Studying your manager and determining what is important to him is a great way not only to learn about his leadership style but also to discern what is important to him and to your organization. Even if—and perhaps particularly if—you're several rungs down the corporate ladder, it's never a bad idea to learn how to anticipate what your manager needs and how he likes to receive information. It's never too early to start thinking and acting like a leader. When it comes to becoming a leader, "[t]he key is to take on opportunities now, regardless of your tenure or role."[5]

Of course, taking on opportunities extends beyond working directly with your boss. As *Harvard Business Review* notes, it's also important to "[r]aise your hand for new initiatives, espe-

---

5. Amy Gallo. "Act Like a Leader Before You Are One," *Harvard Business Review*, May 20, 2013. Retrieved May 11, 2015, from https://hbr.org/2013/05/act-like-a-leader-before-you-a.

cially ones that might be visible to those outside your unit. . . .
It doesn't have to be an intense, months-long project. It might
be something as simple as facilitating a meeting, offering to
help with recruiting events, or stepping in to negotiate a conflict
between peers."[6]

Similarly, leadership opportunities can come outside of
work. Organizations you volunteer for, community events you
help coordinate, church functions you help facilitate, and so
on offer any number of situations where you can take on leadership responsibilities. The key is to be the one who not only
creates followership, as we discussed in Chapter 5, but who is
able to solve those problems that others can't (or won't or don't
want to) take on.

Whatever opportunities you pursue, give yourself a chance
to become a well-rounded leader. If you tend toward transactional leadership, challenge yourself by undertaking a role
that will allow you the opportunity to test your abilities to
be a more transformational leader. If you're a pedigree who
tends to work with teams comprised of other pedigrees, look
for opportunities to work alongside some junkyard dogs. If you
tend toward support roles, take on an assignment that gives
you some P&L responsibility. Of course, you'll want to be careful to avoid stepping so outside your comfort zone that you set
yourself up for failure. But you shouldn't shy away from risks
that test your mettle in new ways.

LEADERSHIP AND GENDER

Few would dispute the leadership gap that exists between men and
women. Despite the fact that women make up about 51 percent of
the population and earn 60 percent of all master's degrees, they
hold less than 17 percent of Fortune 500 board seats and make

---

6. *Ibid.*

up only "14.6 percent of executive officers, 8.1 percent of top earners, and 4.6 percent of Fortune 500 CEOs."[7] Those are some hard numbers to quarrel with.

Numerous studies and countless anecdotes seek to explain why the leadership-and-gender gap exists. Some studies look at the effectiveness of female leaders (e.g., "at every level, more women were rated by their peers, their bosses, their direct reports, and their other associates as better overall leaders than their male counterparts"[8]) while some have examined a variety of possible reasons behind the dearth of women in executive positions.[9]

Despite all the studies and conjecture and debate, the fact is that the question is not one that will be resolved anytime soon. So what does that mean for women in the workplace, particularly for women who want a spot in the C Suite? In short, it means you have to decide what you really want—and you have to decide what it's worth to get it.

As we discussed in Chapter 3, few people—male or female—make it to the top of the corporate ladder without strategizing their career, from start to finish. If you want a spot in the C Suite, you have to work for it. You have to want it, claim it, and own it, from your entry-level gig all the way up to the position you hope to retire from.

Some studies have shown that women simply don't want C Suite positions as much as men do. By one measure, 69 percent of women desire to advance to the next level in their organizations,

7. Judith Warner. "Fact Sheet: The Women's Leadership Gap—Women's Leadership by the Numbers," *Center for American Progress*, March 7, 2014. Retrieved May 12, 2015, from https://www.americanprogress.org/issues/women/report/2014/03/07/85457/fact-sheet-the-womens-leadership-gap.

8. Jack Zenger and Joseph Folkman. "Are Women Better Leaders Than Men?" *Harvard Business Review*, March 15, 2012. Retrieved May 12, 2015, from https://hbr.org/2012/03/a-study-in-leadership-women-do.

9. See, for example, Robin J. Ely, Pamela Stone, and Colleen Ammerman. "Rethink What You 'Know' About High-Achieving Women," *Harvard Business Review*, December 2014. Retrieved May 12, 2015, from https://hbr.org/2014/12/rethink-what-you-know-about-high-achieving-women.

yet only 18 percent desire a seat in the C Suite.[10] But what if you do want that seat in the suite?

You have to work on developing good followership and leadership skills. You have to understand the business of business. You have to seek out opportunities and take calculated risks. You have to gain the skills to do what it takes, and then you have to believe that you do, in fact, have what it takes to get to the top.

Although society and business are changing, it's up to you to climb the corporate ladder. Some might argue that, "companies need to move beyond regarding flextime and other 'family-friendly' policies as sufficient for retaining and developing high-potential women. Women *are* leaning in. Most women who have achieved top management positions have done so while managing family responsibilities—and, like their male counterparts, while working long hours. Women want *more* meaningful work, *more* challenging assignments, and *more* opportunities for career growth."[11] But the fact remains that no one can count on companies adjusting to meet women where they want to be. Instead, women who want to make it to the top have to lead themselves up the corporate ladder. Remember that you are the leader of your own career.

Develop Your Leadership Style

Just as it's important to recognize (and take) leadership opportunities and to understand the various leadership styles of the managers you will have to follow during the course of your career, so is it important to develop your own leadership style.

Which leadership style do you tend toward? Studies have shown that while men are more likely to adopt a transactional

10. Bob Sherwin. "Why Women Vanish as They Move Up the Career Ladder," *Business Insider*, January 27, 2014. Retrieved May 12, 2015, from http://www.businessinsider.com/women-and-career-advancement-leadership-2014-1.

11. Ely, Stone, & Ammerman. "Rethink What You 'Know' About High-Achieving Women."

leadership style, women tend to assume a transformational leadership style. This means that women naturally work at building consensus and encouraging teamwork, which can go a long way in getting effective, long-term, sustained results. That doesn't mean that transactional leadership can't be useful, particularly in the short term, but it does mean that women have a natural tendency to employ an effective leadership style.

Similarly, pedigrees tend toward transformational leadership while junkyard dogs tend to be transactional leaders. This often is a result of education: pedigrees who attend college prep schools, earn their degrees at Ivy League schools, and then continue on to get their MBAs come up in a world that is focused on creating vision, long-term planning, and big-picture thinking. Junkyard dogs who come up through the School of Hard Knocks often learn leadership through the lens of short-term goals, bottom-line thinking, and following the rules.

As we've mentioned, one style isn't necessarily better than the other; different situations call for different approaches. What's important is knowing when to use each approach and knowing how to develop the leadership style that will help you most in your career.

Developing your leadership style and perfecting leadership skills isn't always easy. If it were, Amazon wouldn't offer nearly 25,000 books on the subject. Just about every thought leader, pundit, scholar, and guru has his or her own take on what makes for good leadership. But there are some elements that most people would agree are common to effective leaders.

For starters, good leaders understand their industry, their organization, and their department, and they understand how they all work together. Before you can even hope to fulfill a mission or carry out a vision, you have to have a basic understanding of how all the cogs in the wheels work together to keep everything in motion. I've said it before, and I'll say it again: You have to keep educating yourself if you want your career to grow.

It's also crucial to understand the culture of your organization and of your division, and to understand your manager's leadership style, as noted above. Employees who really know what makes their offices and their managers tick can be better followers, and good followers often make the best leaders. Getting a handle on the fundamentals of your organization as well as understanding the culture of your organization are two critical steps when it comes to developing your leadership acumen. If you don't get these two things right, there's little chance you'll be able to build a solid foundation on which to grow your career.

Just as it's important to understand what's going on around you, it's crucial to understand yourself. A lot of employees miss this important step when it comes to professional growth. They spend so much time trying to figure out everyone and everything else that they forget to focus on themselves. But it's absolutely imperative that you understand how you work best and how you go about accomplishing your goals.

So think about it: Do you demand compliance from those you work with? Do you create bonds and build consensus? Do you value self-direction? Do you thrive when helping others reach their potential?

There is any number of self-evaluation tools and quizzes available that can help you identify and develop your leadership style.[12] These tools can help you determine which leadership style you tend toward. Of course, that's only a first step in the process of developing your leadership acumen. You have to work on building those skills that will help you know which leadership style to use for any given situation. You'll also have to learn how to recognize the styles of those around you so that you can lead them in the ways that will help them reach their full potential and help you and your organization reach its goals. And you have to determine your strengths and weaknesses.

12. See, for example, http://www.yourleadershiplegacy.com/assessment.html, http://www.teamtechnology.co.uk/personality/test/mmdi, http://psychology.about.com/library/quiz/bl-leadershipquiz.htm, and http://www.sagepub.com/northouseintro2e/study/resources/questionnaires/89527_03q.pdf.

Determining your strengths and weaknesses—and then committing yourself to work on areas that need improvement—is an important part of the process when it comes to being a good leader. For many of us (and perhaps especially for us junkyard dogs), the skills associated with being a transactional leader are inherent. As junkyard dogs, many of us came up painfully aware of the need to make budget, to ensure cost savings, to do more with less. Many of us learned how important it was to play by the rules, and many of us strived hard to fit in. As such, many junkyard dogs will find that they need to work on developing the skills associated with transformational leadership.

On the flip side, many pedigrees came up in a world where money wasn't an issue, and so it can be a challenge to embrace the kind of bottom-line thinking that characterizes so many transactional leaders. Pedigrees often are rewarded for breaking the rules and taking chances, both characteristics of transformational leadership. As such, many pedigrees will find that they need to work on developing the skills associated with transactional leadership.

INEQUALITY EQUALIZER

Learn how to play chess. This thoughtful game will help you develop skills that allow you to become better at strategizing, at seeing the big picture, and at anticipating your competitor's next move—all of which will help you in business.

Regardless of which style you tend toward, for whatever reason, it's important to know when to use which style. This is very much an important key to success. In fact, "research indicates that leaders with the best results do not rely on only one leadership style; they use most of them in a given week—

seamlessly and in different measure—depending on the business situation."[13]

Of course, leaders with the best results also understand what makes business tick—and not just their business, but their competition's business, their industry, and business in general. We'll look at the importance of understanding the business of business next, in Chapter 7.

13. Daniel Goleman. "Leadership That Gets Results," *Harvard Business Review*, March–April 2000. Retrieved May 12, 2015, from https://hbr.org/2000/03/leadership-that-gets-results.

Tough-Love Lessons for Making the Most of Leadership Opportunities

- Top employees understand the importance of being able to recognize the leadership styles of their managers. Doing so allows them to be better followers, which makes both their bosses and themselves look good. It also helps them become better leaders themselves.
- The best employees learn how to recognize which leadership styles fit which situations, and they learn how to adapt their approaches to each situation. Whether a transformational approach is needed, or whether a more transactional style will suit the situation, employees who make it to the top are able to recognize what's needed and to employ the right approach for the right job.
- Being able to recognize leadership styles and when to use whichever style is important, but it won't do much good if you're also not able to recognize a leadership opportunity when you see one. The best employees see leadership opportunities in just about any situation, whether at the office, at a volunteer gig, at church, etc. Whether junkyard dog or pedigree, it's important to take those chances that will allow you to develop your leadership skills.
- Developing leadership skills is an ongoing process for any employee, whether male or female, junkyard dog or pedigree, and no matter where you are on the career ladder. The best leaders identify their strengths and weaknesses and work on developing both, paying special attention to those skills that will help them grow as well-rounded leaders.

= 7 =

Knowing the Business of Business

From: "Jena Abernathy" <jabernathy@email.com>

To: "Megan Watson" <mwatson@email.com>

Subject: Understanding Business

Megan,

As you continue to make the most of new leadership opportunities, it's also important to make sure that you learn from these experiences, understanding what makes your team tick, what makes your department tick, and what makes the company tick. It's important to know where the organization fits in among our competitors, too. One of the best ways to level the playing field is to understand the business of business. That means it's time for some homework.

—Jena

"The business of business is business."

This famous dictum, alternately attributed to University of Chicago economist Milton Friedman and to Alfred P. Sloan, the long-time president and CEO of General Motors, remains as relevant today (and as controversial) as it was decades ago. While pundits and gurus argue whether the business of business today is still business or whether it is corporate responsibility or social responsibility or global accountability or continual improvement or whatever, the truth of the matter is that business is still at the core of business.

What does that mean? Well, Friedman wrote nearly five decades ago that,

> In a free-enterprise, private-property system, a corporate executive is an employee of the owners of the business. He has direct responsibility to his employers. That responsibility is to conduct the business in accordance with their desires, which generally will be to make as much money as possible while conforming to the basic rules of the society, both those embodied in law and those embodied in ethical custom.[1]

More recently, the editorial board of *The Washington Post* opined that, "even though the world has changed, earning a profit by getting excellent goods to customers at the lowest possible cost remains the central purpose of business."[2]

There's a lot of lofty talk around what business is actually about and what it should be about. But when it comes to

---

1. Milton Friedman. "The Social Responsibility of Business Is to Increase Its Profits," *The New York Times Magazine*. September 13, 1970. Retrieved May 21, 2015, from http://www.colorado.edu/studentgroups/libertarians/issues/friedman-soc-resp-business.html.
2. "The Business of Business," *The Washington Post*, June 26, 2006. Retrieved May 21, 2015, from http://www.washingtonpost.com/wp-dyn/content/article/2006/06/25/AR2006062500687.html.

the business of managing your career, I would advise you to think of the business of business as understanding what makes business tick—that is, what makes your business tick, your industry tick, and your competition tick. It means you have to understand mission and margins, Wall Street and Main Street. It means you have to understand market share, service lines, product offerings, and customers. You have to have a handle on what drives stakeholder value for your organization. You have to understand where your organization fits in its industry, and where you fit in your organization. You have to understand how your company achieves its bottom-line objectives, and what your effect is on that bottom line.

These fundamentals get to the business of business—and they have nothing to do with gender or pedigree or tenure. When it comes to your career, the business of business has everything to do with knowledge and understanding and your ability to articulate that comprehension. This means you have to do your homework, you have to keep educating yourself, and you have to be prepared to knowledgeably discuss what makes business tick, what makes your particular business tick, and what your role is in making all of that happen.

Understand Business

They say that you can't manage what you can't measure. I'd like to add to that that you can't even begin to fulfill your organization's mission if you don't understand your organization's margins.

For those of us who come to the world of business without degrees in finance or accounting or without MBAs, understanding the business of business has to be a key priority. It's crucial to educate yourself about the business of business if you want to claim a seat in the C Suite. Whether you attend an Ivy League university or the School of Hard Knocks, understanding what makes business tick is a surefire way to level the playing field.

=====

INEQUALITY EQUALIZER

Educating yourself should be a lifelong pursuit of knowledge—but that doesn't necessarily mean you have to have an advanced degree. Obtain professional development credits, earn certifications relevant to your field, and work toward pertinent professional licensures.

=====

You'd be right to guess that, as a junkyard dog, much of my education was gained in the School of Hard Knocks. I made it a point to learn from every job I ever had, from my first retail gig in a clothing store, where I learned about sales, customer service, margins, and discounts, to an early job in a bank, where I learned about the costs associated with personnel, about resource management, and about cost savings and efficiency.

As I progressed in my career, I made it a point to understand key business fundamentals like cash flow and earnings before interest, taxes, depreciation, and amortization (EBITDA); how to read a P&L; how to compute basic business statistics; how to follow other basic finance and accounting measures; and how to measure risk. Studying these issues—in general and in relation to my field—helped me understand the business issues that affected the economy, my industry, and my organization.

Junkyard dogs like me often don't have easy access to that kind of information. We typically have to seek it out on our own. But just because it takes a little work to educate yourself doesn't mean you shouldn't do it. It's not rocket science—it's business. Don't not educate yourself because you're intimidated or because you're afraid you won't understand it. You can't be afraid to learn. Education is the key to leveling the playing field. It's the great inequality equalizer.

STUDY THE FUNDAMENTALS OF BUSINESS

With the high cost of education, there's been a lot of talk of late about whether getting an MBA or other advanced degree is worth it—that is, whether the return on investment is there. That's a good question, and likely one that will be debated for years to come. If you can afford to attend an executive MBA program (at an accredited university) at night and on the weekends, I would encourage you to do so (especially if your employer will foot part of the bill). But that's not always a viable option.

That does not mean, however, that you can forgo an education. If you want to level the playing field—especially if you're a junkyard dog—it's absolutely crucial that you educate yourself as to the fundamentals of business. Read some classic business books. Subscribe to the leading business publications. Take free online business courses. Complete a certificate program at your local community college. However you do it, you have to study business if you want to understand business. You can't hope that you'll learn by osmosis, simply soaking up helpful tidbits of information here and there.

Where to start? With the basics. Study the fundamentals of corporate strategy, finance and accounting, marketing and publicity, risk management, and sales management. Dig a little deeper to learn about issues related to corporate governance, macro and microeconomics, mergers and acquisitions, operations management, and venture capital.

If you have a financial background, focus first on the more creative side of business by studying the fundamentals of marketing. Same thing goes the other way around: If your job is a creative one, bone-up on finance. Similarly, if you work in the nonprofit field, study the for-profit sector, and vice versa. If you work in government, study NGOs.

No one makes it to the C Suite without understanding how the margins affect the bottom line and developing a strong financial acumen. It's up to you to educate yourself so that you understand the business of business. How you go about getting that education is less important than actually getting it. Remember that it's not so much about where you go to school or where you get your degree but about what you know and how well you can translate that knowledge into real-world practice. As Pulitzer Prize-winning author Thomas L. Friedman has written, "Your degree is not a proxy for your ability to do any job. The world only cares about—and pays off on—what you can do with what you know (and it doesn't care how you learned it)."[3]

Understand Your Business

So often, we get completely caught up in our day-to-day duties. We handle the tasks that are assigned to us. We focus on what's coming across our desks. We look at what's happening in our department. Heck, it's enough just to keep up with e-mail and voice mail and social media. As a result, we all too often fail to focus more broadly on how the work we do actually affects the business we're in. We don't think about business in general. And, more often than not, we don't actually think about our own particular business at all.

Business is so much bigger than your desk in your office in your corner of the building on the floor where you work. It's important to look more broadly, to consider not just what your department is doing but also how that fits in with your

---

3. Thomas L. Friedman. "How to Get a Job at Google," *The New York Times*, February 22, 2014. Retrieved May 21, 2015, from http://www.nytimes.com/2014/02/23/opinion/sunday/friedman-how-to-get-a-job-at-google.html?_r=0.

organization's overall mission. You also need to understand how your organization affects your industry. And you have to understand your industry in general.

What new service lines or product offerings are under discussion in your organization? What's your market share? What's your competitors' market share? Who's best in class in your industry? How does your organization stack up? What regulations and reforms are affecting your organization and your industry?

I didn't necessarily know back at the start of my career where to find information about retail or banking or health care. So I immersed myself in my industry. I learned everything I could about my business. I didn't grow up in a family that was discussing stocks and investments over the dinner table every night; we were eating macaroni and cheese and wondering how we were going to pay for the car insurance. But I leveled the playing field by educating myself. I rode with sales reps, I sat in on client calls, I shadowed tenured professionals to learn from their experience. I created my own orientation program to learn from our closest customers and clients. I understood that I couldn't contribute to the business unless—and until—I really understood the business.

133

Understanding the business you work for, whether it's a for-profit or a nonprofit, begins before you even get the job. The best employees—and the best prospective employees—do their homework before their first day at work (and, even better, as soon as they learn they're going to have an interview). They research everything they can to learn about the company and its vision and mission, what its strategy is, what its primary line of business is, what its leading service or product is, what acquisitions it has undertaken, who its main competitors are, what its bottom line looks like, and so on.

That research shouldn't stop when you get your customized nameplate hung on the outside wall of your new cubicle. Just as it's important to understand the business of business, you really have to know what makes your specific company tick.

Where do you get that information? If your company is public, read its annual report and other public financial documents, such as 8K, 10K, 10Q, or 20F filings (and if you don't know what those are, look it up!). Sit in on quarterly earnings calls with the CEO. Read your company's press releases. Frequently browse your company's website, which will provide some insight into what your corporate leaders think is most important. Attend every lunch-and-learn session you can, even if it might not directly pertain to your department or your specific position. Set up Google alerts for your company (and for your competition) so you can learn about what's happening with your organization and how it's being portrayed in the media. Follow your company on social media, whether Facebook or LinkedIn or Twitter. Read all the white papers published by your company's leaders.

The ways in which you can educate yourself about your own organization are limitless. But you have to actually take the time to educate yourself. This is easier said than done, so you have to make it a priority. Whether it's thirty minutes at the end of the day every Friday or an hour one night a week or a couple hours every weekend, if you want to understand what makes your business tick, you have to study it.

Understanding your organization is crucial, but you also have to be able to put it in context. How does your company stack up to the competition? Where does it fit in your industry? What best practices are your competitors employing that you could adapt for your own organization? Which of their mistakes can you learn from? What changes are your competitors making in light of industry trends, new regulations, or other reforms?

You can use many of the same tools and approaches to research the competition as you would for studying your own organization. In addition, make it a point to attend industry-related conferences where you can learn about the issues and trends that leaders in your field are concerned about. Talk to your clients, customers, and suppliers about how they view your organization in light of the competition. Subscribe to industry-specific journals. Follow the blogs of subject-matter experts and thought leaders in your field.

It's important to think about your business, and it's important to be proactive about it. Make it a point to learn about what's going on in your industry, regardless of where you sit on the corporate ladder. Make a point, too, to keep studying your organization and your industry—because neither is static. Business is always changing and evolving. Because of that, researching your organization and your competitors' organizations isn't a one-time thing you do so you can check it off your to-do list. In order to fully understand your own business, you have to keep studying. If you really want to understand your business, your industry, and your competition, "[c]onducting a competitive assessment should be an ongoing process, one in which you continue to deepen your understanding of the strengths and weaknesses of your competitors."[4]

135

INEQUALITY EQUALIZER

Be prepared for every meeting and for every assignment. When you've done your homework—and done it well—you will gain a thorough understanding of your business, your industry, and your own role and responsibilities. Consider what it will take to meet your goals and objectives and how doing so will help your department in particular and your organization as a whole fulfill its mission.

4. "How to Conduct Competitive Research," *Inc. Magazine*, May 10, 2010. Retrieved May 21, 2015, from http://www.inc.com/guides/2010/05/conducting-competitive -research.html.

When you understand the strengths and weaknesses of your competitors and of your own organization, and when you understand which trends and issues are of most concern to leadership, you are privy to important—and useful—information. Not only that, but that understanding separates you from your colleagues, most of whom likely haven't done much research into the company you all work for or the industry you all work in. In fact, by some measures, for example, only 14 percent of employees have a solid understanding of their company's strategy.[5] That's not cool—and there's really no excuse for it.

You want to be one of those 14 percent who understand their company's strategy—and their company's financials. Remember that knowledge is power. When you're sitting in a meeting and you've taken the time to do your homework ahead of time, it will quickly become clear to your colleagues that you're prepared and that you know what you're talking about. Because of that, people will listen to you. When people listen to you, your power and prestige will grow. And that has nothing to do with gender or pedigree or tenure. Preparation is a great equalizer.

UNDERSTAND THE BUSINESS CULTURE

Every organization has its own culture. This business culture (sometimes called "company culture," "corporate culture," or "organizational culture") goes beyond the organization's finances or strategy to the vision, values, and activities of the people who carry out the organization's mission. Corporate culture also includes everything from the dress code to the jargon to the behavior that employees

5. David Witt. "Only 14 percent of Employees Understand Their Company's Strategy and Direction," *Blanchard LeaderChat*, May 21, 2012. Retrieved May 21, 2015, from http://leaderchat.org/2012/05/21/only-14-of-employees-understand-their-companys-strategy-and-direction.

engage in. We'll talk about this at length in Chapter 8, but let's stick our toes in for a minute here.

Rarely is company culture defined outright or in writing; rather, it's often something more abstract, and usually something discerned over time. But that doesn't make it any less important. In fact, by some measures, "culture can account for 20–30 percent of the differential in corporate performance."[6]

Most of us spend a good part of our careers trying to fit into—or at least figure out—our organization's culture. (And by "culture," I'm not talking "politics," which is a whole other subject.) Understanding this aspect of business is in many ways no less important than understanding the business of business itself.

Regardless of gender or pedigree or tenure, feeling like you don't fit into an organization—despite the fact that you know you can do the job—can be absolute hell. It's best to try to get a handle on your organization's—and your department's—culture as quickly as possible. This means paying attention to things like dress code, work ethic, and communication styles. It means watching the behavior of those you work with, looking at everything from whether they celebrate colleagues' birthdays and what kinds of jokes they tell to what values they articulate and how they carry them out and what symbols or narratives they use to tell the company's story.

At a time when record numbers of employees are dissatisfied with their jobs, a good portion of that dissatisfaction can be attributed to culture. When we don't fit in, we're not happy. And when we're not happy, we're not productive.

So, getting a handle on the culture of your business is crucial as you climb the corporate ladder, regardless of whether you spend your entire career in one organization or move to other companies (of course, industries have their own cultures, too, so it's important to study culture at that level as well).

6. Diedre H. Campbell. "What Great Companies Know About Culture," *Harvard Business Review*, December 14, 2011. Retrieved May 21, 2015, from https://hbr.org/2011/12/what-great-companies-know-abou. See also: James Heskett. *The Culture Cycle: How to Shape the Unseen Force That Transforms Performance*. Upper Saddle River, NJ: FT Press, 2012.

How do you go about studying culture? Follow your organization on social media and look at not only what is said but how it's said. Use the Internet to find out what customers, clients, suppliers, and former employees are saying about your organization. Observe how your colleagues interact with one another and how they interact with fellow employees across all levels of the organization. Avoid playing politics, which all too often is based on gossip, rumor, and innuendo, and instead study the behaviors, customs, jargon, lingo, mottoes, sayings, slogans, and symbols used by the people in your organization.

Understand Your Own Role

How well you understand your industry, your own business, and business in general matters little if you don't understand where you fit in all of that. If you're not certain how you and your job keep your company moving forward, it's nearly impossible to do your job well or to stay motivated and productive in doing it.

Oddly enough, most of us pay little attention to how our particular positions affect our companies. We might have a pretty good appreciation of how our jobs affect our departments, but few of us really think about where we fit in the overall organization. This is shameful for a few reasons, not least of which is that it's important for the bottom line and because it's important for morale.

Not many of us would be happy toiling away in a job that we don't understand. It's not much fun to work eight or nine or ten hours a day at a job without understanding why the work we do is important, how it affects our department, or what it means for the bottom line. It can be pretty demoralizing to think that we're just a cog in a wheel, slaving at tasks that don't really matter.

Understanding your own role in your organization in general and, more broadly, in your industry can help you on your march toward the C Suite in any number of ways. For example, job clarity—that is, what tasks and assignments you're expected to accomplish, what performance measures you're expected to achieve, and how those tasks, assignments, and performance measures are connected to the broader goals and mission of the organization—goes a long way in improving employee engagement and productivity. In fact, by some measures, job clarity is crucial when it comes to employee engagement: "Highly engaged employees respond 96 percent favorable to the question, 'I have a very clear idea of my job responsibilities.'"[7]

How do you get the kind of job clarity that will help you to be more engaged and more productive? You ask for it.

The first step is to get a copy of your job description—not the description that was in the employment ad you responded to, but the organization's description of the responsibilities, performance measures, and goals of your position. (You can usually get this from your manager or from your organization's HR department.) Ask for the organizational charts of your department, your division, and your entire organization so you can see where exactly you fit. Make sure you understand the criteria by which you'll be reviewed, as well as any requirements for bonus or incentive programs. Understand, too, that not all of your responsibilities will be listed in the job description. That catch-all phrase "and all other duties as assigned" can mean just about anything. The more flexible you are, the better. The key is to understand expectations.

This is another reason why it's so important to have a conversation with your manager, discussing exactly what she expects of you, how she expects you to go about fulfilling your assignments, and how she views your role in light of the entire department.

---

7. "8 Tips to Engage Your Employees," *TNS Employee Insights: Measuring and Inspiring Higher Performance*, June 2014. Retrieved May 21, 2015, from http://qualtrics.com/wp-content/uploads/2014/06/TNS_2703-14_ManagerTipsBook_EMAIL.pdf.

We talked a little in Chapter 5 about the importance of communicating with your manager, and this is exactly one of those times to have one of those crucial conversations. Don't be afraid to ask your boss—shortly after you're hired and periodically thereafter—what her expectations are of you and of the position you're in. Explain to her that you want to make both a qualitative and a quantitative difference to the company, and ask what you can do to achieve that. Ask her for recommendations as to where you and your department can generate more revenue and make cost savings. Discuss with her the financial impact you can make. Have a conversation about how you can have a positive effect on your department's bottom line.

Come to this conversation armed with the information you gathered during your research into your company and your industry. Make it clear to your manager that you understand your business and the business of business. Chances are she'll appreciate your initiative and will view you as a highly engaged employee, which helps level the playing field.

MAKE IT YOUR BUSINESS

Knowing the business of business, understanding the organization you work for, and understanding how you fit into your organization and your industry is crucial if you want to make it to the C Suite. You have to study these things if you want to have a successful career. There's no two ways about it. You have to make it your business.

I want to repeat that: *You* have to make it *your* business.

Although a lot of management and leadership gurus will say that it's a manager's job to make sure their employees understand their role, to define their jobs, and to clearly articulate expectations, the truth is that it's your job to figure out those things. In an ideal world, your manager would take the time to carefully walk you through your job description and your performance measures. But in the real world, your manager is busy doing other things—managing other employees, meeting performance measures of his own, making the bottom line. He might very well have the best intentions of holding your hand and guiding you through your career, but the truth is that it's your responsibility to manage your own career. You have to do it. You can't count on anyone else to learn the business of business, to study your organization and report back to you, to do a competitive analysis on other players in your industry and fill you in on the details. You have to do it.

When you take the initiative to educate yourself, it pays off. Your colleagues will come to recognize you as someone who knows her stuff. Your manager will know he can count on you to execute on the mission because you understand not only what the mission is but also what it will take to fulfill it. Your industry peers will think of you as a subject-matter expert who can offer sage advice and keen insight. All of this will help propel your career.

But what happens if you don't do what it takes to understand the business of business?

You won't understand where you fit into the organization. You won't appreciate how your responsibilities affect the bottom line. You won't fully understand how to meet the performance measures that have been set for you. You won't be as capable when it comes to contributing to the bottom line. You won't have a holistic view of your industry, your organization, or your department. You will not be viewed as an expert. And you will soon find yourself excluded from important conversations.

Furthermore, you won't understand the impact you have on your department and on your organization. You won't be able to keep score. If you don't understand the business of business, you can't keep score of your own accomplishments. Because of that, you won't be able to have a quality conversation with your manager when it comes time for your annual review. Your résumé then becomes nothing more than anecdotal evidence of your career highlights because you won't be able to explain the ways in which you improved bottom-line revenue or achieved double-digit growth.

> The truth is that you will never be able to climb the corporate ladder if you don't understand the business of business, the business of your own organization, or the business of your own position within that organization. So, you have to make it your business to educate yourself, regardless of pedigree, gender, or tenure.

I want to end this discussion about knowing the business of business with a real-world example. Kat Cole is the former president of Cinnabon, which has more than $1 billion in sales and a presence in more than thirty countries. Just around her thirty-seventh birthday in 2015, Cole was promoted to group president of Focus Brands, the parent of Cinnabon as well as Auntie Anne's, Carvel, Moe's Southwest Grill, McAlister's Deli, and Schlotzsky's.[8]

Nothing was handed to Cole on a silver platter, and major portions of her education were self-taught. At the age of eighteen, as the eldest daughter of a single mom, Cole entered the University of North Florida while working part-time as a Hooters girl. When the restaurant's cook quit, she learned to cook; when the manager quit, she learned to handle finances. By age nineteen, Cole was on a plane (a first for her) and on her way to open the first Hooters restaurant in Australia. Soon she was traveling to Central America, South America, Asia, Africa, and Canada.

As you might imagine, this wreaked havoc on Cole's academic progress, so she dropped out of college. But she never abandoned the goal of gaining a traditional education. So, at age twenty-nine, by then a vice president of a billion-dollar company, Cole "applied and was accepted to Georgia State's executive MBA program, without ever going back to finish her

---

8. Trent Gillies. "Kat Cole Reflects on Sweet Success at Cinnabon and Beyond," *CNBC On the Money*, February 28, 2015. Retrieved May 21, 2015, from http://www.cnbc.com/id/102463257.

bachelor's degree."[9] Today, Cole can claim dual degrees: one from a university and one from the School of Hard Knocks.

Cole attributes much of her success to her willingness to leap at every opportunity, to ask for assignments that she knew would teach her something new, and to learn from every experience. By continually educating herself about the business of business, about her specific business, and about the business surrounding each assignment, Cole has ascended to the top of the business world.

No one makes it to the C Suite without knowing the business of business—from strategy and finance to mission and vision to industry trends to corporate culture to specific roles and responsibilities. The best employees take the time to educate themselves, whether formally through an accredited graduate program or informally by reading everything they can get their hands on and researching what it is that makes business—and their own business—tick. Remember that where or by what means you gain your education is less important than how you put that education to use. And, finally, remember, too, that no one but you can educate yourself.

A big part of that education is about the business of business. Also important in your professional education is corporate etiquette and cultural competency. We'll tackle that next, in Chapter 8.

9. Catherine Clifford. "How Kat Cole Went from Hooters Girl to President of Cinnabon by Age 32," *Entrepreneur Magazine*, August 19, 2013. Retrieved May 21, 2015, from http://www.entrepreneur.com/article/227970.

Tough-Love Lessons for Knowing the Business of Business

- C Suite-caliber employees recognize the value—and necessity—of lifelong learning and continuing education, regardless of what form that takes or by what means one educates oneself. Education is a requirement if you want to ascend the corporate ladder—a strong work ethic and positive demeanor aren't enough.
- If you want a seat in the C Suite, you have to understand the business of business—everything from corporate strategy to finance and accounting to sales and marketing . . . and beyond. No one makes it to the top without understanding each of these key areas and how they all interact.
- Understanding business isn't enough if you want to succeed. You have to know what your competition is doing, and you have to understand what's going on in your industry. Top employees make a point to conduct regular research into their own organizations, their competitors, and their industry as a whole, learning what the key issues are, what's trending, and what best practices are evolving.
- It's crucial that you understand how your position and its related roles and responsibilities fit into your organization. Where are you in the organizational structure? What's your job description? What does your manager expect of you? Leadership-quality employees aren't afraid to discuss these important issues with their managers.

144

= 8 =

Understanding Corporate Culture and Business Etiquette

From: "Jena Abernathy" <jabernathy@email.com>

To: "Megan Watson" <mwatson@email.com>

Subject: Etiquette and Culture

Megan,

You've learned how understanding the business of business is crucial when it comes to advancing your career. But business isn't only about figures and data. You also have to understand the culture of business and the rules of business etiquette, because too many *faux pas* can sabotage your career—and you'd be surprised to learn how easy it is to commit career suicide.

—Jena

You might remember back to Chapter 1 when I shared my story about dropping the F-bomb during an executive committee meeting. It was that outburst that bought my ticket to corporate charm school.

Not only did that outburst get me a free trip to Minnesota in the middle of winter, but it also confirmed my status as a junkyard dog—or, as I might prefer, as a pedigree in the making. It did something else, too: That *faux pas* taught me an important lesson about corporate culture and how important it is to understand how culture varies from one industry to the next, from one company to the next, from one department to the next, from one team to the next.

I had assumed, in moving from one organization to another, that because I was in a similar industry, working on similar projects with like-minded professionals, the culture would be the same. In my previous organization, four-letter words were part of the corporate lexicon, and no one batted an eye when anyone cursed. Such was not the case in my new organization.

That's just one example of how ignorance about corporate culture can be damaging. The same goes for business etiquette, which is closely related. Unfortunately, too many people discount the benefits of mastering corporate culture and business etiquette even though these are crucial skills that are necessary for anyone who aspires to the C Suite. You can't get to the corner office if you don't fit into the culture, if you don't understand the niceties of business, and if you don't mind your manners.

Granted, many consider these to be "soft" skills, not as important as understanding the business of business. But believe you me, mastering these skills matters. Before you can master corporate culture and business etiquette, of course, you first have to understand what they are.

Understand Corporate Culture

Exactly what is corporate culture? Is it the atmosphere in the office? The work environment? Or is it something more?

To many people, corporate culture is a nebulous concept, one that varies depending on who's defining it. *Inc. Magazine*, for example, defines corporate culture as

> the shared values, attitudes, standards, and beliefs that characterize members of an organization and define its nature. Corporate culture is rooted in an organization's goals, strategies, structure, and approaches to labor, customers, investors, and the greater community. As such, it is an essential component in any business's ultimate success or failure.[1]

Entrepreneur Magazine offers a more concise definition of corporate culture, calling it a "blend of the values, beliefs, taboos, symbols, rituals and myths all companies develop over time."[2] Business author John Coleman writes in *Harvard Business Review* that corporate culture consists of six key elements: vision, values, practices, people, narrative, and place.[3]

We can see some commonalities here, values and beliefs chief among them. So, how do you know what the values and beliefs of your organization are? Some among us might work for organizations that actually codify those values and beliefs in writing, perhaps as part of their mission and vision statements. Many companies list the makings of their corporate culture on their websites. New employees might be briefed on an organi-

---

1. _____. "Corporate Culture," *Inc. Magazine*, n.d. Retrieved July 1, 2015, from http://www.inc.com/encyclopedia/corporate-culture.html.
2. Entrepreneur Staff. "Small Business Encyclopedia: Corporate Culture," *Entrepreneur.com*, n.d. Retrieved July 1, 2015, from http://www.entrepreneur.com/encyclopedia/corporate-culture.
3. John Coleman. "Six Components of a Great Corporate Culture," *Harvard Business Review*, May 6, 2013. Retrieved July 1, 2015, from https://hbr.org/2013/05/six-components-of-culture.

zation's corporate culture during orientation sessions. But for most of us, getting a handle on these intangibles often comes through osmosis. We learn over time and from the actions of those we work with what the organization's values and beliefs are and what its overall corporate culture is.

In fact, it is in actions and behaviors that a corporate culture truly reveals itself. Researchers have found that "proclaimed values appear irrelevant" and that it is the actions of leaders that really matters when it comes to corporate culture. In examining, for example, the values listed on corporate websites of a number of S&P 500 companies, researchers found "very little evidence that advertised values are correlated with performance" and that it's possible that "many of these advertised values are simply cheap talk."[4]

Corporate culture might well be cheap talk, though it even could be "the secret sauce"[5] that makes a company what it is. Perhaps it's both or maybe something in between. But, whether codified or unwritten, the actions, behaviors, values, beliefs, and attitudes that shape an organization's culture are important, not least of which because culture affects both how people work and how they feel about their work. Indeed, studies find a direct link between corporate culture and job satisfaction. Some note that, "[i]n many cases, a company's culture can affect the overall job experience as much as the work itself or the salary."[6] Others note that corporate culture affects not only job satisfaction but morale and performance as well.[7] As such, understanding and being able to adapt to corporate culture,

---

4. Luigi Guiso, Paola Sapienza, and Luigi Zingales. *The Value of Corporate Culture*, Working Paper 19557, October 2013. Cambridge, MA: National Bureau of Economic Research.

5. *Ibid.*

6. Dennis McCafferty. "How Corporate Culture Affects Job Satisfaction," *BaseLine*, April 29, 2015. Retrieved July 3, 2015, from http://www.baselinemag.com/careers/slideshows/how-corporate-culture-affects-job-satisfaction.html.

7. Judy H. Gray, Iain L. Densten, and James C. Sarros. *A Matter of Size: Does Organisational Culture Predict Job Satisfaction in Small Organisations?* Working Paper 65/03, September 2003. Retrieved July 3, 2015, from http://www.buseco.monash.edu.au/mgt/research/working-papers/2003/wp65-03.pdf.

both in general and as it relates specifically to the organization for which you work, is crucial for employees who wish to make it to the C Suite—and to do so happily and productively.

Regardless of how corporate culture is defined, it's important to figure out what it actually is—meaning that employees have to get a sense of what an organization's culture is like in order to really thrive. Corporate culture reveals itself in myriad ways, often in seemingly little things. This can range from stated policies, procedures, and processes to unofficial norms and customs that guide the behavior of an organization's leaders and employees. We get a sense of an organization's true corporate culture from its dress code, vacation policy, and T&E procedure as much as from, say, the channels through which and even how often employees communicate with each other. How or whether department successes are celebrated; when, where, and for how long staff members take (or don't take) lunch; when, where, and how meetings are held—all of these speak to corporate culture.

149

UNCOVER CORPORATE CULTURE

Although it's important and often necessary to learn by doing, when it comes to corporate culture, you can do more than just learn by the ropes. In fact, it's never too early to uncover the corporate culture of an organization—whether it's a company you want to work for, one you've just started your career with, or even one of your competitors.

You can start to get a feel for an organization's culture before you even walk in the door for your first interview. In fact, even before you apply for a job, you should do a little research to see if the company fits not only your professional goals but your work style as well. Find out what you can about policies. Learn about the organization's leaders and key stakeholders. Look into the organization's numbers: How is its stock doing? How does it compare to competitors? Doing your due diligence will help fill in some of those crucial blanks.

That concrete stuff is usually pretty easy to dig up. Uncovering what the working environment is like, however, can be another matter altogether. But that doesn't mean that sussing out the corporate culture of an organization is impossible. You just have to know where to look.

- **Look to Social and Traditional Media.** See what people are saying on LinkedIn, Twitter, and Facebook about the company, its employees, and its products and services. Check out sites like Glassdoor to see what former employees have to say. Investigate what business media are saying about the organization and its key stakeholders.
- **Use Your Networking Skills.** Touch base with current and former employees by working your networks and connections. Ask if you can chat with them about the organization. See what they enjoy and what they dislike about working there. Inquire about working conditions and employee morale. Ask them how they would characterize the organization and its reputation.
- **Ask Key Questions.** When interviewing with HR, the person who would be your boss, and potential colleagues, ask them about their work habits, about team dynamics, about company policies. Listen to what they say and how they say it—and to what they don't say or won't comment on.
- **Look and Learn.** When visiting the office for an interview, pay attention to whether people are eating lunch at their desks, whether they have personal photos and other items on their desks and walls, whether people are chatting and smiling and laughing, whether staff members are wearing jeans or khakis or suits. Paying attention to these details will give you a sense of what the office atmosphere is like.

Understanding corporate culture takes time—and a little legwork. Numerous facets play a part in creating culture, so it's important to do what you can as soon as you can in order to uncover corporate culture.

I recently attended an onsite meeting at a large multinational corporation. As soon as I walked into the offices, I could tell the corporate culture was traditional (and perhaps a bit stodgy). Dark, heavy paneling adorned the walls. Executive assistants sat in cubicles outside each executive office. Small signs with the word "Quiet" were stationed around the office. I found myself talking to everyone in a whisper and tiptoeing every time I went anywhere.

At one point, one of the administrative assistants pulled me aside and said, "I want to let you know that our 'No Pantyhose' policy will not go into effect until next week." This was her diplomatic way of telling me that, even though I was a visitor, I was in violation of company policy by coming to the office in bare legs—this despite the fact that I was wearing a classic St. John suit and conservative heels.

Oftentimes, corporate culture boils down to a lot of little things—from dress code to expected decorum and beyond. All of those little things add up—and in an important way. Misunderstand an organization's culture, and you might just misunderstand the organization in general, making it much more difficult for you to contribute to the organization's mission in a positive way and to keep moving up the corporate ladder.

Most of us probably recognize this, whether we've thought much about it or not. We kind of understand that culture is intangible, that it reveals itself through numerous aspects and does so over time. We also get that culture varies among industries, organizations, and departments. No one would argue, for instance, that the corporate culture at, say, General Motors is just like the culture at General Electric or that the culture at Baker and McKenzie is the same as the corporate culture at McKinsey & Company. Indeed, corporate culture is so nuanced and so specific to each particular organization that it has led many a merger to failure. Daimler and Chrysler, AOL and Time Warner, Quaker and Snapple—each of these mergers ended in disaster, thanks largely to clashing corporate cultures.

These organizations learned the hard way that the little things matter. Although abstract, corporate culture speaks to the heart of an organization. Failing to recognize what makes a culture what it is can be devastating. Indeed, Greg Urban, a professor at University of Pennsylvania, has noted that, "very small things can catch you off guard. They can become something much more important than you originally thought."[8]

Whether it's dropping the F-Bomb at an inopportune moment, taking a too-long lunch, sitting in the wrong chair during an important meeting, working a forty-hour week when everyone else is working sixty hours, arriving at work at 9 a.m. when typically all the executives arrive at 7:30 a.m., leaning in when you should have leaned back, or anything else, committing a *faux pas* related to corporate culture can have lasting effects. Commit one too many of these mistakes, and you just might find yourself looking for a new job.

INEQUALITY EQUALIZER

Understand that there is a gray area between your professional life and your social life—and be careful about merging those lives. Remember that work is where you go to work, not where you go to socialize, even during social business functions where lines are blurred.

---

8. "The Power of Corporate Culture—And How to Harness It," *Wharton@Work*, July 2014. Retrieved July 1, 2015, from http://executiveeducation.wharton.upenn .edu/thought-leadership/wharton-at-work/2014/07/the-power-of-corporate-culture.

LEAN IN TO CORPORATE CULTURE

Why is understanding corporate culture so important? Because even if you can do all the assigned tasks and hit all your performance measures, if you don't fit in, if you can't get on board with the norms and customs, if you don't understand the way things really work—the unwritten rules—well, then, you really won't be able to perform at your best.

One of the most challenging unwritten rules, and one that can be especially tricky to navigate, is when to speak up. In some organizations, employees are encouraged to speak up, to share their ideas and opinions, to ask challenging questions—regardless of gender or title or tenure. In other organizations, however, leaning in in such a manner can get you noticed for all the wrong reasons.

The notion of leaning in is a popular one these days, with various arguments for and against the concept of taking a seat at the table, speaking up, being heard, and getting noticed. But before you can lean in, you have to understand the culture of your organization— because not every organization encourages every employee to lean in. Corporate culture varies drastically on this point. Facebook is not Wells Fargo, and Wells Fargo isn't Walmart—what you can get away with at one organization might be strictly taboo at another.

The truth is that, in some organizations, corporate culture actually dictates that you lean back sometimes. Sometimes you have to be invited to sit at the table; you can't just grab a seat. Whether related to title or tenure, or even to social or demographic aspects, when to lean in and when to lean back can very often be dependent on corporate culture. This requires you to understand nuances particular to your specific organization and its culture. You have to learn to gauge how assertive you can be, at what moments, with which colleagues, and under which circumstances.

Although there's been much chatter of late of the importance and benefits of—especially for women—leaning in, it can be equally important to know when to lean back at key moments, because sometimes the best strategy is to sit back and listen rather than to lean in and voice your opinion. It all depends on the culture of the organization you're working in, the people you're working with, and the project you're working on.

Understand Business Etiquette

Closely related to corporate culture is business etiquette. Whereas corporate culture embodies the values, beliefs, attitudes, and practices of an organization, business etiquette speaks to the behaviors, manners, and customs that govern the actions of employees. Although certain good manners apply across the board, different industries and organizations might well have their own rules for business etiquette, rules which very often evolve over time.

To a lot of people, etiquette is another one of those nebulous concepts, an unwritten set of vague rules intended to guide behavior. To many of us, the very concept of etiquette feels stuffy and stodgy, an old-fashioned way of doing things. In a day when wearing flip-flops, torn jeans, and faded T-shirts to work has become the norm for so many offices, at a time when posting snarky tweets is fashionable, and in an age when virtual conversations have replaced face-to-face meetings, the very notion of etiquette seems to have gone the way of the fax machine.

But the truth is that good manners never go out of style. How you behave and the manners you employ say a lot about you, and you'd likely be surprised at the extent to which your colleagues and your supervisors judge you by your manners. As Barbara Pachter notes in her book *The Essentials of Business Etiquette*:

> Just doing your job in our competitive, global business environment isn't enough. . . . Your ability to get along

with people, to exhibit good manners, to project an impressive image, and to make others feel comfortable are key components of your success. In today's fast-paced, digital, multicultural world, these business etiquette skills can sometimes get lost in the shuffle. But without them, your organization may lose business, your colleagues may lose respect for you, and your bosses may not promote you.[9]

Being passed over for a promotion because you don't know which fork to use during a business lunch might sound extreme, but the reality is that etiquette is a sign of competency. As such, business etiquette, along with corporate culture, is a skillset you need to master.

I can tell you from experience that this can be especially tricky for junkyard dogs. I didn't grow up in a world where I learned which fork to use, when to use a black napkin instead of a white napkin, or how to pair wine. Hell—I thought wine was a special beverage that came out of a jug or a box and was served only at the holidays.

Of course, I'm not the only one who has ever struggled with etiquette. Many of us simply never learn these things. We're not taught. We're not exposed to situations where the rules of business etiquette are needed. Such was the case with one of my colleagues.

One particular instance with my colleague Jay was so bad that it would have been hilarious—had we not been in the presence of our CEO, who came from old money, with Emily Post-style rules of etiquette drilled into him from childhood.

In his mid-twenties, Jay was a new hire, eager to get ahead, with movie-star looks coupled with a huge ego. My boss had invited Jay, his newest hire, to join us as we both met our company's CEO for the first time during a business dinner at one

155

---

9. Barbara Pachter. *The Essentials of Business Etiquette: How to Eat, Greet, and Tweet Your Way to Success.* New York: McGraw-Hill Education, 2013, pp. 1–2.

of the finest restaurants in the city. I began to have misgivings about how well the evening might go when Jay kept rehashing his college football glory days as we drove to the restaurant. We arrived at the restaurant entrance almost simultaneously with the CEO. My boss made the introductions all around, and as Jay shook the CEO's hand, he said, "Nice to meet you. I've heard a lot about you." With that, Jay whirled around toward the restaurant entrance and bounded in ahead of all of us. The CEO's perplexed expression captured all our feelings as we all stared ahead trying to figure out why Jay had darted out in front, even gliding past an elderly couple who had been waiting patiently in line.

By the time the three of us caught up to Jay, he was telling the maître d' who we were and where we wanted to be seated. As the maître d' led the four of us to the table, my boss slipped a bill into the maître d's hand and Jay said, "You should hand that over to me—I got us the table." All three of us stared at Jay and smiled (awkwardly), but the CEO was not impressed. While Jay was feeling like he was in his element, he proceeded to dominate the conversation right from the start instead of allowing the CEO to determine the topics and warm up to meeting us for the first time. When the waiter asked for our drink order, Jay asked for the wine list. My boss immediately winced and sent "the look" over and then interjected that perhaps we might want to have a drink first. Jay then proceeded to order a shot with a Jack Daniels Black on the rocks. My boss glared. And the evening continued downhill.

Jay was no longer obnoxious; he had become awkward. He had no idea about dining basics, such as using one's utensils in order, from the outside in. And he'd forgotten to turn off his cell phone; it blared Queen's "Another One Bites the Dust" (I kid you not. I couldn't make this stuff up.). He answered the call, while the CEO was in mid-conversation. Time and again, my boss gave Jay "the look."

Jay really tried to mind his manners for the remainder of the evening, but the damage was done. He just didn't know how to behave appropriately at a business dinner—apparently no one had ever taught him anything about etiquette. I'd never eaten with Jay or with this CEO before, so I had no way of anticipating the business etiquette debacle that was to unfold over that dinner. The next day, the CEO commented that Jay had quite a few gaps that needed to be closed in order for him to be successful as a senior leader. Jay never recovered, and in one dinner what was a promising career was derailed, all because he wasn't aware of the importance of mastering the social graces and the ability to blend in at the most senior level. What could have been a shining moment turned into a tarnished occasion.

Jay could have benefitted from a few pointers so he could have been better prepared for this important business dinner:

1. Let the senior-most person choose the restaurant, select the table, and pick up the tab.
2. Defer to the host and other senior executives throughout the course of the meal.
3. Do not order a bottle of wine for the table unless asked to.
4. Turn off all electronic devices such as cell phones before entering the establishment.
5. Sit up straight, don't hunch over, and keep your elbows off the table.
6. Wait until everyone at the table is served before you begin to eat.
7. Use your utensils from the outside in, and do not place a utensil you've used back on the table; if it isn't in your hand, it should be placed carefully on your plate.
8. Don't talk with your mouth full. Don't shovel food into your mouth (it's not a race!). And never overindulge in alcohol or food.

9. Be courteous to the waitstaff.
10. Do not ask for a "doggie bag."

Stuff like this might seem like nothing more than needless and outmoded social niceties. But putting such niceties to use not only shows you in a good light, doing so also makes those around you feel comfortable. Following the rules of etiquette actually helps you put those around you at ease. Treating people with politeness lets them know you respect them. Knowing what to say and how to behave in a given situation helps put everyone at ease and shows you to be a well-mannered professional.

No one wants to sit through a business dinner with an ill-mannered loudmouth who chews with his mouth open, smacks his lips, and slurps his wine. No one likes to have their conversation interrupted by an obnoxious ringtone or constantly buzzing cell phone. No one wants to have a *Pretty Woman* moment and end up flinging a snail across the room when eating escargot.

It's all too easy to commit *faux pas* like these, and I could write an entire book filled with my own social blunders through the years. Early on in my career, for example, I was out with my boss and some clients at a really nice restaurant. It was the first time I was served sorbet between courses to cleanse my palate, and I blurted out, "I can't believe they're serving dessert already!"

Another time, when I was a vice president of a bank at a very young age, I was invited to play golf and have dinner along with some members of our law firm at the local country club.

I had never belonged to a country club.

The event was a month away, so I went out and bought some golf clubs. I was taking lessons, too, so I knew enough to muddle my way through a round of golf. Even so, I was awful, and it was very humbling. Eighteen holes later, we wrapped up and my colleagues suggested we all go ahead and change for dinner. "What do you mean?" I asked, dumbfounded.

Having never belonged to a country club, it never dawned on me that I'd need an extra set of clothes to change into after golfing and showering.

I had no clue.

But because I was a senior executive, everyone just assumed I would know what's what.

We ended up eating dinner outside on the veranda at the clubhouse, me in my golf attire and everyone else in their fresh, clean business casual clothes.

I was mortified. They were very kind, and the world didn't end (nor did my career). But I had to fake my way through the entire dinner, feeling like I didn't belong.

I've learned the hard way that etiquette is absolutely critical in business. Most people don't realize how often, for instance, they'll have to socialize as part of business during the course of their careers. From the interview process to the C Suite, as you wine and dine colleagues, customers, and clients, you'll have to demonstrate your finesse in all manner of business etiquette.

Etiquette, in fact, is an equalizer. It helps to level the playing field if you can demonstrate that you know how to dress appropriately, behave appropriately, and communicate appropriately. Whether junkyard dog or pedigree, you want to be professional and elegant in every situation, behaving correctly in light of the corporate culture or your organization.

INEQUALITY EQUALIZER

Remember that even in the most casual workplaces, business is still business. Even if you might work in an informal setting, understand that most offices still adhere to some level of formality, so remember that manners matter.

MASTER SOME BUSINESS ETIQUETTE BASICS

Changing times and changing technology can make it challenging to keep up with changing customs. That said, countless social graces are timeless. Although good manners might go unnoticed by some, remember that everyone will recognize it when you display bad manners. You don't want to be remembered for your bad manners. Mastering these basics can help you present yourself as a polished, poised professional who is confident in any situation.

- **Master the Business Dinner.** Conducting yourself well during a business dinner is crucial. Bumbling your way through a meal with the boss and a group of clients can deflate your career faster than a fallen soufflé. So, get to know your utensils and stemware. Know when and where to sit. Know the proper way to use your napkin, when to fold it, where to place it, and when to request a black napkin instead of a white one. Know when, what, and how much to order. Know how to butter your dinner roll. Know how to pace your meal with others at the table.

- **Master the Social Sporting Event.** Participating in sports outings provides an opportunity to demonstrate stress-management skills, communication skills, and all manner of social graces. Whether you get invited to play a round of golf, a game of squash, or a frame of bocce, learn the rules of play as well as the culture around the sport. Know what to wear so that you are dressed appropriately. If, for instance, you get invited to join your boss in his box seats for a hockey game, you should know not to show up in your Jonathan Toews jersey. If you're a landlubber and have been invited to go sailing on a client's Oyster 625, be smart enough to ask for guidance and direction while on the vessel—don't just fake your way through the outing.

- **Master the Art of Wine.** As *The Wall Street Journal* has noted, "Ordering the wine at a business function is not unimportant. Business people are judged by just about everything they do, and an ability to order wine crisply and well probably takes on far more significance than it should."[10] In addition, know that wine collecting is a hobby well loved by many C Suite executives, so getting to know this world is a good idea. So, learn about vintages and vintners. Know how to sip and savor a good wine. Explore various wine and food pairings. Become conversant in the subject of wine, labels, varietals, and so on.

- **Master the Art of Communication.** Technology has changed the ways in which we communicate. How we communicate in face-to-face get-togethers, during departmental meetings, via e-mail, and so on says a lot about us. Many of us communicate via e-mails, texts, tweets, and IMs. Doing so is quick and easy—but that doesn't mean it shouldn't also be professional. Whether talking with someone or messaging someone, it is essential to communicate effectively and professionally. This goes beyond avoiding the "reply all" button or not using all caps in an e-mail message. It speaks to what you say and how you say it, from the words you use to the volume in which you address someone. It speaks to how you communicate in writing, whether memo, e-mail, text, or post. Key here is corporate culture and understanding how those in your organization prefer to communicate, via which methods and how frequently. Entire books, countless articles, and innumerable posts deal with this subject—which should be an indication of how important the topic is. The best employees, regardless of title, tenure, or pedigree, master the art of communication.

---

10. Dorothy J. Gaiter and John Brecher. "How to Order Wine at a Business Dinner," *The Wall Street Journal*, October 2009. Retrieved July 2, 2015, from http://guides. wsj.com/wine/dining-with-wine/how-to-order-wine-at-a-business-dinner.

Codes of conduct and rules of etiquette abound. Some of these guidelines are universal, some are unique to your industry and to your organization. How you behave not only reflects on your background but also shines a light on your professionalism—and your potential.

Make no mistake: Every organization has a code. The organization's corporate culture often dictates the unwritten, unspoken rules that inform the business etiquette that employees at every level are expected to adhere to. How you conduct yourself during a meeting, how you communicate with colleagues and customers, how you dress for a business social function—all of that matters, because people are watching. Maintaining a professional decorum at all times is crucial if you want your career to lead you to the C Suite.

Knowing that you should bring a change of clothes when invited to play a round of golf with clients, knowing how to order a bottle of wine during a business dinner, knowing how and when to use e-mail appropriately—all of that might seem superficial. But those who ignore the rules of business etiquette or the codes of conduct surrounding corporate culture are putting their careers in jeopardy. On the other hand, those who do follow these rules and codes make positive impressions on colleagues and clients. They help make those around them feel comfortable and respected. They exhibit a level of self-assurance that, in turn, makes people feel confident in them and their abilities.

When coupled together, understanding business etiquette and corporate culture and understanding the business of business serves as a positive double whammy. Employees who master the skills surrounding both prove themselves to be polished, effective, well-rounded individuals who not only can get the job done but can do so in a way that reflects well on themselves and their organizations. It's in developing this kind of competency that they can distinguish themselves.

═══

INEQUALITY EQUALIZER

You have to know the rules before you can break them. Learning the rules of business etiquette can help junkyard dogs earn pedigree status, breaking down the barriers of perception that might limit their professional growth.

═══

Tough-Love Lessons for Understanding Business Etiquette and Cultural Competency

- Don't assume that culture is the same from one industry to the next, one organization to the next, or even one department to the next. Every group has its own cultural identity, which reflects the shared values, beliefs, and behaviors of its members. Top employees research, study, and learn about an organization's various cultural cues and expectations in order to act accordingly.
- Leaning in may all be well and good in some organizations, but, more often than not, the truth is that you have to pick key moments to do so. Being able to distinguish those times when you can lean in and when you should lean back is a crucial skill that employees must learn, regardless of title or pedigree.
- Etiquette might seem old-fashioned, but the truth is that good manners never go out of style. Business professionals who aspire to the C Suite must be able to master the rules of etiquette that allow them to function in social, business, and hybrid situations with grace and confidence.
- How you dress, how you communicate, and how you behave speak to who you are as a person and as a professional. People with bad manners get noticed—and remembered—for all the wrong reasons. The most successful employees make a point of learning the code of conduct that governs their organizations, following the customs that guide behavior.

= 9 =

Developing Intuition and Trust

From: "Jena Abernathy" <jabernathy@email.com>

To: "Megan Watson" <mwatson@email.com>

Subject: Intuition and Trust

Megan,

Figures, data, and statistics, along with culture, manners, and etiquette can help you progress in your career. But, as you'll likely find out, it's crucial to develop intuition and trust, too. It's this combination of hard skills and soft skills that will help you become the kind of well-rounded employee that makes it to the executive suite.

—Jena

Intuition is a concept we refer to often but might not really understand. It's actually logical, though, that we speak of and even use intuition without fully understanding it. By definition intuition is intuitive: knowing something to be true without having all the available empirical evidence about it. I know something simply because I know it, not because I've studied it or because I've seen it or heard it firsthand, or even because all the big data out there tell me it's true.

Sometimes, you've just got to trust your gut.

Intuition is one of those soft skills that can't be taught—but it can be learned. (We'll get to that later.) And if you want to succeed in business, you have to learn how to develop your intuition and your ability to trust—to trust your gut and to trust the people around you.

While it's crucial to understand the business of business and it's essential to understand corporate culture and the rules of business etiquette, so too is it necessary to develop intuition and trust. It's that mixture of hard skills and soft skills like these that can help propel employees up the career ladder, regardless of tenure or pedigree. In fact, as business columnist Dan Schwabel writes:

> To be perfectly blunt, people with hard skills are a dime a dozen. A high school kid can probably learn most of the hard skills that would be required to do just about any job, but it's doubtful that he or she would have the emotional maturity and the people skills to make it in a Fortune 200 company.[1]

That said, some people still pooh-pooh the idea of developing soft skills like trust and intuition, believing it's better to rely on facts, evidence, and data when making decisions, especially in

1. Dan Schwabel. *Promote Yourself: The New Rules for Career Success*. New York: St. Martin's Press, 2013, p. 74.

this era of big data, which some would argue has revolutionized business management. But facts aren't necessarily always the be-all and end-all of decision making. As Lynn Robinson writes in her book *Trust Your Gut*:

> Is intuition better than cold, hard facts? That depends! There are decisions that require logic and analysis. You may have the rational information necessary to easily make the right decision. But there are times when you have nothing to go on, no information on which to base your determination. That's when knowing how to access your intuition can be most helpful.[2]

Schwabel and Robinson aren't alone in their thinking. Some really smart people believe in intuition. Albert Einstein, for instance, kept in his office a wall-hanging that said, "Not everything that can be counted counts, and not everything that counts can be counted." I don't want to analyze this to pieces in an attempt to answer whether certain types of knowledge can or must be gained only apart from the physical senses. We'll leave that to the philosophers of the world. But from a practical standpoint, it's important to know that, no matter our role or title or age or gender, we have to make decisions every day— many of them small and seemingly insignificant, but some of them crucial, and often on the spur of the moment—without the benefit of every factual detail. When that happens, we have little choice but to go with our gut feelings.

And, as it turns out, there's really nothing wrong with that. Or is there?

---

2. Lynn A. Robinson. *Trust Your Gut: How the Power of Intuition Can Grow Your Business*. Chicago: Kaplan Publishing, 2006, p. viii.

Intuition vs. Evidence

Some experts believe that going with our gut can be beneficial. Others, however, believe that, in the era of big data, or "long data," we should rely less on intuition. Let's take a closer look at this.

The late, great Steve Jobs said that, "Intuition is a very powerful thing, more powerful than intellect" and that he valued "experiential wisdom over empirical analysis."[3] Jobs wasn't alone in this belief. According to *Harvard Business Review*, "a survey that was conducted in May 2002 by executive search firm Christian & Timbers reveals that fully 45 percent of corporate executives now rely more on instinct than on facts and figures in running their businesses."[4]

Jobs and countless other leaders might well place their trust in intuition, but many others argue that evidence should rule when it comes to decision making, especially in this age of big data. Andrew McAfee, codirector of the Initiative on the Digital Economy at the MIT Sloan School of Management, for example, argues that, "we should turn many of our decisions, predictions, diagnoses, and judgments—both the trivial and the consequential—over to the algorithms."[5] McAfee and Erik Brynjolfsson further argue that, "throughout the business world today, people rely too much on experience and intuition and not enough on data."[6]

---

3. Walter Isaacson. "The Genius of Jobs," *The New York Times*, October 29, 2011. Retrieved July 8, 2015, from http://www.nytimes.com/2011/10/30/opinion/sunday/steve-jobss-genius.html.

4. Eric Bonabeau. "Don't Trust Your Gut," *Harvard Business Review*, May 2003. Retrieved July 8, 2015, from https://hbr.org/2003/05/dont-trust-your-gut.

5. Andrew McAfee. "Big Data's Biggest Challenge? Convincing People Not to Trust Their Judgment," *Harvard Business Review*, December 9, 2013. Retrieved July 8, 2015, from https://hbr.org/2013/12/big-datas-biggest-challenge-convincing-people-not-to-trust-their-judgment.

6. Andrew McAfee and Erik Brynjolfsson. "Big Data: The Management Revolution," *Harvard Business Review*, October 2012. Retrieved July 8, 2015, from https://hbr.org/2012/10/big-data-the-management-revolution/ar.

So which is it? When luminaries like Steve Jobs extoll the virtues of intuition while experts like McAfee and Brynjolfsson argue persuasively for evidence, facts, and data, what does that mean for the soft skill of developing intuition and trust?

It turns out there's no easy answer to this question. In fact, leading academics have argued the issue at length. For example, Daniel Kahneman, professor emeritus at Woodrow Wilson School of Public and International Affairs at Princeton University, and Gary Klein, senior scientist at Applied Research Associates, have found that a number of factors come into play when determining when and under what circumstances managers should use intuition or evidence to make decisions. Among the many findings of their study, the authors note that, "[v]alidity and uncertainty are not incompatible"[7] and that intuition is more reliable under certain circumstances, while evidence is more reliable in others.[8]

So where does this leave us? While the debate over intuition versus evidence will continue to rage, the bottom line is that both intuition and data matter. Knowing when to use either or both is the key. It's important to note that acting on intuition is not akin to taking a shot in the dark. Being intuitive is not the same as being uninformed.

This is important. Although it might seem capricious when leaders appear to make decisions on gut instinct alone, much more goes into this kind of decision making. Instinct might be considered a sixth sense, but experience and expertise are in the mix as well. So when someone makes a snap judgment, it's not necessarily a crapshoot. Chances are that business and life experience as well as subject-matter expertise are coming into play, even if the decision maker might not be conscious of it.

---

7. Daniel Kahneman and Gary Klein. "Conditions for Intuitive Expertise: A Failure to Disagree," *American Psychologist*, September 2009, Vol. 64, No. 6, pp. 515–26. Retrieved July 8, 2015, from http://www.hansfagt.dk/Kahneman_and_Klein(2009).pdf.

8. "Strategic Decisions: When Can You Trust Your Gut?," *McKinsey Quarterly*, March 2010. Retrieved July 8, 2015, from http://www.mckinsey.com/insights/strategy/strategic_decisions_when_can_you_trust_your_gut.

Acquiring the kind of experience and developing the kind of expertise needed to make effective decisions based at least in part on intuition takes some doing. Making the most of intuition isn't necessarily done without training or without thinking. Although some leaders might be considered talented decision makers, that talent doesn't come by chance. By some measures, "[m]any characteristics once believed to reflect innate talent are actually the result of intense practice extended for a minimum of 10 years."[9] Indeed, it was this notion that author Malcolm Gladwell popularized in his book *Outliers*, in which he noted that it takes about 10,000 hours for most people to achieve what he called "greatness"[10] (an argument that has since been debated extensively).

Whether 10 years or 10,000 hours, the point is that no one becomes great at what they do without practice. Some people might be natural-born talents, but that doesn't mean they don't have to study their craft. This is why, for those who want to make it to the C Suite, it's so important to understand the business of business, to understand corporate culture, and to keep score so that you know what works and what doesn't. In fact, I once read about a business leader who kept a "hunch-log" to track the success of his gut-level decisions, which is a great way to keep track of your wins and losses.

Keeping score of decisions is a great idea, and not just to measure whether intuition or evidence plays a more effective role in positive outcomes. It also can help you develop your intuition so that it does, indeed, become a mixture of that sixth sense along with experience and expertise. And the more you develop your intuition, the better you'll become at listening to it.

---

9. K. Anders Ericsson, Ralf Th. Krampe, and Clemens Tesch-Romer. "The Role of Deliberate Practice in the Acquisition of Expert Performance," *Psychological Review*, 1993, Vol. 100, No. 3, pp. 363–406. Retrieved July 8, 2015, from http://projects.ict.usc.edu/itw/gel/EricssonDeliberatePracticePR93.pdf.
10. Malcolm Gladwell. *Outliers: The Story of Success*. New York: Little, Brown & Co., 2008, p. 41.

Listen to Your Instincts

When it comes to decision making, we all sometimes rely on instinct and intuition, just as we all sometimes rely on evidence and data. Sometimes we rely on both. How effective those decisions are—that is, what kind of results they generate—will vary from situation to situation. But no one can make effective decisions if they don't actually learn to listen to their intuition. You have to trust your gut, because if you don't, chances are that bad things will happen.

I know this firsthand. Earlier in my career, I was offered a position in which I would head the HR department of a very successful corporation. The offer was for a job that would be a promotion for me in title, and it included a sizable raise from my current salary as well as some impressive stock options. My head was telling me, "More money, more influence, more prestige . . . there's no logical reason to decline this offer." But my heart was telling me to walk away. My instincts told me to resist the temptation. But the dollar signs loomed as large as roadside billboards, and, ultimately, the big money was just too enticing, so I suppressed my intuition and made the leap.

It turned out to be the worst job of my career.

Here's the short-story version. My initial interview was on a Saturday morning. That didn't bother me, because it meant I didn't have to miss any time from work. But what was strange was that the office was busy. It was nine o'clock on a Saturday morning, and everybody was there working.

Then, when I was ushered into the CEO's office, I noticed that the whole place was decorated with lions. Pictures and paintings of lions decorated the walls. Lion tchotchkes lined the bookshelves. Lions were everywhere—even the CEO's hair was sort of leonine, a wavy mane of flowing locks. I remember thinking, "Wow. Big game hunter?" So I asked. He told me that the decorations were there because "the lion is the king of the jungle"—the implication being that he wanted everyone who came into his office to know that he was the king of his particular jungle.

The hair on the back of my neck was standing up, so I called three people in the industry who had inside knowledge of the company and its leader, and they all told me to stay away from the organization. But soon enough, I was fielding an offer, with that big title and that big salary. Despite the warnings I had heard, it was all too enticing. I accepted.

Within just three days of my first day on the job, I knew I'd made a terrible mistake.

I didn't listen to the advice I'd received from the mentors I had connected with. I didn't pay attention to the corporate culture I witnessed during the interview process. I didn't heed the due diligence I had conducted that told me the CEO would be a challenge to work with. I discounted all of my instincts and disregarded my intuition.

This job turned out to be one of the most traumatic experiences of my career. It was horrible—I cried on the way home almost every day. I tried to figure out what I could do to make this successful; I had never failed and was determined to make this work. Making it successful meant working every Saturday along with the rest of the team, sacrificing valuable family time. It meant sitting through weekly tirades from the CEO and watching divisive tactics among the leadership team. It meant constant micromanagement from the CEO to the point that I did not recognize myself when I looked in the mirror and saw only the reflection of a truly miserable human being. I did not fit the culture, and I needed to figure out an exit strategy. So, I identified a candidate who would be a better fit and then I quit, after just six months on the job. It was a horrible move from a résumé perspective, but as I also tell candidates and mentees, you are allowed one "growth" experience in your career.

I learned a lot from that experience. One of those lessons has become a key tenet of my life: Listen to your intuition; it will be your best guide in life, and especially in your career.

INEQUALITY EQUALIZER

Listening to your intuition can be a powerful equalizer. No matter your title, pedigree, or gender, learning to trust your gut and pay attention to your instincts can be an effective tool throughout your career.

How you go about learning to listen to your instincts can be challenging. Even though it's something we should learn and develop, intuition isn't something that's really taught in MBA school. To the contrary, "[e]ducational institutions give little attention to how to develop intuition implying that it is not highly valued," notes Kaylene C. Williams, professor of Marketing at California State University, Stanislaus. "Rather the opposite, effort has been given to showing that intuitions systematically ignore important information and that judgments can be improved when individuals are pressed to reason more carefully."[11]

This is especially interesting when we consider the fact that most business executives admit to using intuition in at least some of their decision making. Williams, for example, notes that "approximately 89 percent of marketing professionals frequently use their intuition to direct some part of their decision making and, hence, competitive impact."[12]

So what are all these professionals doing in order to boost their intuition acumen? They're tapping into their experience and expertise. They're learning from what works and what

---

11. Kaylene C. Williams. "Business Intuition: The Mortar Among the Bricks of Analysis," *Journal of Management Policy and Practice*, 2012, Vol. 13(5), p. 55. Retrieved July 8, 2015, from http://www.na-businesspress.com/JMPP/Williams KC_Web13_5_.pdf.
12. *Ibid.*, p. 48.

doesn't, from their own mistakes and from the mistakes of others. They learn to recognize patterns. As Gary Klein, PhD, senior scientist at MacroCognition LLC, explains, "[i]ntuition is the way we translate our experience into action." Klein further notes that "[i]ntuitive decision making improves as we acquire more patterns, larger repertoires of action scripts, and richer mental models."[13]

The more experience we gain, the more we can develop our intuition—a useful skill regardless of title, tenure, pedigree, or gender. But it's not just about getting experience, it's also about assessing and analyzing those experiences—we have to learn from what we do as well as from what others do. When it comes to developing business intuition, we have to study what's going on not only in our departments or our organizations, but in our industries in general. We have to take note of what's working and what's not, what's trending and what's fading. We have to keep practicing our hard skills and our soft skills. We have to learn how to listen to warning signals, whether overt or abstract. We have to consider the facts, too, because the best decisions take both intuition and evidence into consideration.

Various experts promote any number of ways to hone intuition skills, from playing word games to building models, from listening to music to keeping a dream journal. Mindfulness and meditation—both experiencing a surge in popularity these days—also are tools often referenced by those touting ways to develop intuition. But perhaps among the most important tricks of the intuition trade is learning to listen to yourself and to trust your gut. Because, as it happens, developing trust is another one of those crucial soft skills that the most successful employees learn to master.

---

13. Gary Klein, PhD. *Intuition at Work: Why Developing Your Gut Instincts Will Make You Better at What You Do.* New York: Currency/Doubleday, 2002, p. 8.

Put Your Trust in Trust

Trust is a tricky wicket, especially in business. Trusting your gut, trusting in yourself, trusting your colleagues, trusting the leaders and managers around you—it can be challenging to allow yourself to rely on yourself and on others, to put your faith in yourself and others. Trust is difficult to develop in yourself and to nurture in others. Trust, in fact, is a double-edged sword: place too little trust in yourself and your abilities, and you sell yourself short; but place too much trust in yourself or others, and you risk making mistakes that could derail your career.

Developing trust is another one of those soft skills that is crucial to master. Much that relates to trust is intuitive—you get a gut feeling about whom you can trust, you get a sense of what works and what doesn't. Oftentimes, the ability to trust, like intuition, comes from experience.

So let's talk a bit about trust, as it relates to intuition and instinct, as it relates to yourself and your skills, and as it relates to those around you.

Trust Your Gut

We've talked a lot about intuition and instinct in this chapter, why it's important to nurture your intuition, and how you can learn to listen to your instincts. We've seen how the best decisions are based on both intuition and evidence. We've seen how experience and expertise play a role in informing intuition so that making gut-based decisions isn't based solely on feeling but on all the knowledge and know-how you've gained over the years. It takes time to learn how to trust your gut.

How do you find the confidence to trust your gut? By paying attention to yourself. They don't say "trust your gut" for no reason. They don't tell you to take it as a warning when the hair on the back of your neck stands up. It might sound kooky, but the truth is that your body will tell you when your instinct is speaking up—even if your head isn't listening. Logic

175

and reason might be telling you one thing, but if your heart and your head are telling you another thing—by making you feel physically uneasy in many cases—you need to listen. Your intuition is talking to you.

It's important to pay attention when your sixth sense is shouting at you. Part of learning to trust your gut involves learning to listen to yourself. In a day and age when big data is all the rage and at a time when technology rules, it can be easy to shush the little voice in your head that tells you that, despite all the evidence to the contrary, you're about to make a bad decision.

Sometimes, everything looks great on paper. All the facts are there, all the data point in one direction, and all the evidence forecasts a sure outcome. But there's that niggling feeling poking you in the back of your mind, telling you "Don't do it!"

In a world that values technology and data and analysis and logic, it can be difficult to listen to that visceral part of you. But you should. In fact, when making difficult or important decisions, doing so is imperative. "[L]earning to harness one's instincts and intuition helps individuals make better decisions in all areas of their lives, personal and professional."[14]

When making decisions, listen to that little voice in your head. Pay attention to what your gut is telling you. That flutter in your stomach, the prickly sensation on the back of your neck, the quickening of your heartbeat—that tells you something. Listen.

Remember, though, that trusting your gut doesn't mean ignoring all the available information. So, when making decisions, listen to what your intuition is telling you. Write down the first thoughts that jump into your mind. But also dig deeper by making a pro–con list. Solicit feedback from trusted advisors, colleagues, and mentors. Ask yourself what would hap-

---

14. Meridith Levinson. "How to Harness Instinct and Intuition to Make Better Business and Career Decisions," *CIO Magazine*, April 7, 2009. Retrieved July 9, 2015, from http://www.cio.com/article/2429366/careers-staffing/how-to-harness-instinct-and-intuition-to-make-better-business-and-career-decisions.html.

pen if you did the opposite. Predict the worst-case scenario if the decision goes wrong. Then decide whether to trust your intuition or the evidence.

And then own it—embrace that decision and follow through. Doing so proves you to be a leader of conviction and one in whom followers can trust.

And keep score—keep a record of whether your intuition paid off or where you got it wrong. Doing so will help you further develop your intuition as you gain confidence in your decision-making abilities.

Trust Yourself

Closely connected to trusting your gut is trusting in yourself, your skills, and your abilities. In fact, it could be easily argued that you can't trust your gut until you trust yourself.

Trusting yourself means you have to conquer self-doubt and nurture self-confidence. This can be easier said than done, especially for us junkyard dogs.

But learning to trust in yourself is also crucial if you want to make it to the C Suite. No one becomes a CEO by living a life full of self-doubt, by waffling on major decisions, or by avoiding important situations. Trusting in yourself is a key component of nurturing a successful, fulfilling career. As leadership expert Glenn Llopis notes, "to trust yourself is also the most empowering decision that you can make. It is one of the most critical success factors in your career and work."[15]

Llopis goes on to argue that, "[t]rusting yourself is a learned skill. It requires a deep understanding and acceptance of who you are and what you represent."[16] I couldn't agree more. Learning to trust in yourself and develop your intuition very much requires no small measure of self-awareness. It's impor-

---

15. Glenn Llopis. "You Must Trust Yourself in Order to Make a Real Difference," *Forbes*, September 26, 2011. Retrieved July 9, 2015, from http://www.forbes.com/sites/glennllopis/2011/09/26/you-must-trust-yourself-in-order-to-make-a-real-difference.
16. *Ibid*.

tant to listen to what's going on around you. It's important to learn from your experiences. Keeping score can help with this.

In fact, I keep a record of my accomplishments—and of my mistakes and failures—and I review this list periodically. I also keep a folder of all the encouraging cards and notes I've received over the years, and I go back and read them whenever I need an ego boost or a gut-check. Doing so helps me identify the themes that characterize my career, and it helps me ensure that I'm being true to myself in pursuing my goals.

You can do the same. Keep track of where you've made a difference. Take stock of the type of people you work well with. Keep notes on what you've done well and what you've done not so well, of what you like and don't like. Learn what your professional storyline is and pay attention to how your career trajectory is progressing.

All of this will help you learn to listen to your intuition, trust your gut, and trust in yourself, building the kind of self-assurance that will help you progress successfully and confidently in your career.

Trust Those Around You

Let me start right off here with an example that illustrates how important the issue of trust—and knowing whom to trust—is.

Jim was working as a plant manager at a manufacturing company. A PhD in engineering, he had been with the organization for more than thirty years when the company brought in a new CEO who was coming from a different industry. The new top man was considered something of a leadership guru, and it was a big deal for the company to have snagged this well-known executive.

As far as Jim was concerned, however, this was by no means a match made in heaven. He was really struggling because he was not at all getting along with his new CEO. Jim had been with the organization for several decades, the CEO for just a few months, and the transition was difficult to say the least. Change can be hard, of course, but this was more than that.

After the new CEO had been on the job for a few months, the organization's HR department contacted Jim and solicited his feedback about how well the new CEO was assimilating into the company. They asked for a meeting with Jim so they could "discuss things."

Jim's intuition told him that this was a sign of nothing good. He could tell he was about to be put between a rock and a hard place, and he asked me what to do. I advised him not to say anything negative and to avoid undermining the new CEO in any way. I also advised him to start keeping records of all his accomplishments, all his assignments, and all his interactions with the CEO. I suggested he keep minutes of every meeting that involved the both of them. I reminded him of the importance of managing up and keeping score.

The senior vice president of HR came in from out of town to meet with Jim, along with a witness (i.e., a colleague who would sit in on the meeting). Jim really couldn't stand working with the new CEO, but he knew he couldn't say so. He instinctively understood that placing his trust in the company representatives and opening up about all the faults of his new boss would be self-destructive.

Keep in mind that the new CEO was hired by the system CEO with input from key stakeholders. No one wants to see "their pick" or "their person" fail within the first year, and they expect some turmoil will occur as the new CEO tries to implement change. Therefore, you need to be careful with your feedback and constructive with your messaging. Whatever you say will be documented (hence the witness), so remember who the HR representatives work for: the company. It's important for you to know that discussing an issue with someone from the company isn't at all like confiding in your BFF. You need to assume that your feedback will be shared in some format with the individual in question. You can't take the risk that negative feedback might be shared with the individual, nor can you take the risk of how it will be interpreted.

Jim knew this, and so he was cautious going into the meeting with the representatives, keeping his comments measured and framing the issues carefully. He left the meeting and returned to work, keeping his head down and keeping score.

As it happened, within fifteen months, the new CEO was let go—but before he was, many employees left the company. Jim is still with the company, feeling positive about his continued future with the new current CEO.

INEQUALITY EQUALIZER

Recognize that trust is a two-way street. You have to be careful about whom you trust in the workplace because competition is fierce. Accept the fact that you can't be everybody's buddy; sometimes you have to settle for respect.

When it comes to business, trust is a challenging issue. It's important to create a culture of trust so that colleagues can work effectively together, but it's also important to remember that your coworkers are not your best friends. It's important to develop professional trust while not getting too personal.

Trusting in those around you, particularly when it comes to business, means that you demonstrate confidence that the people you work with will do their jobs well, on time, and with integrity. It means you can discuss openly the issues of the day without being ignored, punished, or ridiculed. It means you can believe that colleagues and managers will honor their commitments.

Learning to trust those around you can be something of a balancing act. Intuition plays a big role here—we often know instinctively and right away whether we like and can trust someone. But trust is one of those things that you have to keep on earning, not the least of which because it can be so easily eroded. One poorly phrased sentence, one instance of not following through, one incendiary "reply all" e-mail with a cc to the boss—anything can destroy in an instant trust that was built up over years.

I know this first hand. I had been working for a healthcare organization for a while when it was bought by another company. With that change came a new boss, one who had never managed a woman before (at one point, he made me go out and buy a skirt because he didn't believe a pantsuit was appropriate for an outside meeting). It turned out he would be one of the most difficult bosses I would ever work for.

This new CEO knew his business and had a reputation for being an effective leader. I found him to be competent, but with a foul, abrasive personality. After he had been with the organization for a while, he asked me how I thought he was doing. Of course, junkyard dog that I am, I decided to tell him the truth.

This was a huge mistake.

I told him—after we'd had a few drinks together during a conference (I thought this was "bonding time")—that I thought he was a bulldog, that he was difficult, that I thought he was boorish. I brought up an incident in which I had to escort him to his hotel room to keep him from doing or saying anything embarrassing because he'd had way too much to drink at a company function.

I didn't let up, either. The next day, I proceeded to "share" with him what I had left out the night before, thinking I was advising him. I felt that, as the head of Human Resources, I had a responsibility to tell him how out of line his behavior had been.

As you can imagine, he never forgot this. Our work relationship was never the same. Rewinding time is never an option, and erasing your actions is not reality.

When I finally decided to leave the organization for another role, I told the CEO that I was resigning, and I am sure he was thrilled but knew the organization would be surprised. Then he asked me not to tell anyone yet.

I decided to forgo this request and tell my senior direct reports that I was leaving. I trusted my top lieutenants to keep the news under wraps, and I wanted them to know what was happening. Most important, I wanted them to hear it from me. I disregarded the request of my current CEO and put my own interests above the company's best interest.

Of course, it soon became known that I had disregarded the CEO's request, which displeased him greatly. And I realized that one of my trusted colleagues had betrayed me as well, telling my CEO what I had told them.

All of this affected my career in many ways, including events which still come back to bite me to this day, since we still travel in some of the same business circles. The business relationship was never repaired.

As happens with life, I learned a lot of lessons from this experience. I learned that you need to respect the hierarchy of the organization on the way out just as you would on the way into the company. I also learned that being transparent doesn't mean sharing everything you know. Sometimes the best favor you can do for employees is to not share information that will put them in a compromising position. Loyalty is fickle—in the end, your team members will be loyal to themselves and to the organization they work for more than they'll be loyal to you. I learned that it's awfully easy to destroy relationships when trust is betrayed in all directions. I learned that trusting in others doesn't mean that you can say whatever you want whenever you want. No one will tolerate a case of Truth Tourette's where you blurt out every thought you have every moment that you have them.

Trust is as important as it is fragile. You have to trust people to get their job done. You have to trust that people will be supportive of you. You need to trust that your colleagues will treat you and each other with respect. You have to trust that those who lead you know what they're doing and how to get the job done—and that you don't always need to know everything. But you also have to realize that trust can be shattered in an instant.

Even so, at some point in your life (professional and personal), you likely will simply have to decide to place your trust in the people around you—especially if you want them to trust you as well. Few of us can go it alone, and no one's career is built in a vacuum, so it's both important and necessary to learn how to trust others.

As with my own examples, you'll likely find that developing trust—in your intuition, in yourself, and in others—comes with experience. So long as you're open and willing to learn from your experiences, you will be well equipped to develop the kind of trust and intuition that will help guide you throughout your career.

INSTILL TRUST IN OTHERS

Just as it's important to place your trust in those around you, it's important to instill trust as well. You can't expect anyone to trust you if you don't trust them—and vice versa.

Trust is a big issue. By some measures, roughly 80 percent of us have little to no faith in the people who lead our major corporations.[17] Bankers, lawyers, politicians—the majority of us don't place much trust in these professionals.[18] This at a time when "trust is the new core of leadership," argues *Forbes*, which notes that, "[l]eaders can no longer trust in power; instead, they rely on the power of trust."[19]

Few would doubt the importance of trust in the workplace. In fact, CEO Jim Dougherty writes that,

17. Robert F. Hurley. "The Decision to Trust," *Harvard Business Review*, September 2006. Retrieved July 9, 2015, from https://hbr.org/2006/09/the-decision-to-trust.
18. Rebecca Riffkin. "Americans Rate Nurses Highest on Honesty, Ethical Standards," *Gallup*, December 18, 2014. Retrieved July 9, 2015, from http://www.gallup.com/poll/180260/americans-rate-nurses-highest-honesty-ethical-standards.aspx.
19. Charles Green. "Why Trust Is the New Core of Leadership," *Forbes*, April 3, 2012. Retrieved July 9, 2015, from http://www.forbes.com/sites/trustedadvisor/2012/04/03/why-trust-is-the-new-core-of-leadership.

establishing trust is *the* top priority. Whether you are taking over a small department, an entire division, a company, or even a Boy Scout troop, the first thing you must get is the trust of the members of that entity. . . . Without trust, it is *very* unlikely you will learn the truth [about] what is *really* going on in that organization and in the market place. Without trust, employees won't level with you—at best, you'll learn either non-truths or part truths.[20]

So how do you go about making people trust you? In addition to showing your colleagues that you trust them, you also have to demonstrate that you're worthy of their trust. There is no shortage of ways to build trust, including:

- **Be Loyal to Yourself.** If you want people to trust you, you have to have enough self-confidence and self-assurance to be true to yourself, your goals, and your ethics. You have to act with integrity. And you also have to understand that your colleagues have to be loyal to themselves as well. So, don't ask them to do anything unsavory, anything that they would be uncomfortable with, or anything that would undermine their own integrity.
- **Be Truthful.** People can't trust you if they don't believe you—what you say or what you do. If you want people to trust you, you have to be trustworthy, and that starts with keeping your word, speaking truthfully, and being honest and open. Remember, though, that this doesn't mean you can or should say anything you want whenever you want.
- **Be Present and Available.** Being trusted means that you show up when you're supposed to and that you pitch in as expected. It means you keep your door open to colleagues and staff as well as clients and customers. It also means

---

20. Jim Dougherty. "The Best Way for New Leaders to Build Trust," *Harvard Business Review*, December 13, 2013. Retrieved July 9, 2015, from https://hbr.org/2013/12/the-best-way-for-new-leaders-to-build-trust.

you pay attention when people are talking to you and that you take the time to actually hear what they're saying. No one builds trust by multitasking during a meeting or by answering a cell phone in the middle of a business dinner.

- **Be Accountable.** Instilling trust means that you have to follow through, keep your promises, and do what you say you will. It also means you have to take responsibility for your actions, including admitting when you're wrong or when you've made a mistake.

No organization can function with any success if it is mired in mistrust and suspicion, and no leader can succeed if she doesn't treat trust as a two-way street. Just as it's crucial to learn to trust those around you, it's equally important to work hard at earning the trust of those you work with. When it comes to building trust, everything you say and do matters.

Developing intuition and trust is a crucial component of a successful career, one of those soft skills that no one can do without. Building trust is key when it comes to building relationships, and no career-minded professional can make it to the C Suite without creating some healthy, positive relationships with colleagues at every level. Those relationships will be crucial throughout your career, and we'll look at that next, when we discuss networking in Chapter 10.

Tough-Love Lessons for Developing Intuition and Trust

- Professionals who dismiss intuition as unreliable mumbo-jumbo miss out on mastering a crucial soft skill that can help them advance their careers. Intuition, when used effectively, often proves to be a winning tool in any decision-maker's arsenal.

- Making the most of intuition requires professionals to keep score and learn from both their accomplishments and their mistakes because the best intuition-based decision making is built on experience and expertise. Top professionals understand that using intuition isn't the same as ignoring evidence.

- No one can make effective intuition-based decisions if they're not in tune with themselves. Listening to your intuition can be one of the most effective skills in your career—and ignoring your intuition can prove damaging.

- Developing your intuition means you have to learn to trust your gut and trust yourself. High-level executives don't waste time on self-doubt, second-guessing every decision. Instead, they learn to foster the kind of self-confidence that allows them to trust themselves and their abilities.

- A successful career means you have to learn how to put your trust in others. Few of us work in a vacuum, hermits without any human contact. As such, we have to learn how to trust others—and we have to learn how to recognize whom we can trust, to what extent, and in which circumstances. Top professionals learn to recognize those individuals in whom they can confide.

- Trust is a two-way street, and you can't expect someone to trust you if you don't trust them. In order to instill trust in others, you have to be loyal, truthful, present, and accountable. You have to walk the talk.

= 10 =

Networking for Success

From: "Jena Abernathy" <jabernathy@email.com>

To: "Megan Watson" <mwatson@email.com>

Subject: Networking

Megan,

So much of what we accomplish in business isn't about how well we complete the tasks we work on but on how well we work with others, the kind of relationships we build, and the connections we forge. We talked about how important developing intuition and trust is, and that plays a big part in knowing whom you can trust—and when. Because building relationships and networking with your connections is crucial as you progress through your career.

—Jena

You know that person on the plane in the seat next to you who smiles when you sit down after you hoist your roller-bag up into the tiny carry-on compartment and then goes back to her book or her iPad or her white paper and never talks to you again for the rest of the flight?

Yeah . . . that's not me.

No, I'm the one who will smile and then say hello and ask why you're heading to wherever it is we're both flying. I might ask how long you've been at your company, what you do there, and how well you like it. I might ask about your interests. In fact, I'm likely going to interview you. And, I'm probably going to give you advice that you never asked for and may not even want. But I'm also going to listen to you. I'm going to spend some time with you. Chances are, if you're sitting next to me, we'll have a pretty good conversation that will make it feel like that was the shortest flight you ever took to New York or Los Angeles or Chicago or Dallas or wherever.

Was that lovely, three-hour-long airplane conversation we just had a networking opportunity? You bet. Was it also a nice way to pass the time? Absolutely. Because you never know whom you might be sitting next to on an airplane or a train or during a conference session—unless you smile and say hello and start a conversation.

A lot of people cringe at the notion of networking, as though it's an onerous task to be conducted with dread. When we think "networking," many of us picture having to ham it up at a cocktail party during a business conference, walking into the room alone, nursing a weak gin and tonic, and hoping, simultaneously, that no one will approach us and that someone will. We psyche ourselves up to be "on" in order to say the right thing and act the right way so that we sound savvy and charming and knowledgeable.

When we do that, we forget about how nice it can be— fun, even!—just to have a conversation with someone. We also forget that relationships aren't built on the simple act of exchanging business cards during a two-day conference down in Miami in January. Relationships are built on conversations, and networking can't happen effectively unless you've been able to forge some quality relationships.

When it comes to business, few of us build our careers without working our contacts, without benefitting from referrals, or without making introductions. Networking helps us do that. It helps us expand our sphere of influence, which we discussed in Chapter 5. Remember that your sphere of influence includes direct reports, support staff, colleagues, and team members, as well as industry peers, competitors, clients, and customers. The people who are in your sphere of influence reflect the relationships you have with the people in your organization and in your industry. Your sphere of influence is in large part made up of your connections—your network.

It is with these people that you will work throughout your career. Some may come and some may go at various points during your professional life. You might lose touch with some of them. But there also will be connections to whom you turn again and again, whether for referrals or mentoring or other advice and insight. You might want to call on them for the favor of an introduction. Someone in your network might call on you to provide a reference. You might look to people in your sphere of influence to help you find a new business partner or to reach a key new customer. This is networking—having conversations, building relationships, and working together to accomplish more than anyone could do alone.

I enjoy meeting new people, so networking comes naturally to me. I recognize, however, that networking is far from easy for most people. Fear and shyness can cripple some people to the point that networking feels like a terrible chore, one to be avoided at all costs. Many of us—and especially junkyard dogs, who often haven't been schooled in the finer points of schmoozing—are reluctant to build and work our connections. But learning how to be savvy, effective networkers is crucial if you want to make it to the C Suite. No one ever

189

makes it to the corner office by sitting behind her desk all day avoiding people.

So let's talk a bit about the benefits of networking, ways to go about it—and not go about it—and where to start building your sphere of influence.

Embrace the Power of Networking

I think that part of the challenge with networking is to reframe it. A lot of people think of networking as this kind of schmarmy, glad-handing, what's-in-it-for-me approach to working acquaintances in the hope of getting new business.

Do I need to tell you that that's not at all what networking is about?

First and foremost, networking is about building relationships. Those relationships might well turn into something more. That person you're sitting next to on the plane, the stranger you approached at a conference—she could be your next mentor, your next client, or even your next boss. But if you never talk to anyone, if you never introduce yourself, you're missing out on what might turn into lifelong relationships that could do wonders for you and your career—and for the people in your life.

Years ago, I was on a flight and struck up a conversation with the guy sitting next to me. He, too, was a consultant, and, as it turned out, his brother was a chief executive for a major healthcare company. As we got to talking, it turned out that we worked in related industries, shared similar interests, and knew some people in common. We kept in touch, and over the years, he has sent potential candidates my way for key job openings. He also has sent some potential clients my way, and I have done the same for him. That networking conversation, held so long ago, has benefitted both of us for years as we've built a lasting professional relationship.

Experiences like that prove that the old adage "it's not what you know, it's who you know" is true. None other than former General Electric CEO and business guru Jack Welch has said, "Forget the MBA. Learn to network."

Jack Welch is right about that. Networking can be a powerful business tool, helping to propel you up the corporate ladder. In fact, this is something that pedigrees seem to have an innate understanding of. So many Ivy Leaguers have come up in a world where they all get to know each other, and they trade on that familiarity, giving each other references (and preference), helping provide a leg up on a great job or an important contract, and making the kind of introductions that opens doors to leading companies, desirable clubs and associations, and influential thought leaders. Learning how to network effectively can help junkyard dogs level the playing field.

———

191

INEQUALITY EQUALIZER

Top-performing employees are also often the best networkers, people-persons who know how to make introductions and build relationships. Whether junkyard dog or pedigree, those professionals who understand the nuances of networking have a leg up on the competition.

———

Before you can understand how to network effectively, though, you first have to embrace the power of networking. Understanding the power of networking means recognizing the benefits, both short-term and long-term, that networking can bring not only you but those in your sphere of influence as well. The benefits of networking are myriad, so I'll just list a few here:

- Networking can introduce you to any number of people who will be influential throughout your career, from potential clients and customers to potential colleagues and bosses.
- Networking can put you in touch with mentors who can offer sage advice, industry insight, and priceless expertise that can help you navigate your career, particularly at key junctures.
- Networking can lead to opportunities that help you build a community of followers that will help position you as a thought leader and subject-matter expert.
- Networking can help open doors to new business contacts who can help you grow your business, get new contracts, provide seed money for a new venture, or otherwise invest in you and your organization.
- Networking can provide entrée into situations that will help you further your career, such as membership into important clubs and associations or seats on boards of directors.
- Networking can help position you as a person of influence who can help others connect with new people by brokering introductions.
- Networking can help build your self-confidence as you become more adept at working a room, making introductions, connecting with new people, and discussing issues related to your industry.
- Networking can help you build lasting, fulfilling relationships with like-minded individuals who share your goals and interests.

No matter how you look at it, networking can be a powerful tool to help you grow your professional life and propel your career. As Michael Dulworth writes in his book *The Connect Effect,*

When you have a network of thoughtful, experienced, and smart people, you actually have a cadre of "consultants" you can call on to help you deal with difficult personal and professional issues. . . . There is significant comfort in knowing that you have a group of trusted and objective colleagues you can call on when you need help, advice, and support.[1]

As we discussed in Chapter 9, developing trust is a crucial component to your professional success, and tapping into a network of trusted colleagues and advisors can help you do just that. It's a virtuous circle. The benefits of networking are numerous, and those who make the most of this important skill will find it a powerful tool to help them throughout their careers.

Build Your Sphere of Influence

Networking goes well beyond exchanging business cards or racking up another connection on LinkedIn. Effective networking isn't so much about how many people you know as it is about what you do with the relationships you have. Being connected to 500+ strangers on a social media site could never help you in the way that having fifty meaningful relationships can. Networking isn't about quantity; it's about quality.

"[H]aving a lot of networks doesn't necessarily lead to measurable change," says Erica Dhawan, coauthor of *Get Big Things Done*, in a *Huffington Post* article. "The key is how you combine your networks, your resources, your ideas and people to get something big done."[2] I couldn't agree more.

1. Michael Dulworth. *The Connect Effect: Building Strong Personal, Professional, and Virtual Networks*. San Francisco: Berrett-Koehler Publishers, Inc., 2008, p. 9.
2. Alena Hall. "Why Quality over Quantity Is the Key to Productive Networking," *Huffington Post*, February 25, 2015. Retrieved July 16, 2015, from http://www.huffingtonpost.com/2015/02/25/networking-tips_n_6753976.html.

Amassing hundreds of connections on LinkedIn or thousands of followers on Twitter does little good if you rarely ever actually interact with those people. Networking is about building relationships, and few of us have the time to have meaningful or productive conversations with 10,000 fans or followers. It takes time to meet people, establish trust, and build strong relationships. Clicking "accept invitation" and becoming "friends" with someone through a social media platform isn't quite the same as having a series of face-to-face meetings and follow-up conversations with a person with whom you, together, nurture a relationship.

So how do you build your sphere of influence and expand your network? Where do you find the people with whom you can grow meaningful relationships? The short answer is that you build your sphere of influence by making connections within and without. By "within," I mean within your own organization. By "without," I mean outside of your company or industry to other venues. Let's look at both.

Building Your Network from Within

When we think about networking, most of us tend to think about reaching beyond the walls of our own organizations, meeting new people at conferences or other industry events. All too often, though, we forget about networking among our own teams or departments and beyond to the numerous other colleagues in our own companies. This never ceases to amaze me, and it's too bad, really, because most organizations offer a wealth of experts who can become trusted colleagues in our networks.

We've talked a little already throughout these pages about the importance of making yourself known at corporate headquarters and of volunteering for cross-departmental assignments. Doing so isn't just about getting face time with the higher-ups in your company, but about building relationships across the organization. Networking within your own organization is a great way to meet people, build relationships, and build your reputation.

There are other benefits as well to networking within. Among these is the increased ability to work the back channels in order to gather support for key projects you're working on. Let's say, for example, that you are about to present a new product proposal to everyone who sits on your new product development board. You might know a handful of people with whom you work directly, but those team members aren't in decision-making positions and likely won't have much say. The key decision makers are directors and vice presidents from the likes of the R&D, sales, marketing, and publicity departments. If you've never met these people, you're likely going to have a tough sell. If, on the other hand, you've made a point to introduce yourself to these individuals, to chat with them about the project ahead of time, to discuss pros and cons, to earn their trust, and to build your reputation with them, you'll have a much better chance of success. Working the back channels like this and gathering support ahead of the meeting is just one of the benefits of networking within your organization.

Networking from within (sometimes called "internal networking") also can help improve teamwork, reduce gossip and office politics, and help you identify potential mentors who have institutional knowledge you can learn from. In addition, of course, networking with your coworkers can help you build your reputation as you become better known across the organization, which also helps keep you top of mind for plum assignments and promotions.

When networking within your organization, it's important to do so strategically. You shouldn't be stalking senior management or interrupting a meeting in order to introduce yourself, but you should be willing and able to talk to strangers and acquaintances. Chit-chat can be helpful to break the ice, but be careful about spending too much time jabbering away in someone's cubicle: You don't want to be intrusive and hog their time, and you don't want to give the impression that you're a chatterbox more intent on socializing than on actually working. Instead, ask your colleague if you can pick her brain over breakfast or lunch. When you have that meeting, avoid veering into gossip or office politics. Instead, stay on topic, discussing with your colleague a particular assignment, procedure, or industry trend that relates to your organization. Keep it professional.

This isn't at all to say you should shy away from being sociable at work. You should, in fact, make a point to be pleasant to everyone at every level, saying hello, asking about how a project is going, or discussing the results of a new product launch. Remember here that the goal isn't just to make sure you're talking to people—you also have to listen to them. The best networkers are good connectors, good communicators, and good listeners—not just good talkers.

INEQUALITY EQUALIZER

When networking, let people talk. People love to tell their stories, and everyone wants to be heard. The best networkers are those who take the time not only to ask questions but also to listen to the answers, because they're willing to learn from and are interested in people and what they have to say.

I want to reiterate here how important it is to network with people at every level. You can tell a lot about a person by how he treats everyone from the CEO to vice presidents to directors to assistants—even to the janitors who clean the offices long after most of the staffers have left for the night. People at every level of the organization can share all kinds of institutional knowledge, and there is insight to be gained from employees across the organization. Just as we discussed in Chapter 5 the importance of managing up, down, and sideways, you also should be networking in all directions.

As Miranda Brawn, Esq., a London-based attorney and investment banker, writes in *The Glass Hammer*,

> Take an interest in people from greeting the receptionist and potentially stopping for 15 seconds to take a moment to look into their eyes and listen to their answer when you ask "how are you?" which is what networking is all about. This is not just networking upwards with the senior people in your organization but everyone![3]

Throughout your career, you will undoubtedly work with some amazing people. But you won't get to know them if you don't make an effort to reach out across teams, departments, and silos. Especially early in your career, as you're building your sphere of influence, networking from within can be a particularly effective way to meet influential people who will help shape your professional life.

Building Your Network from Without

Networking outside our own organizations is what most of us think about when we think about networking. We think about having to do the small-talk thing with strangers during the pre-conference cocktail hour. We think about handing out business cards and chatting with attendees in the exhibit hall during an industry trade show. We think about working the room during the hour-long meet-and-greet before an association workshop. We think about these events, and we hate them.

Most of us know we should network, but we hate the idea of having to schmooze like this. We might hate it because we're

3. Miranda K. Brawn. "Building the Talent Pipeline: Developing Your Networking Skills Within Your Organization," *The Glass Hammer*, June 3, 2014. Retrieved July 16, 2015, from http://theglasshammer.com/2014/06/03/building-the-talent-pipeline-developing-your-networking-skills-within-your-organization.

shy or introverted. Or maybe because we don't like the idea of having to be "on" in a room full of strangers after a long day at work. Or maybe because we've done it before and it hasn't led to anything beneficial. All too often, we feel like networking isn't the best use of our time. But networking can, in fact, be an effective use of time, with both short-term and long-term payoffs.

In the short term, networking at minimum introduces us to new people from whom we can learn about the company and industry in which we work, related fields, new trends, and so on. In the long term, the benefits, some of which we noted above, are myriad, any of which can help us grow professionally and personally as we develop lasting relationships.

INEQUALITY EQUALIZER

There's practically no limit to the avenues through which anyone can network, although it is important to keep in mind the culture of particular organizations. When networking, always be professional and courteous—and remember that your brand and your reputation are at stake.

So, in addition to networking from within, it's important to look outside your organization to find people with whom you can build professional relationships. Certainly one route to this is via social media platforms such as LinkedIn or apps like Hashable. Other venues include conferences and other industry functions, events hosted by local professional associations and organizations, meetings held by civic groups such as the local chamber of commerce, and volunteer organizations you work with.

Volunteering, in fact, is one of my favorite ways to network. Not only do you get to work for a good cause, but you also often make contact with people from other companies and industries, which widens your network while you're doing a good deed. Volunteering is a great way to level the playing field, too, because anyone can do it, regardless of title or pedigree. It can be especially effective for younger professionals and junk-yard dogs who might not otherwise have access to influential thought-leaders at, say, country clubs, where they can make new connections.

NETWORK WITH RECRUITERS

As someone who has spent a long time in human resources and executive search, I've seen the good, the bad, and the ugly when it comes to working with recruiters. Search firms (sometimes called "executive search firms" or "executive recruiters" or, in the olden days, "headhunters") can be a great way to network with high-level professionals.

Of course, most people turn to recruiters or search consultants if and when they want to find a new position. And that's okay. But it's actually better to introduce yourself to a search consultant before you're desperate for a new job. Becoming familiar with a recruiter allows you to develop a stronger relationship so that, when opportunities do arise, you both can work in a more targeted fashion to find the best position.

Top-performing professionals who build relationships with search consultants also are able to help them by referring others. Doing so is a win–win–win: it helps the recruiter place more candidates, it helps candidates (i.e., your connections) find new positions, and it keeps you front of mind so that the recruiter thinks of you first when the next new job comes around.

Networking with search consultants can open any number of doors—to new positions, to new organizations, even to new fields. Finding the right recruiter might require a bit of research, but it can pay off in spades. Let me share some tips when working with search consultants:

- **Research the Leading Recruiters in Your Field.** Some search firms are limited to certain industries or even organizations they can or do work with. Find a few firms that specialize in your field and connect with them. Make sure your résumé/CV is in their databases. Ask your connections for recommendations (but be careful about even hinting that you might be looking for a new job).
- **Keep Your Search Consultant Updated.** If you take on new responsibilities (or even a new position), win an award, keynote an event, etc., let your recruiter know so she can update her database. That way she's sure to have at her fingertips the most current information about you, your responsibilities, and your accomplishments when she chats you up to prospective employers.
- **Stay in Touch.** Along the same lines as keeping your search consultant updated is to keep in touch with her. Return her calls and e-mails. Even if you're not interested in a position she suggests, be courteous enough to reply to her messages. If she's taking the time to get in touch with you, the least you can do is to return the favor. But do not appear desperate, and don't call continuously to check on opportunities.
- **Don't Argue with Your Recruiter.** If you don't get an offer, or if a negotiation falls through, or if your search consultant opts against putting you forth for a position, don't argue with her. Don't argue with her when things don't go your way. Don't threaten her in any way. Remain professional at all times. If you've established a trusting relationship with your recruiter, you should feel confident in her abilities and her decisions.
- **Say Thank You.** Even when you're going through the interview process thanks to the help of a search consultant,

it's important to thank the people you interact with. E-mail each point of contact a note thanking them for their time and reiterating why you'd be a great fit for the job. And don't forget to thank your recruiter for all the work she does on your behalf.

Recruiters can be great tools in your networking arsenal. But remember that they're human, too, and so, as with all networking, keep in mind that the success of the interaction depends on the strength of the relationship.

No matter which avenues you go through, networking doesn't stop with "hello." The goal in networking isn't simply to exchange contact information or to amass connections. No one wins a prize at the end of a long career for acquiring the most business cards. The key is what you do with them.

Remember that networking is about building relationships. Although it certainly can help you build your career—and is instrumental, in many cases, in doing so—networking shouldn't be thought of as a conduit for favors. In fact, one of the reasons so many people are loath to network is because we're afraid of the inevitable ask that follows. We don't want a simple exchange of business cards to lead directly to a request to do a favor for someone we barely know.

This is networking done wrong. Most of us think about networking when we want something—typically a new job. But no one should go about networking as a way to find people who can do favors for you. In fact, researchers have found that this kind of networking, sometimes referred to as "instrumental networking," is exactly what makes many of us hate the very notion of networking. "[I]nstrumental networking in pursuit of professional goals can impinge on an individual's moral purity—a psychological state that results from viewing the self as clean from a moral standpoint—and make an individual feel dirty."[4]

Instead, networking should always be about the relationship first. Don't connect with someone on LinkedIn and immediately ask for an introduction to one of her connections. Don't exchange business cards with someone at a meeting only to get back to your office two days later and ask if he can put in a good word for you for a job at his firm. Instead, work first on getting to know those people. Follow them for a while on social media and comment on the articles they post. Congratulate them on an especially interesting white paper they've written. Invite them to coffee or drinks during an upcoming industry event that you'll both be attending.

Perhaps most important when it comes to networking is to think not about what your contacts can do for you, but what you can do for them. As psychotherapist Amy Morin writes in *Forbes*, "Think about what you have to offer, not just what you want to gain. If you only view networking as a self-serving promotional tool, you're likely to feel a little sleazy. Before you approach your next networking opportunity, think about what you can give, not just what you want to gain."[5]

So, when meeting new people and starting to build relationships, think about what you can offer them that will help them professionally. Maybe you can introduce them to potential new clients. Perhaps you can connect them to an industry thought-leader they've been dying to meet. Or maybe you can point them in the direction of a new job, either at your own firm or at one of your connection's firms. You might well know someone who knows someone who could help your new connection with a project she's working on. (Just remember that

4. Tiziana Casciaro, Francesca Gino, and Maryam Kouchaki. *The Contaminating Effects of Building Instrumental Ties: How Networking Can Make Us Feel Dirty.* Harvard Business School, Working Paper No. 14-108, April 2014. Retrieved July 16, 2015, from http://www.hbs.edu/faculty/Publication percent20Files/14-108_dacbf869-fbc1-4ff8-b927-d77ca54d93d8.pdf.
5. Amy Morin. "How to Network Without Feeling 'Dirty,'" *Forbes Magazine*, September 11, 2014. Retrieved July 16, 2015, from http://www.forbes.com/sites/amymorin/2014/09/11/how-to-network-without-feeling-dirty/

if you offer to help someone, you have to follow through on that promise.)

HOW NOT TO NETWORK

Networking has a bad reputation—largely in part due to the fact that so many people do it wrong. In addition to forgetting that networking is about building relationships rather than about asking for favors, too many people approach networking as a means to amass a large quantity of connections while failing to pay attention to the quality of those connections. Let's look at some of the things to avoid when networking.

- **Don't Go After the Big Fish.** If you're at a conference and the industry's top CEO is the keynote speaker, think twice about trying to introduce yourself, especially if you're an entry-level or even mid-level employee. Remember that networking is very much about what you can do for your new connection—and chances are there's little early on in your career that you could do for a leading CEO.
- **Don't Waste Your Connection's Time.** Whether cornering a coveted contact at a conference cocktail party or barraging her with e-mail, it's crucial to respect her time. Remember that your priority is very likely not her priority, and so be careful about taking up too much of her time in the hope of furthering your own agenda.
- **Don't Go in for the Big Ask.** All too often, people equate networking with asking for a favor. This is especially dangerous when reaching out to new connections—no one likes to be asked for a job seconds after meeting someone new. But it can be just as troublesome to ask someone you know only a little for a big favor, such as making an important introduction or participating in a billboard event. Remember to keep in perspective the quality of the relationship before asking any connection for a favor.

- **Don't Interrupt.** When networking, remember to harness all the cultural and etiquette lessons you've learned. Part of that means that you should never interrupt someone in order to introduce yourself. Don't barge into a group of people and stop their conversation so you can speak to a coveted contact. Don't interrupt a new contact by interjecting your own two cents' worth or by diverting your attention to someone else you'd like to meet. Remember that good networking is about good communicating—and good communicators are careful not to interrupt.
- **Don't Forget to Follow Up.** Whether it's keeping a promise, thanking someone for his time, or simply letting a new connection know how much you enjoyed talking with her, it's important to keep the dialog going. Networking isn't a one-and-done event; it's an ongoing relationship. So, if you want to build lasting relationships that result in effective networking, it's important to keep in touch with your connections.

There are a million ways networking can go wrong. So, perhaps, the Golden Rule applies here: Treat others as you would like to be treated. Be kind, respectful, and courteous. Keep your word. Be polite. Give of yourself without expecting anything in return. And work on building relationships rather than asking for favors.

Networking is one of business's great equalizers. Whether junkyard dog or pedigree, male or female, entry-level employee or C Suite executive, networking provides opportunities to meet new people who can influence your career in important ways. Tenure, title, or gender—it doesn't really matter when it comes to networking; anyone can—and everyone should—do it. Of course, there are differences in the way people approach networking, as there is with everything else in business. We'll look at some of those differences next, in Chapter 11, when we discuss gender issues.

Tough-Love Lessons for Networking for Success

- Top professionals don't shy away from networking just because it might make them feel socially awkward or because they don't feel like being "on." Instead, they view networking as an opportunity to build relationships.
- High-level executives consider networking a crucial soft skill and an important component of their professional toolkit. They understand that anyone can learn how to do a task, but it takes finesse and practice to learn how to network effectively.
- The best employees take the time to network within their own organizations, connecting with people across and throughout all levels of the company so that they network in all directions—not just up.
- Successful professionals see networking opportunities just about everywhere, anytime—in large part because they understand that networking is about having conversations with interesting people who have like interests, whether at work, at the club, at industry functions, at volunteer gigs, or wherever.

= 11 =

Dealing with Gender Issues

From: "Jena Abernathy" <jabernathy@email.com>

To: "Megan Watson" <mwatson@email.com>

Subject: Gender at Work

Megan,

Hard skills, soft skills . . . I know there's a lot to figure out, especially when you're at the beginning of your career. As you study the business of business and develop your networking skills, another thing to think about is gender at work. You'd think gender wouldn't still matter now, nearly two decades into the new millennium, but it does. It still does. Men and women simply come at some things differently—and we perceive each other differently. It's important to be aware of gender issues as you navigate your way through your career.

—Jena

Regardless of how much we might like to think that everyone believes that men and women are equal, the truth is that every woman (and most men) will face a variety of gender issues throughout her career. Among those challenges is simply getting to the top spot. We see this every day when we witness the dearth of women in leadership positions. A recent CNNMoney analysis revealed that, of the top five positions in S&P 500 companies (i.e., C Suite roles), only 14.2 percent are held by women. Of those 500 companies, only 24 are led by female CEOs.[1] The numbers are roughly the same for Fortune 500 companies, where only 25 women are in the top spot.[2]

These figures are better than they were two decades ago when no women led either any Fortune 500 or S&P 500 companies. But we still have a ways to go. And by "we," I don't mean just women—men and women alike need to rethink what it takes to be a leader. We need to recognize that men and women lead in different ways (as we discussed in Chapter 6). We also need to make sure that we're not working under different standards for the same job and that we're judging, treating, and evaluating each other with fairness and equity.

Rethinking needs to happen both from the top down and from the bottom up. But it might help most if some of today's most well-respected business executives would do more to lead the way. For instance, at a Women in the Economy Conference in 2012, former General Electric CEO Jack Welch told a gathering of women executives from a range of industries that, in matters of career track, it is results and performance that chart the way. "Overdeliver!" Mr. Welch advised. "Performance is it!"[3]

1. "Still Missing: Female Business Leaders," *CNNMoney*, March 24, 2015. Retrieved July 21, 2015, from http://money.cnn.com/2015/03/24/investing/female-ceo-pipeline-leadership.

2. Colleen Leahey and Caroline Fairchild. "Women CEOs in the Fortune 500," *Fortune Magazine*, May 9, 2013; updated January 6, 2015. Retrieved July 21, 2015, from http://fortune.com/2013/05/09/women-ceos-in-the-fortune-500.

3. John Bussey. "Women, Welch Clash at Forum," *The Wall Street Journal*, May 4, 2012. Retrieved July 21, 2015, from http://www.wsj.com/articles/SB10001424052702303877604577382321364803912.

Welch took a lot of flak for that comment. The perception that Welch—and, one can assume, scores of other leaders—believes that women simply don't work hard enough to make it to the C Suite or that, for some reason, women don't understand that hard work is essential caused an uproar that could be heard all across the business community. Understandably, many women balked at the notion that they simply don't put in the hours, deliver the goods, outperform colleagues, or get results. Indeed, counterarguments surfaced almost immediately, with scores of business professionals, thought leaders, and journalists chiming in with statistics and data that prove that women perform equally as well as (and, in some cases, better than) their male colleagues.[4]

Here's the thing, though: I don't necessarily disagree with what Welch was saying. In fact, I believe he didn't go far enough: It's not just women who need to overdeliver. Everyone at every organization could stand to overdeliver and focus on knocking performance measures out of the park, particularly if they want to make it to the C Suite. But we also all need to get past the stereotype that women are of a "lesser" gender, that women continually need to prove their worth, and that women constantly need to show that they're willing to sacrifice their family, their time, their everything in order to get ahead. The fact is that anyone who wants to achieve must overdeliver, regardless of gender.

As an executive recruiter, I've seen firsthand the many gender issues that are at play in the corporate world. I've felt the frustration of watching women who were really great candidates not be selected for high-level positions for which they were eminently qualified. I've seen countless times that when a male candidate has CEO experience at even the smallest organization, he will get preference over a female candidate

209

---

4. Jenna Goudreau. "Why Jack Welch Is Spectacularly Stupid When It Comes to Women," *Forbes Magazine*, May 4, 2012. Retrieved July 21, 2015, from http://www.forbes.com/sites/jennagoudreau/2012/05/04/why-jack-welch-is-spectacularly-stupid-when-it-comes-to-women.

who has C-level but not CEO experience at a leading company. They should be considered equal, but most organizations will ultimately choose the man.

Why is this? A lot of times, it's simply bias. Whether consciously or not, most of us still tend to envision a man in the CEO's chair. This despite all the talk about gender equality and leveling the playing field. The truth is that "women are still less likely than men to be associated with leadership positions."[5] In addition, a recent Pew Research survey found that, "34 percent of the respondents believe that male executives are better than women at assuming risk."[6]

Again, why is this? According to Pew,

> topping the list of reasons, about four-in-ten Americans point to a double standard for women seeking to climb to the highest levels of either politics or business, where they have to do more than their male counterparts to prove themselves. Similar shares say the electorate and Corporate America are just not ready to put more women in top leadership positions.[7]

So what does this mean for women in the workplace—and for men? How can we all overcome issues of gender bias at work? Just as there are myriad reasons for why women face barriers to top-level jobs, there are countless ways to confront the issues. Part of that starts with simply recognizing that there

---

5. Abigail Player. "Gender Equality: Why Women Are Still Held Back," *The Guardian*, December 6, 2013. Retrieved July 21, 2015, from http://www.theguardian.com/business/economics-blog/2013/dec/06/gender-equality-women-stereotypes-stop-progress.

6. Caroline Fairchild. "Why So Few Women Are CEOs," *Fortune Magazine*, January 14, 2015. Retrieved July 21, 2015, from http://fortune.com/2015/01/14/why-so-few-women-ceos.

7. Claudia Deane, Rich Morin, Kim Parker, et al. *Women and Leadership: Public Says Women Are Equally Qualified, but Barriers Persist*. Washington, DC: Pew Research Center, January 14, 2015. Retrieved July 21, 2015, from http://www.pewsocialtrends.org/2015/01/14/women-and-leadership.

is, in fact, a gender issue in Corporate America. That recognition goes beyond the fact that women still only earn seventy-eight cents for every dollar a man earns. It means we have to recognize that men and women lead in different ways, that we confront challenges in different ways, and that we tackle problems in different ways—and that one way might not necessarily be better than the other; they're just different. We have to recognize and embrace those differences.

As women, we have to get down to brass tacks and claim what we want, as we discussed in Chapter 3. We can't be afraid of a desire to get ahead, of ambition, or of success. (Nor should we be punished if we decide that reaching mid-level management is enough.) We also have to come to terms that it's not just women who have to overdeliver their way to the C Suite—it's men, too. All of us, male or female, junkyard dog or pedigree, have to blow our performance measures out of the water, consistently, if we have any hope of making it to the top rung of the corporate ladder.

As women, we also might well have to accept that, yes, there might be some bias there and that we have to overcome gender issues in order to get ahead—but so what? That doesn't mean we can whine our way to the C Suite. So what if "most Americans say it is easier for men to get into top positions in business as well as politics" and "two thirds of Americans overall believe men have an advantage and three quarters of women say men have a better chance"[8] at winning top leadership spots? It's not as though that information gives women carte blanche to give up. Maybe it does mean that we have to work harder in general or even harder than men. But who cares? So we keep working harder. Resolving gender bias won't mean that we as women suddenly get to work less hard in order to succeed in business. We'll still have to work hard and overdeliver, and so will men.

---

8. Fairchild. "Why So Few Women Are CEOs."

====

INEQUALITY EQUALIZER

Women have to work on becoming one of the guys without sacrificing their gender. Women also need to know how to take credit for their ideas versus giving their ideas to others to accept as their own. Want it, claim it, own it—and keep score!

====

I'm not saying that gender bias doesn't matter. It absolutely does. But as much as we might all like to wish it away with good intentions, we can't. No one can. So until gender bias somehow magically resolves itself and ceases to be an issue, we do have to accept the fact that we have to work with it, we have to work around it, and we have to work through it.

For women, this often means we just have to deal with it (of course, that doesn't mean we have to like it—or put up with anything that even feels remotely like sexual harassment). We have to put our heads down and do the work, without complaining. Results are what levels the playing field. For men, it means that it's time to recognize that no gender has cornered the market on hard work—or on the corner office. No doubt there are plenty of things both women and men can do to subvert and overcome gender bias. As mentioned, it starts with recognition. And then we have to change the way we work—and the way we think.

LEAVE YOUR INNER GIRLY-GIRL AT HOME

It's a fine line, discussions about gender and bias and sexism and feminism. It's awfully easy these days to offend individuals and groups, especially when we start stereotyping and lumping individuals into categories. It's easy to say "men always do this" or "women always do that" as a way of either explaining or excusing certain behavior.

Of course we should avoid stereotyping, and of course we should avoid assigning behavior to particular groups.

But, that said, and at the risk of offense, I do want to share some observations, particularly about women in the workplace.

In many respects, we are well beyond the *Mad Men* days when so many women were treated as pieces of eye candy who also happened to type and take shorthand. But we still have a way to go yet, and, unfortunately, I see too many women doing things that reflect badly not just on themselves but on women in the workplace in general. And so, at the risk of stereotyping, I offer some advice to women as they climb the corporate ladder.

- **Don't Be a Girly-Girl.** If I had a nickel for every pink Post-It note covered in hearts and smiley faces and exclamation points that I've gotten from a female colleague, I'd be rich. Never once have I received such a note from a male colleague. Hearts and smiley faces and stickers and glitter and pink ink don't belong in the office, no matter where you are on the corporate ladder.

- **Don't Bring Me Flowers.** Bouquets are beautiful, and unless you're prone to allergies, pretty much all of us women enjoy getting flowers on special occasions or even for no reason at all. But don't bring them to work. Rarely have I ever seen the office of a male colleague adorned in two dozen long-stemmed roses for his anniversary or with a birthday bouquet full of daisies and balloons. Unless your organization dispenses bouquets for the office, leave the flowers at home.

- **Put Away That Purse.** People are weird about handbags. Do not carry one into an interview; it's distracting and can be cumbersome. If you must tote your purse with you everywhere you go, never ever set it on a conference table or someone else's desk. Men don't like it, and neither do women. It's not just a gender issue; it's a gut-level territorial instinct: When you plop your purse (or briefcase or tote bag) onto a desk or conference table, people feel as if you are usurping mutual territory, claiming an area that is not yours alone. And they don't like it.

- **Use Scent Sparingly.** I can't tell you how many meetings and interviews I've sat through during which I was practically asphyxiated by a dense cloud of perfume. Rarely have I been ambushed by men's cologne. This is much more often a women's issue, ladies coming to the office bathed in scent. It's never wise to make your colleagues choke and gag because your perfume is too strong, so go easy on it. If you wear scent, use a light touch. (In fact, one of my favorite tips for women is actually to wear men's cologne. Men feel more comfortable around scents they recognize.)

- **Be Careful with Cosmetics.** That smoky cat eye might be gorgeous when you're out clubbing, but it has no place in the office. Same goes for the fingernail decals. And the glittery lip gloss (which you should never reapply during a meeting or business meal). Unless your office is extremely creative or very casual, it's important to keep your workday appearance separate from your weekend style. Colorful mascara, glittery blush, neon lipstick—save those trends for your nights out.

As much as we each want to portray ourselves as individuals with style, it's important to remember that our personal style reflects on our professional reputation. It might be fun to bring a Hello Kitty tote bag to work, but what does that say about you as a professional? If you want to be taken seriously as a professional—and as a professional woman—it's important to play that part, which usually means you have to leave your inner girly-girl at home.

Recognize Gender Bias

Gender bias is one of those things that most of us would agree exists but few would admit to being guilty of. As Pew notes, "[w]omen are far more likely than men to see gender discrimination in today's society. About two-thirds (65 percent) of women say their gender faces at least some discrimination in society today, compared with 48 percent of men who believe women face some discrimination."[9]

Okay, so, most of us acknowledge that gender bias exists, at least to some extent. Let's just all agree on that one. But when we discuss gender bias at work, what exactly are we talking about? We might not all agree on what gender bias entails. So, what do we mean when we say "gender bias"? Researchers note that

[g]ender bias is a prominent and pressing issue within corporate leadership today. This bias includes denying equal opportunity to certain positions because of gender, but it also includes negatively altering our treatment and expectations of individuals based on their gender and its associated stereotypes.[10]

215

Gender bias might be more subtle these days than it was even a few decades ago—most women today aren't being slapped on the tush and asked to get their male bosses a cup of coffee (thank goodness)—but it's still out there. It might reveal itself in, say, a woman being told by her male boss to wear a skirt to a meeting instead of a pantsuit, a story I've already related in these pages. It could come in the form of a male boss addressing a young female staffer as "young lady," although he would never call a male colleague of similar age or title "young man." It could take the shape of a hiring committee that leans more toward a C-level male executive than a C-level female executive, even though their achievements, accomplishments, and experience are on par.

---

9. Claudia Deane et al. *Women and Leadership.*
10. Devora Shapiro and Marilea Bramer. "Gender Issues in Corporate Leadership" in *Handbook of the Philosophical Foundations of Business Ethics* (Christoph Luetge, ed.). New York: Springer Science + Business Media, 2012, p. 1178.

Whether it's in the form of assigning stereotypical characteristics (e.g., women are compassionate, nurturing, and warm while men are competitive, driven, and ambitious) or assuming certain genders prevail in certain industries (e.g., women make great teachers or nurses while men make great investors or politicians), gender bias is a part of life. In fact, some researchers note that, "the problem is so well hidden in the social psyche that it's hard to spot let alone change. After all, no one wants to think of themselves as a sexist these days (or at least not sexist enough to be called on it)."[11]

Few people want to be called a sexist, and fewer still want to consider themselves sexists. Few of us even want to have to talk about gender bias at all, much less think about it. But nothing will happen if we don't do exactly that. Because when we think about gender bias and gender equality, and when we commit to doing something about it, only then can we start to change things.

I know this firsthand. During my first national sales meeting for a major healthcare company, I experienced what would be one of the biggest "aha" moments of my professional life. These were the days when vendors paid for access, and our sales meetings were huge and elaborate. The biggest night of the multiday meeting was when we gave out awards. As the awards were unfolding, I was thinking, "Wow. All these winners look the same." They looked the same because they essentially were the same: white, middle-aged males. The only women who were represented on the stage worked for the company as support staff. They had been asked to dress up in nice cocktail attire and play Vanna White while handing out the awards to their male colleagues.

After the national sales meeting, the CEO called me into his office to ask me to share my thoughts about the meeting. I told him that I thought I had a lot of job security. My boss asked

11. Eric Jaffe. "The New Subtle Sexism Toward Women in the Workplace," *Fast Company*, June 2, 2014. Retrieved July 21, 2015, from http://www.fastcompany .com/3031101/the-future-of-work/the-new-subtle-sexism-toward-women-in-the -workplace.

me what I meant by that, and I explained that we had a lot of work to do in order to recruit a more diverse pool candidates and to mentor women so that more women could make it to the awards stage—on the merits of their accomplishments rather than on the merits of their stilettos. I told him that we had succumbed to stereotyping—and avoiding hiring—women, assuming that they wouldn't relocate to regions where they could take on more lucrative, more important, and more visible sales jobs. We weren't doing enough to ensure that women were becoming successful sales reps. We weren't doing enough to provide them with mentors or partners in order to grow their careers. I told him that the women who were up on that stage during the meeting were just eye candy.

I then asked my boss if he had a daughter, and he said that he did. I asked him what role he would want his daughter to play if she were on that stage. He shook his head and gave me a knowing grin. "You don't need to say anything else," he said. "This needs to be a priority." Three years later, at the next national sales meeting, more than half of the top award winners were women.

I was so proud of that moment. I still count it as one of my biggest achievements. But I don't share this story to boast. I share this story because it serves as an important example of why we do need to speak up and why we do need to think about—and talk about—gender equality. Had I not said anything, chances are high that nothing would have changed and our sales force would have gone on being predominantly male and our awards events would have featured women as nothing more than eye candy. But because I chose to speak up and confront the issue directly, we were able to, together, take the steps necessary to level the playing field.

Deal with Gender Bias

One of the reasons gender issues persist is because men and women are different. We think differently, we manage differently, we communicate differently. There's something to that whole Venus–Mars thing.

It doesn't help anything to ignore these differences. In fact, it's important to be aware of them. While we want to avoid stereotyping and we want to change the kind of thinking that equates "different" with "unequal," we also need to be aware of commonalities that persist. For instance, some people think that women talk in pink tones while men talk in blue tones. There may well be some truth to that, as much as we hate to admit it.

Women do, for example, tend to apologize too often, saying "I'm sorry" for any number of reasons even when an apology isn't necessary. We say "I'm sorry" when we want someone's attention but are afraid we might be interrupting. We say "I'm sorry" as a sort of generic preamble when delivering news we fear might be hurtful or misconstrued. We say things like "I'm sorry, but . . ." or "with all due respect . . ." or "I hate to say this, but . . . ."

We shouldn't do that. No one should.

Truth be told, though, I'm just as guilty as the next woman of doing this very thing. I've found myself saying things like, "I'm sorry I didn't meet your expectations," even when I know that the approach I've taken to, say, finding candidates for an executive search is the right approach. In that instance, the man I was working with told the team something along the lines of "How dare you question our approach. We are experts in this field." I was defensive; he went on the offensive (which is what I should have done).

Too often, women can have such an unbelievable need to be liked that we feel that we don't measure up, and so we're always wanting to please—and apologizing when we think we've fallen short. (This is often true for junkyard dogs, too.)

When we apologize for no good reason, we relinquish our power and authority. Women too often give away their power, leaning back and taking second chair even when we're supposed to be taking the lead. This is another thing we shouldn't do. Because when we adopt an apologetic tone and give away our power and authority, we create a situation in which we sell ourselves short and make ourselves subservient by the very way we ourselves communicate.

Often we do this out of politeness. We learn as young girls that speaking up and butting in is rude. We learn that being ambitious is unwelcome. We learn that being assertive is unsightly. And so we all too often, whether consciously or not, try to couch our communication, both verbal and nonverbal, in language and behavior that inadvertently portrays us as weaker—not necessarily as less smart or less savvy or less talented, but as submissive.

I see this all the time. I see women raise their hands during a meeting, hoping that the leader will call on them, as though everyone is still in the fifth grade and needs to be invited by the teacher to speak before sharing some insight or asking a question. Men don't do this. Men just jump into the conversation. I recently experienced this myself, raising my hand during a meeting. I was trying to be polite. But what I really needed to do was just to find the opening in the conversation and go for it.

219

INEQUALITY EQUALIZER

When you have something to say or need to ask a question, go for it. Don't sit back and wait to be called on, hoping that whoever is leading the meeting will realize that you want to say something, especially if the culture or your organization isn't that formal or hierarchical. Remember that you're not being judged on how polite you are; you're being judged on what you add to the conversation.

On the flip side of this coin is what might be considered the masculine communication style, which is generally more assertive. Again, although we don't want to subscribe to stereotypes, I'm not going out on a limb when I say that men rarely preface a statement with any kind of apologetic preamble, that they don't worry about whether a colleague will like them as a person in light of something they might say during a meeting, and that they tend to interrupt more often.

In fact, studies have shown that men do a lot of interrupting (although, to be fair, so do women)—and that it is women who are most frequently interrupted. Interestingly, recent research shows that "men interrupt women more frequently than they interrupt men" and that "[b]oth men and women feel entitled to interrupt women more frequently than they interrupt men."[12]

Most of us have seen this happen at one time or another. A female colleague might pipe up in a conversation with an idea about a project and another colleague—oftentimes male, but sometimes female—will jump on the idea and run with it. As a result, the woman usually shuts up and withdraws from the conversation, often out of simple frustration of having her comments hijacked yet again.

When it comes to interrupting, let's all agree that it isn't nice. Interrupting limits discussion, diverts attention, and derails conversation—and often makes the person being interrupted feel like she (or he!) doesn't matter, that her opinions aren't valid, or that her ideas aren't worthy. In short, no one likes being interrupted—and no one really benefits from interruptions, either.

As it happens, curtailing interruptions can be a key step in dealing with gender issues. If, for instance, we can learn to recognize when interruptions have, in fact, derailed a conversation or prohibited someone from speaking up, then we also can learn to circle back and make sure that that person is invited to speak. Effective leaders make a point of doing this, monitoring conversations to ensure that all points of view have been addressed. It might be as simple as saying something like,

---

12. Zawn Villines. "Study Finds Women More Likely to Be Interrupted," *GoodTherapy.org*, May 26, 2014. Retrieved July 22, 2015, from http://www.goodtherapy.org/blog/study-finds-women-more-likely-to-be-interrupted-052614.

"Jane, it looked like you wanted to say something a minute ago. Did you have some insight you wanted to share?"

INEQUALITY EQUALIZER

Dealing with gender issues includes recognizing that it's important to hear everyone out, regardless of gender, pedigree, title, or tenure. It means being proactive about curtailing interruptions, and it means being aware that different people communicate in different ways.

Of course, interrupting is but one example of the ways in which gender issues manifest in the workplace. Gender bias can be overt or more subtle, and oftentimes we're not even aware that we're being biased or sexist. I worked with one CEO, for instance, who realized an unconscious—and unintended—bias only when called on it. This CEO made a point to meet regularly with colleagues and direct reports. He frequently scheduled dinner meetings with his male counterparts and direct reports, but with the women, he scheduled only breakfast or lunch meetings. The dinner meetings with the male colleagues became more social, with business conducted over drinks and cigars; for the women, however, the lunch was much more formal. As a result, the male colleagues bonded with the CEO in a way that the female colleagues could not.

He hadn't even realized he was doing this. He was doing it subconsciously, until one of his female direct reports finally asked him about it. From that point forward, this CEO made it a point to hold dinner meetings only when with the entire group; all other meetings held over meals took place during breakfast or lunch. In doing this, he took an important step in leveling the playing field and creating equal access.

221

Sometimes we're lucky enough to be called out when we display bias. I say "lucky" because it is, indeed, so often done unintentionally. Were no one to ever call us out, chances are we might never realize that what we're doing is offensive or counterproductive. The challenge, though, is in actually having those conversations. Because all too often no one wants to even talk about gender bias. And if we can't talk about it, resolving the issue becomes just that much more difficult.

As with so many things, communication is crucial when it comes to confronting gender bias (or any kind of bias, for that matter). Whether on a grand scale or in everyday tasks, it's important to be able to find ways to talk about these things. Case in point, I was recently working with a male CEO candidate who wasn't selected for a particular position. This individual has excellent credentials, but accepting constructive criticism isn't one of his core skills. After he wasn't selected for the position, he refused to call me back so that we could discuss the situation and so I could give him feedback that would help him prepare for the next position he would be considered for. Because of this, he was at a disadvantage for that next opportunity.

I discussed the situation with my male partner, and he suggested I write up a document that he would then deliver to the candidate. He thought that it might be more palatable for the candidate to hear the news "guy to guy."

We certainly could have gone this route, but why should we have? Why would guy-to-guy constructive criticism be more palatable than gal-to-guy feedback? Shouldn't men and women be able to discuss such issues with each other? How do we get to a point where gender doesn't matter?

It's a problem that we can't even talk about gender equality in much more than a whisper. Most of us are loath to have the conversation about who can say what to whom, when, and under which circumstances, particularly when gender is at issue. We're afraid of stepping on toes or hurting feelings or getting called down to HR for a different but related conversation.

Thankfully, that conversation has been started. Companies like Facebook and Google are spending many millions of dollars a year on bias training and diversity initiatives.[13] Learning institutions like Harvard University are offering courses on gender and women in the workplace. People like Ellen Pao, Sheryl Sandberg, Anne-Marie Slaughter, and Joan Williams are raising awareness and tackling issues surrounding gender bias.

All of this is definitely a start—and a good one at that. Because if we as a society really want to deal with gender bias, then we have to talk about it. We have to talk about things like maternity and paternity leave. We have to talk about equal pay. We have to talk about making our places of work true meritocracies. But we also have to deal with gender issues on a daily basis, in countless small but important ways, as we navigate our careers—and that goes for men and women, junkyard dogs and pedigrees.

So what does that mean? Obviously, every workplace is different. Cultural norms vary from one organization to the next and from one industry to the next—Sidley Austin isn't Hewlett-Packard, and Goldman Sachs isn't Ernst & Young. Dispensing generic advice that applies to everyone in every place of business at all times is fraught with disaster. What one expert suggests for women (and men) as to how to behave, how to dress, or what to say another guru dismisses as ridiculous. But there are, perhaps, some commonalities that both men and women, junkyard dogs and pedigrees, should consider when it comes to dealing with gender issues in business, including:

223

- **Be Aware of Bias.** In order to deal with gender bias, we each have to recognize that it exists—and that we're likely guilty of bias and even sexism at least sometimes. This

---

13. Jessica Guynn. "Exclusive: Google Raising Stakes on Diversity," *USA Today*, May 6, 2015. Retrieved July 22, 2015, from http://www.usatoday.com/story/tech/2015/05/05/google-raises-stakes-diversity-spending/26868359.

means each of us has to avoid lumping people together into stereotypes and expecting, anticipating, or assigning certain behaviors to or from certain people. This takes conscious effort and practice as well as a level of self-awareness in order to change our own behavior.

- **Communicate with Care.** Remember that different people communicate in different ways. We've discussed in these pages the importance of asking colleagues how they prefer to be communicated with. It's also important to study patterns of communication and behavior, watching what people say and don't say, and what their body language conveys. This can help reduce interruptions, which are especially damaging for women, and it can help in delivering constructive criticism.

- **Keep Keeping Score.** I've said it before, and I'll say it again: Keeping score is crucial in business. If you have a clear and comprehensive record of your achievements and accomplishments, you are better positioned to defend yourself against gender bias in performance reviews. Being able to point to solid evidence puts you in good stead to counteract any vague comments that might, in fact, be based more on gender-related perceptions than on actual performance.

- **Be One of the Guys—and Be True to Yourself.** While it can be helpful to study sports or cars or wine, particularly if that's what the C Suite executives in your organization are into, that doesn't mean you have to smoke a cigar with the men after a business dinner. (I've done that before, and, believe me, it wasn't pretty.) It's important to fit in professionally and to adapt to the corporate culture, but you should never compromise your own values or sacrifice your own interests. You can skip the after-dinner cigar and still be part of the team. But remember, too, that business should be androgynous. Make a point of studying the interests of the people you report to, but don't eschew traditionally masculine interests if you're a woman and don't shy away from traditionally feminine interests if you're a man.

- **Stop Mothering, and Don't Expect to Be Mothered.** Oftentimes, women automatically shift into mother mode when at work. This can involve anything from bringing in bagels every Friday morning to wiping the crumbs of the conference room table after a meeting to trying to mediate minor conflicts between coworkers. It might even include cleaning out the office refrigerator or watering all the office plants. No woman with her eye on the C Suite should take on the role of room mother—and no enlightened male colleague should expect a female coworker to do so.

Gender issues are pervasive, and they're not going away anytime soon. As much as we might wish, none of us can solve this enormous issue on our own. But we can tackle, each in our own small ways, the daily displays of gender bias that infiltrate the workplace, often in insidious although unintended ways. Becoming aware of gender bias and recognizing where it exists is the first step. Dealing with specific instances is the next. How each of us goes about doing so will depend in large part on the organization we work for and the people we work with. Regardless, being aware, communicating carefully, keeping score, being true to ourselves, and avoiding mother mode can help alleviate the kind of everyday bias that shows up in so many organizations. This is true for junkyard dogs and pedigrees as well as for men and women alike.

When we work individually and collectively on both the little things and the big things, together we can help alleviate gender bias. Doing so helps the organization itself and everyone in it. In helping each other, we give each other confidence and pull each other up. We'll talk about that more in the next chapter when we look at the ins and outs of lending a helping hand to colleagues.

Tough-Love Lessons for Dealing with Gender Issues

- The best employees recognize that, although we're making progress toward gender equality, there remains a lot of progress to be made. We might like to think that everyone agrees that men and women are equal, but the real world doesn't always play out that way. This means we have to get over it, deal with it, and keep moving forward.
- Professionals who want to make it to the C Suite understand that performance is what really matters and that everyone—regardless of gender or pedigree—has to overdeliver. It also means that everyone has to keep score of their achievements and accomplishments, especially if it becomes necessary to overcome gender-related perceptions with hard data.
- Sometimes you have to call your colleagues (and even yourself!) on the carpet when it comes to gender bias. So often we do and say things that are hurtful or offensive or sexist without even realizing it. But unless and until someone says something, that behavior usually goes uncorrected. Sometimes you have to speak up in order to deal with gender issues.
- Top employees avoid stereotyping or expecting certain behavior from certain people. They communicate with colleagues as individuals and respect their differences regardless of gender.

= 12 =

Lending a Helping Hand

From: "Jena Abernathy" <jabernathy@email.com>

To: "Megan Watson" <mwatson@email.com>

Subject: Find Mentors and Lend a Helping Hand

Megan,

You've come a long way since we began our e-mail mentoring—developing hard and soft skills, understanding the business of business, making the most of networking, and learning how to deal with gender issues. Along the lines of gender is another issue: Feline Syndrome, which derails too many opportunities for mentoring. Throughout your career, it will be important to be mentored—and to mentor others. Because no one gets ahead without a helping hand now and then.

—Jena

I sometimes look back over my career and wonder "What if . . ." I think most of us do this at one time or another, wondering whether making a different choice, following a different path, or choosing a different approach would have changed things. What would have happened if I hadn't taken the job with the Lion King boss who demanded I work every Saturday? Where would I be now had, early in my career, my boss not sent me to corporate charm school in Minnesota?

What, for instance, might have happened had I not told another boss that we needed to expand our pool of candidates in order to have a more diverse staff of employees? By opening more opportunities for other women, we ushered in a new wave of success for the entire organization. I received many notes from women thanking me and my team for our support and obvious commitment to their success. It was one of my proudest moments.

During my career, I've been proud and grateful to have been both mentor and mentee. I've been lent countless helping hands, and I've lent a few helping hands myself. I can't imagine where my career might have gone had I not sought mentors, found advocates, and expanded my sphere of influence, or where I might have ended up had I not returned favors by mentoring and helping others. I have established mentoring programs and career development opportunities throughout my career, not because I should have or was required to because I was a C-level HR executive or an executive consultant or a career coach, but because I truly believe it is a calling to help those who seek to advance their careers—even beyond their own expectations.

When we're able to share our experiences and give back, we can pull each other up the corporate ladder. As they say, a rising tide lifts all boats. When one of us wins, we all win. The success of one woman helps open the door for many others. I have always believed this. If you have the chance to mentor, be generous of your spirit, your time, your expertise, and your insight. If you have the chance to help others in their careers, do so. And, when helping someone up the ladder, remember where you came from. Remember what it was like earlier in your own career and think about how much help you received. No one wants to be crushed by a sharp stiletto while trying to climb the ladder.

None of us makes it to the C Suite alone.

My charm school boss could easily have muddled along with me as is—or given up on me and fired me. But he saw something in me that was worth investing in. He became a gentle, helpful mentor without whose guidance my career would have suffered. Without him, who knows if I would have survived the executive suite and built a successful track record.

It's a good thing I've been open to receiving that kind of guidance, and I'm grateful every day for him and all the other professionals who have served as mentors for me at various points in my career. Because had I not sought their advice and benefitted from their insight, my career would likely have been very different.

All of us can—and should—benefit from mentors. These individuals become important members of our spheres of influence, people whose insight, advice, and guidance help us become better employees—and better people. In fact, some of the world's top CEOs frequently turn to mentors for any manner of help. Andy Grove of Intel often shared advice with Apple's Steve Jobs, who, in turn, mentored Facebook's Mark Zuckerberg. Richard Branson, founder of Virgin, frequently turned to British airline entrepreneur Sir Freddie Laker for guidance.[1] Yahoo! CEO Marissa Mayer has counted Larry Page, Sergey Brin, Eric Schmidt, Jonathan Rosenberg, and Stanford University Professor Eric Roberts among her mentors.[2]

1. "Three Famous Billionaire Entrepreneurs and Their Mentors," *Small Business BC*, September 21, 2014. Retrieved August 3, 2015, from http://smallbusinessbc.ca/article/three-famous-billionaire-entrepreneurs-and-their-mentors.
2. Andrea Huspeni. "Meet Behind-the-Scenes Mentors of 15 Top Tech Executives," *Business Insider*, July 11, 2012. Retrieved August 3, 2015, from http://www.businessinsider.com/meet-the-mentors-behind-the-visionaries-of-tech-2012-7?op=1.

Whether it's imparting keen institutional knowledge, helping to brainstorm around a problem, playing devil's advocate, or simply sharing advice during a critical juncture, mentors can do much to help throughout the span of a career. And, of course, it's not just the mentee who benefits. Studies have shown that mentors get just as much out of mentoring as mentees do, which is something we'll look at later in this chapter.

When it comes to mentoring and lending a helping hand, it's something you should do—and something you should do the whole way: You should find a mentor. You should be a mentor. You should lend a helping hand in any way you can. And, along the way, you should be sure to avoid Feline Syndrome—that nasty proclivity women can succumb to that keeps us from helping each other up the corporate ladder. No matter where you are in your career, mentoring should be a part of your professional life.

Find Mentors and Advocates

As far as I'm concerned, everyone should find a mentor—and a lot of them, if possible. No matter where you are in your career— entry-level gig, mid-level management, or even the C Suite—a mentor can help you in any number of ways.

A mentor is someone who shares expertise, insight, and guidance, usually to a younger and/or less-experienced professional. By some definitions, "a mentor is a special kind of helper who works with others in a positive, constructive way so that both mentor and protégé have the potential to grow through the relationship,"[3] or mentors can be "senior people in your organization. They know where the company is going, they know the system, and they can draw on their experience and wisdom to show you what you should be doing and

3. *About Mentoring: Who Is a Mentor?* Indiana University, n.d. Retrieved August 3, 2015, from http://www.indiana.edu/~omsld/whoismentor.php.

when."[4] A mentor could be a coworker, an industry colleague, or an educator, such as a former professor. It might be someone within your organization or from elsewhere. A mentor is usually someone within your own or a related industry, but that isn't always the case.

You might connect with your mentor on a regular basis or simply every now and then when, perhaps, you need some advice or even just want to touch base. You might work with your mentor in a formal way, through specific training or education, or more casually, perhaps through informal conversation. You might have a defined relationship with a mentor, perhaps through a professional organization to which you belong, or you might simply look to a particular person as a mentor, seeing her as someone whose advice you can rely on.

No matter how formal or informal the mentor–mentee relationship, how often you meet, or the avenues through which you connect, the key is to be open to finding a mentor, to seeking out people who are willing to help you, and to finding fellow professionals who will be advocates for you.

Oddly enough, some people either don't even think about finding a mentor or consciously choose not to. Some people believe they don't need or wouldn't benefit from advice or insight or education from a professional elder. Some people, especially younger employees, think that older, wiser professionals are too out of touch and too old-fashioned to be of any real help. Some people are afraid that asking for help makes them appear weak or ignorant. In fact, some experts have found that "many women say they tend to see asking for a mentor as a sign of weakness. They really fear that, if they raise their hands for additional support, other people will perceive them as unable to succeed on their own."[5] This despite the

---

4. Dan Schwabel. *Promote Yourself: The New Rules for Career Success.* New York: St. Martin's Griffin, 2013, p. 182.

5. Anne Fisher. "Why Young Workers Avoid Mentors," *Fortune Magazine*, September 19, 2014. Retrieved August 3, 2015, from http://fortune.com/2014/09/19/mentoring.

fact that research has shown that, even for junior and mid-level employees, mentoring programs "enable them to advance more quickly, earn higher salaries, and gain more satisfaction in their jobs and lives than people without mentors do."[6]

So, all that talk about appearing weak or knowing enough already to being too busy or whatever—you can forget about that. You have to get over that—and get real about mentoring.

INEQUALITY EQUALIZER

Regardless of gender, pedigree, title, or tenure, mentoring can help propel your career to new heights, leading to better pay and more job satisfaction. Junkyard dogs especially can benefit from being mentored, particularly when they pair up with pedigrees who can show them the ropes, provide them with access to high-placed leaders, and get them into exclusive clubs, associations, or other organizations.

Employees from every level in organizations across industries report how beneficial mentorship programs are, and many of today's leading organizations provide some kind of mentoring programs. Researchers note, for example, that 71 percent of Fortune 500 companies offer mentoring programs to their employees.[7] Those programs are effective, too. The same study reported that of more than one thousand Sun Microsystems employees followed over a five-year period, "mentoring has a

---

6. Suzanne de Janasz and Maury Peiperl. "CEOs Need Mentors Too," *Harvard Business Review*, April 2015. Retrieved August 3, 2015, from https://hbr.org/2015/04/ceos-need-mentors-too.

7. Chronus Corporation. *Why Corporate Mentoring? Five Benefits of a Workplace Mentoring Program*, n.d. Redmond, WA: Author. Retrieved August 3, 2015, from http://www.mentorourkids.org/articles/Five-Benefits-of-a-Workplace-Mentoring-Program.pdf.

positive impact on mentors and mentees, producing employees that are more highly valued by the business."[8]

I can tell you that mentoring has had a positive impact on me, too, both as a mentor and a mentee. In fact, I can't overstate how important it is to find mentors and advocates whom you trust and to whom you can turn throughout the course of your career. (Trust, of course, is a key issue to consider when it comes to mentoring—and to whom you should turn for mentoring—so be sure to look back to the discussion in Chapter 9 about developing trust and intuition.)

So just how do you find these people, these professionals who will be your mentor? Where do you find someone whom you can trust to be an advocate for you? And once you find these people, what should you expect of them? Let's look at all of that.

Where to Find Mentors

In short, mentors are everywhere. It might be a trusted colleague from whom you've learned a lot. It might be a client who has shared keen industry insight with you. It might be a fellow member of a professional association to which you belong with whom you've discussed everything from sweeping industry trends to everyday work-related minutiae. Mentors can be found anywhere—as long as you're open-minded about receiving insight, advice, and guidance from them.

Oftentimes, the mentor–mentee (sometimes called "mentor–protégé") relationship isn't necessarily a formal, defined relationship. Sometimes you won't even realize that the trusted colleague to whom you've turned again and again for advice has been a mentor until years later when you reflect upon the professionals who have had the most influence on you.

You might find a mentor within your own department or elsewhere within your organization, from another company in your industry, from a professional association to which you

---

8. *Ibid.*

belong, from a group you volunteer for, from a board you sit on . . . the list is endless. A growing number of industries, including finance, healthcare, law, and technology, and organizations, such as AT&T, DHL, IBM, KPMG, and even USGS (the U.S. Geological Survey), have official in-house mentoring programs by which employees are matched with colleagues.

When seeking a mentor, look to the people whom you consider role models. Seek out leaders in your organization, in your field, and in business in general. Turn to the people who have educated you over the years, whether formally or informally, such as your favorite graduate school professors or experts who have led certification courses you've taken. You might find a mentor in a former boss for whom you once worked or in a former colleague who has since moved on to another organization.

Remember, too, that your mentors need not be of the same gender or background or at the same point in their careers. Although most mentors tend to be older or more experienced, it's becoming more common for younger employees to mentor seasoned professionals, particularly when it comes to such issues as technology and social media. Sometimes called "reverse mentoring," the practice is popular across a number of industries and organizations such as Cisco Systems, Hartford Financial Services Group, Mars, Inc., and MasterCard.[9]

Finding a mentor might well require you to practice the networking skills we discussed in Chapter 10, tapping into and building your sphere of influence with people who can help you, advise you, listen to you, and guide you. As with networking, approaching a potential mentor requires you to build trust as you nurture a relationship from which you can both benefit.

---

9. Sue Shellenbarger. "Pairing Up with a Younger Mentor," *The Wall Street Journal*, May 28, 2014. Retrieved August 4, 2015, from http://www.wsj.com/articles/SB100 01424052702303903304579588122552355480.

What to Expect from Mentors

Among the biggest challenges with building a mentor–mentee relationship are knowing who to approach, when and how to approach that person, and what and how much to ask of that person. One of the biggest reasons that mentoring relationships never take off is because the mentee asks for too much too soon of a person who is too busy.

Knowing what you can expect—and what you shouldn't—from a mentor is crucial when it comes to building this kind of relationship. In general, you should expect in a mentor someone who will willingly and generously share time, insight, advice, and guidance. Your mentor might help train you on specific tasks or she might offer more big-picture advice by counseling you about your career in general. In such a relationship, which is built on mutual trust, you should expect your mentor to keep your confidences—just as you should hers.

If the mentor–mentee relationship is more structured and formal, you should expect your mentor to be responsive, keep appointments, follow up as needed, and provide unbiased, objective guidance. In such a relationship, you might wish to set goals and objectives, agreeing on what you both hope to accomplish, within what kind of time frame you wish to do so, and by what criteria you will measure progress. You might also determine whether the relationship will be ongoing or finite, dedicated, perhaps, to a specific challenge, project, or deadline.

You should expect your mentor to be available to you—although not at your beck and call. It's important to respect your mentor's time. Remember that she, too, is busy with work, life, and any number of obligations. Her schedule and the demands placed on her have to come before your needs. "'I tell people whom I mentor all the time: Don't be put off if you call or email me and I don't get back to you immediately, or I don't reach out to you as frequently as you may like,' said Morgan, Lewis & Bockius Partner Sandra Phillips, who previ-

235

ously was SVP and associate general counsel at Pfizer Inc.," in an article in *Inside Counsel*.[10]

In building an effective and fulfilling mentor–mentee relationship, it's crucial to not ask too much from your mentor. You have to manage your expectations and remember that, although your mentor does want to be your advocate and look out for you, she also has to look out for herself. So be careful about asking for too much, especially early on in the relationship. In addition, if the relationship has a defined end date, ask your mentor if you can continue to contact her in the future about related issues. If she agrees, be careful not to inundate her with questions or requests. Bottom line: Don't take advantage of your mentor's generosity. Consider how you would like to be treated if you were the mentor and act accordingly.

HOW TO BE A GOOD MENTEE

When I was sent to charm school, it could have gone either way. I could have been disgruntled, bitter, and surly, shunning the advice and tips that were taught me. Instead, I opted to be open-minded, accepting with grace and gratitude the lessons that were bestowed upon me. I was a good mentee. I chose to be.

When it comes to being a good mentee, the first order of business is to be open-minded, willing to accept advice, knowledge, and insight from a professional who deserves your respect. The mentor–mentee relationship is doomed if the mentee comes to it thinking she knows everything, doesn't need any advice, and won't learn anything from someone a few years or even generation or two older or a few rungs higher on the corporate ladder. Nobody likes to work with a know-it-all.

10. Alex Vorro. "Mentoring Helps Attorneys at All Levels Advance Their Careers," *Inside Counsel*, March 27, 2012. Retrieved August 4, 2015, from http://www.insidecounsel.com/2012/03/27/mentoring-helps-attorneys-at-all-levels-advance-th?page=3.

Being a good mentee means you come to the relationship willing to learn—wanting to learn—and absorb the keen professional insight that only someone with more experience can share. It also means avoiding some relationship killers:

- **Don't Be a Stalker.** When approaching someone about being a mentor to you, handle the situation with care. As with any new relationship, it's important to work up to that question, which can feel like a big request to some people. You're not asking your mentor to move in with you, but you are asking for a major commitment in terms of time, energy, and resources. Be careful not to stalk your potential mentor. Don't barrage her with e-mails, phone calls, or texts. Don't be clingy or needy. Don't force the relationship. Instead, be mindful of how the relationship is naturally developing and then carefully choose the right moment to request a more formal mentoring relationship.

- **Don't Ask for Too Much Too Soon.** Remember that building any relationship takes time. It takes effort to develop the kind of trust that allows both mentor and mentee to feel comfortable enough to share in the kind of open, honest way that's crucial to a successful relationship. So, work first on building trust before making a bunch of requests, before asking for favors, and before demanding extra attention with a lot of meetings, calls, e-mails, or texts. In addition, discuss with your mentor what you hope to learn from her, including any specific goals or challenges that you want to address. This way, you both can manage expectations.

- **Don't Reject Your Mentor's Advice.** As in any relationship, it can be easy to become defensive in the face of criticism. Your mentor might offer advice for improving your performance in one way or another, and that advice might sting. Don't reject it out of hand. Instead of closing your mind to her insight, try to consider her feedback as objectively as possible and discuss honestly with her ways in which you might try to implement her suggestions.

237

- **Don't Forget to Mind Your Manners.** Just as in all your business dealings, it's important to be polite, cordial, gracious, and professional when interacting with your mentor. Be respectful of your mentor's time and make sure you're punctual for appointments with her. Come prepared to your meetings, bringing any documents, files, or other materials as needed. Follow through with any homework that she might request of you before your next meeting. Listen attentively when chatting with your mentor, which means you should turn off and put away any mobile devices, avoid multitasking, and forward phone calls into voice mail. Thank her for her time and for sharing her insights. And let her know how you fare in your business endeavors—it's always nice to let your mentor know that her advice was not only welcome but effective, too.

Building an effective mentor–mentee relationship takes time and effort—on both parts. Being a good mentee is a crucial part of the equation if you want to benefit from what could very well be one of the most influential relationships in your professional life.

Be a Mentor to Others

Over the years, I've benefitted from being both a mentee and a mentor. I feel strongly that the mentor–mentee relationship is a win–win. Not only do mentees tend to earn higher salaries and get bigger promotions, but they also expand their networks, learn new things (often at a faster pace than were they simply to learn on their own), become more self-aware, and become more visible in their organizations. Of course, mentees aren't the only ones who benefit from the relationship.

Mentors reap numerous benefits, too, from the mentor–mentee relationship, not least of which is giving back to their organizations and industries. There's something to be said for mentoring the people who will become the future of your industry. It's good karma. But mentors benefit in other ways as well. They, too, expand their networks, particularly with younger professionals, which can help bridge the generation gap that exists in so many organizations. In mentoring, mentors often improve their leadership skills, their problem-solving skills, and their communication skills. Many mentors reveal themselves to be subject-matter experts and thought leaders who go on to become widely recognized and highly regarded in their fields.

Mentoring can be a satisfying experience as you progress in your career. And it's important to remember that mentors need not be of specific age, title, or tenure. We saw earlier in the chapter how popular reverse mentoring is becoming, with younger, more junior employees mentoring the more seasoned employees within their organizations. Similarly, junior associates can mentor entry-level employees. Mid-level managers can mentor colleagues and direct reports. Professionals can at any point in their careers mentor students who wish to pursue careers in their fields. Even CEOs need mentors. In fact, researchers have found "dozens of executives [accelerate] their learning by engaging the services of high-profile veteran leaders from outside their companies."[11]

With so many people in need of mentors, the opportunities to mentor someone are nearly endless. I've made a point throughout my career to help organizations create cultures where mentoring became ingrained, making it more welcoming and easier for younger professionals, women, minorities, and junkyard dogs to excel. How you go about becoming a mentor depends, of course, on your own situation, but there is any number of ways to connect with a mentee or protégé.

As mentioned, many organizations provide mentoring programs whereby more experienced employees are paired with junior colleagues to help train them in various aspects of their

11. de Janasz and Peiperl. "CEOs Need Mentors Too."

jobs. Check with your HR department about signing up for the program and connecting with a mentee. In addition to the organization where you work, a wide array of professional associations including the American Bar Association, Asian American Professional Association, American Public Health Association, and American Translators Association also offer mentoring programs. (Some regional and local chapters of national associations also might offer mentoring programs closer to home.) Other organizations, such as Business Mentor NY, MicroMentor, Pathbuilders, and Vistage, also offer programs that connect mentors with mentees, either for face-to-face meetings or online sessions.

Once you've decided to be a mentor, you have to be all in—just as you would be in any relationship. That means you have to be dedicated, responsive, and giving. You have to be willing to share your expertise, knowledge, and wisdom. You have to be a good role model, demonstrating by your behavior what it takes to be a better-than-good employee and a successful professional. You have to be compassionate, fair, and objective when helping your mentee work through issues, solve problems, and face career-related challenges. You also have to keep it professional.

There's a lot of talk out there about how easily a mentor–mentee relationship can move beyond one's professional life into one's personal life, where the mentor and the mentee become close friends. That might well happen, particularly if you've built a trusting relationship over time. But be careful of that gray area: It can easily turn into a sticky wicket.

I know because I've made that mistake. Early on in my career, I wanted to be friends with my mentees. I would take them out to dinner now and again and, over time, we'd start to become very open with each other. Soon we knew all sorts of personal things about each other, things that ventured well outside our office walls. Then one of my mentees and I hit the speed bump of relationship hell. My mentee started arriving late to meetings because her car broke down. She wasn't focused on her work because her boyfriend just broke up with her. Her performance at work started to suffer because her personal life was careening off the rails. As her mentor, I knew it was time for a serious conversation about performance and behavior and how her personal problems were affecting her work. But my mentee, who had become my friend, didn't want to hear it. She looked at me like I had two heads. What happened to her BFF? What happened to the girlfriend who was supposed to have her back?

A line had been crossed—that thin gray line between personal and professional.

I'm not saying that building relationships isn't important; it is. But also important is to establish boundaries, making sure that you and your mentee fully understand where that line is. As a mentor, you need to listen to your mentee—but you also have to keep things in check, guiding your mentee back to the issues surrounding her professional goals when things veer into personal territory. When you can do that, you'll be in a much better position to be a helpful, trusted mentor.

241

Help Someone Up by Lending a Hand

When we mentor junior associates, we help them build their careers. We help them gain the skills and knowledge they will need as they climb the corporate ladder. We help them develop their self-confidence and become well-rounded professionals.

We need to help the people coming up the corporate ladder behind us. We need to give them that guidance. We need to give them opportunities. We need to give them our business. We need to share our connections and help them build their spheres of influence. We need to share the information and knowledge we have. We need to be advocates for the younger professionals we believe in and in whom we see potential. We need to support coworkers and colleagues who have the drive and motivation to succeed. If they want it, we have to help them claim it and own it. We need to lend them a helping hand.

Helping junior employees up the corporate ladder doesn't mean doing their work for them. It doesn't mean giving them the easiest or most lucrative assignments or going easy on them when they fall short. It means being a good teammate, being a good colleague, being a good customer.

Oddly enough, a lot of us shy away from being truly helpful. Oftentimes, our competitive natures take over and we jealously guard knowledge and information. We decline to assist an overwhelmed colleague whose workload makes it impossible to meet a deadline. We might refrain from praising someone else's work even when it deserves accolades. The worst among us might even go so far as to actively sabotage a coworker's project.

No doubt, work is competitive. There are only so many seats in the C Suite, and people can get catty when they're clawing their way to the corner office. That competitive spirit can lead some of us to avoid lending a helping hand. In fact, *The Wall Street Journal* reports that "reciprocity, the social norm that compels us to return favors, doesn't apply as strongly at work as it does to life outside the office" and that "people are far more generous when interacting with individuals in a personal context as opposed to an organizational context," according to researchers at Stanford University Graduate School of Business.[12] Furthermore, researchers have found that, "[h]elpfulness must be actively nurtured in organizations . . . because it does not arise automatically among colleagues."[13]

With that, it's important to actively and purposefully lend a helping hand to your coworkers and colleagues. If you have

---

12. Rachel Feintzeig. "Don't Expect Any Favors at the Office," *The Wall Street Journal*, March 9, 2015. Retrieved August 4, 2015, from http://blogs.wsj.com/atwork/2015/03/09/dont-expect-any-favors-at-the-office.
13. Teresa Amabile, Colin M. Fisher, and Julianna Pillemer. "IDEO's Culture of Helping," *Harvard Business Review*, January–February 2014. Retrieved August 4, 2015, from https://hbr.org/2014/01/ideos-culture-of-helping/ar/1.

some spare time and can help an overworked colleague finish a project on deadline, do it. If you can proffer an introduction for someone, do it. If you can send some business to a colleague, do it. If you can answer a question or help solve a problem for a coworker, do it.

And do it without expecting something in return.

Instead, think of lending a helping hand as both a way of giving back to the profession that has treated you so well and of paying it forward. No matter where you are in your career trajectory, you can find ways to be helpful. You might not be rewarded in obvious or material ways, but that doesn't mean there aren't any payoffs.

In fact, people who are helpful tend to be seen as team players. They're considered good collaborators. And, they're often viewed as experts who are willing to share their knowledge. All of that helps build your reputation, which is a great reward for lending someone a helping hand.

Lending a helping hand is by no means restricted to those who are junior to you. Just as you should manage up, down, and sideways (as we discussed in Chapter 5), you should help out in all directions as well. Not only that, but you also should lend a helping hand to colleagues regardless of title, tenure, pedigree, or gender—perhaps especially regardless of gender.

Avoid Feline Syndrome

I don't know why it happens so often, but I have seen countless times women literally kill another woman's career and professional opportunities. It is shameful and shocking because, collectively, we have power and influence. I have heard many female leaders state, "I had to make it up the ladder on my own," and for some reason they can then find a way to rationalize stepping all over their female colleagues in order to get to the top. They tell themselves that their behavior is okay.

It is not okay.

I call this "Feline Syndrome." Sometimes referred to as "Queen Bee Syndrome," Feline Syndrome afflicts women who willingly sabotage the careers of other women. It strikes women who ignore their female colleagues and focus solely on their own careers, regardless of whether that puts other women in jeopardy. It appears in women who outright refuse or passively decline to support their fellow females at work.

Feline Syndrome might appear in some fields more than others. Sometimes it rears its head more often when the female–male ratio is out of balance. In fact, some researchers have found that "women may not support each other's progress specifically in situations where they are outnumbered by men."[14]

Although some have argued that this affliction doesn't really exist at all or at least not to the extent that some people might think,[15] I can tell you I've seen Feline Syndrome in action firsthand. And it is ugly. I've seen female colleagues who once worked well together get into a catastrophic argument that fatally damaged their professional relationship. Neither party trusted each other again. When they were together in the same room, it was uncomfortable for everyone else in there with them. Their own teams felt pressured to take sides. The War of the Felines had commenced.

This does nobody any good.

And it makes everyone involved look bad.

Whether female or male, junkyard dog or pedigree, you never look good when you intentionally sabotage someone else's career. Women who succumb to Feline Syndrome tend to be viewed as emotional, hysterical, unprofessional, vicious,

---

14. Alecia M. Santuzzi, Ph.D., Sarah Bailey, Jasmin Martinez, and Giulia Zanini. "Women Helping Women in the Workplace—or Not?" *Psychology Today*, April 7, 2014. Retrieved August 4, 2015, from https://www.psychologytoday.com/blog/the -wide-wide-world-psychology/201404/women-helping-women-in-the-workplace-or -not.

15. Press Association. "'Queen Bee Syndrome' at Work Is a Myth, Study Finds," *The Guardian*, June 7, 2015. Retrieved August 4, 2015, from http://www.theguard-ian.com/world/2015/jun/07/queen-bee-syndrome-women-work-myth-research -columbia-business-school.

catty, petty, and even bitchy. (Men don't usually get labeled in a similar manner, but that's another discussion for another day.) If you have any aspirations toward landing a seat in the C Suite, among your top priorities should be avoiding Feline Syndrome at all costs.

Indeed, as Stanford University Professor Deborah Gruenfeld says in *Lean In* by Sheryl Sandberg, "We need to look out for one another, work together, and act more like a coalition."[16] So, as you ascend up the corporate ladder, you need to help others who have the drive and motivation to succeed. Coach these eager-to-move-ahead women on how to navigate the political waters in your organization. Counsel them on their appearance and professional demeanor in the workplace. Share opportunities, knowledge, insight, and connections with them.

In the same vein, turn to other professional women for advice and guidance. Consider the strengths and abilities of the female colleagues around you and think about how their knowledge could be valuable to the work you are doing. Find a way to ask for advice from these women, and look for ways to keep them in your sphere of influence. Work toward building positive, productive relationships with the women in your organization and your industry.

As former Secretary of State Madeleine Albright once said, "There is a special place in hell for women who don't help other women." I believe this to be true—but it doesn't go far enough. Women absolutely should be helping other women, and they should be helping their male colleagues as well—just as their male colleagues should be helping others, too, regardless of gender. Because lending a helping hand isn't a gender issue—or at least it shouldn't be. And making it a nonissue starts with you, helping out one colleague at a time, whether male or female. By doing so, you can honor your colleagues and honor yourself, which we'll discuss next, in Chapter 13.

---

16. Sheryl Sandberg. *Lean In: Women, Work, and the Will to Lead*. New York: Alfred A. Knopf, 2014, p. 160.

===

INEQUALITY EQUALIZER

Top professionals lend a hand regardless of gender, pedigree, title, or tenure, and those who do are recognized as collaborative team players who do what it takes to make themselves, their colleagues, and their organizations successful. Women and junkyard dogs in particular who make a point to help others can do much to elevate their professional reputations and get noticed.

===

Tough-Love Lessons for Lending a Helping Hand

- The most successful employees recognize that no one makes it to the top alone. Those who are too arrogant, too shy, or too lazy to ask for help and work with mentors are only denying themselves opportunities for professional growth.
- The best mentees are those who are open-minded and willing to learn from coworkers, colleagues, and professional peers who can share the kind of information, insight, advice, and expertise that only more experienced employees can offer.
- Mentoring provides opportunities not only to help a colleague, but also can be beneficial for the mentor by expanding her sphere of influence, bridging the generation gap at work, and learning to look at problems and challenges in new ways.
- Everyone should be looking for ways to help their colleagues, coworkers, clients, and customers. Lending a helping hand is a win–win, opening doors and providing opportunities in any number of ways, regardless of gender, pedigree, title, or tenure.

= 13 =

Honoring Yourself and Your Values

From: "Jena Abernathy" <jabernathy@email.com>

To: "Megan Watson" <mwatson@email.com>

Subject: Values

Megan,

I know I've given you a lot to think about. From taming your inner junkyard dog to branding yourself to managing in all directions to dealing with gender issues—that's a lot to keep track of as you manage your career. I've given you a lot of advice, and you'll get a lot more from every corner during the course of your career. It can be challenging to know which advice to follow and which to take with a grain of salt. The trick is to stick to your own moral compass. Because none of it matters if you don't honor yourself and your values.

—Jena

We all evolve and change during the course of our careers. We gain new skills. We develop our strengths. We reach new goals. We keep score of our accomplishments, and we learn from our mistakes. We learn to be assertive instead of aggressive, taming our inner junkyard dog while nurturing our inner pedigree.

As we move from one job to the next, we meet all sorts of new people, many of whom do much to influence our careers. We might look to some of these people as mentors and learn from them, considering them role models who guide us as far as what to do and how to do it. We also might come to consider some of the people who come into our lives negative influences—and we learn from them, too, often in what not to do.

No matter what happens, no matter where you work (or for whom), no matter whom you meet as you wind your way up to the C Suite, it's crucial to keep those parts that are essential to your authentic self. Claiming the pedigree in you, for example, doesn't mean that you have to completely muzzle your junkyard dog—that scrappiness, that resourcefulness, and that assertiveness can still come in handy in certain situations. By learning to be constructive instead of critical, assertive instead of aggressive, accepting instead of defensive, you can honor yourself and your values while still making the most of the environment in which you work and of your authentic self.

You should never go against your value system, but it can be difficult sometimes to be truly authentic and true to yourself in every situation. Situations require flexibility. You will be tested. You will be challenged. Sometimes you have to put on the mask and play the role you're being paid to play. But that doesn't mean you should compromise your values. You should never sacrifice your personal integrity for any reason. And, in fact, I can guarantee that, if you do, it will catch up to you one way or another, one day or another.

Bottom line: You have to be able to look yourself in the mirror—every day—and feel comfortable and confident that what you're doing, and how you're doing it, is in keeping with the best version of you.

That means you have to know yourself. You have to know what you want—and you have to know how far you're willing to go to get what you want. You also have to know what you don't want. You have to be yourself.

Get to Know Yourself

What are your values?

It's not often that most of us sit down and really think about our own values. But we should.

Organizations often delineate their corporate values, linking them to mission and vision statements, often as a way of defining who they are, what they stand for, what they do, why they do it, and how they're different (and better) from other organizations. These written statements often articulate that the organization "lives these values."

What values are you living?

251

INEQUALITY EQUALIZER

Regardless of title, tenure, gender, or pedigree, only you can define your values. You have to look yourself in the mirror every day. Your values are something no one else should dictate. Those who take the time to articulate their own values are best positioned to achieve their goals.

Before you can really honor yourself and your values, you have to know what those values are. This requires a bit of self-discovery as well as some soul searching. It requires you to get to know yourself, identifying which values matter most to you, where your moral compass is pointing, what you hope to accomplish, and how you plan to do that.

Early on in my career, when I was admittedly immature and naïve, I burned a few bridges when leaving one of the organizations I worked for. I wanted to save the rest of the employees from experiencing the wrongs I felt I had endured for too long. So, on my way out the door, I gave the leaders a piece of my mind, telling them straight out all the things I thought they were doing wrong. I thought I was being a kind of corporate Joan of Arc, living up to my values (or at least what I thought should have been my values). But really I was just being self-righteous and maybe even a little arrogant (it was that junkyard dog in me). The truth was that I hadn't really stopped to think about what my values actually were. I was just sort of going with the flow, certain that my instincts would keep me pointed in the right direction.

This is what most of us do. We climb the corporate ladder, shape-shifting as necessary depending on what organization we work for, pausing only when something we're told to do sends shivers down our spines. Instead of taking the time to identify our values—to get to know ourselves—we just plod along doing our best to avoid making any terrible mistakes.

A better plan would be to craft a values statement, along with personal mission and vision statements. Doing so can help you get to know yourself, particularly when it comes to identifying the things that are truly important to you. In addition, "[a] personal mission statement is a powerful tool because it provides you with a path for success, and it gives you permission to say no to the things that are distractions."[1] In short, a written values/mission/vision statement helps put into words your moral compass, identifying what is important to you and what your priorities are, what you hope to accomplish, and

---

1. Stephanie Vozza. "Personal Mission Statements of Five Famous CEOs (and Why You Should Write One, Too," *Fast Company*, February 25, 2014. Retrieved August 6, 2015, from http://www.fastcompany.com/3026791/dialed/personal-mission-statements-of-5-famous-ceos-and-why-you-should-write-one-too.

how you plan to do so. So effective is such a tool that some of today's most successful professionals live by them, including Virgin Group Founder Sir Richard Branson, Campbell Soup Company CEO Denise Morrison, DailyWorth.com Founder Amanda Steinberg, and OWN Founder Oprah Winfrey.[2]

Getting to know yourself and crafting a personal statement takes a bit of doing and more than a little self-awareness. This isn't something you do in fifteen minutes over lunch while eating a Lean Cuisine at your desk. It takes some self-reflection. That might sound daunting or even silly or kooky, but becoming self-aware pays off in spades.

Remember how that charm school program helped me become more self-aware? I'm living proof that self-reflection works! And I'm not the only one who thinks so.

Harry Kraemer Jr. is Professor of Management and Strategy at Northwestern University's Kellogg School of Management and an executive partner with Madison Dearborn Partners, one of the largest private equity firms in the United States. He also happens to be a best-selling author. In his book *From Values to Action*, Kraemer writes that, "[e]ngaging in self-reflection on a regular and ongoing basis has made a huge difference in my life as a business leader." He also notes that, "As I became more self-aware, I gained clarity about my values and goals. I was able to focus on what mattered most because I took the time to discern my priorities."[3]

Gaining clarity on your values and goals sounds pretty good, right? It is. Self-reflection and the self-awareness it leads to can also help you identify your strengths and weaknesses and likes and dislikes. It also will help guide you when making decisions, particularly when you're faced with challenging situations that test your mettle. There are times in your career

2. *Ibid.* See also: Drew Hendricks. "Personal Mission Statement of 13 CEOs and Lessons You Need to Learn," *Forbes*, November 10, 2014. Retrieved August 6, 2015, from http://www.forbes.com/sites/drewhendricks/2014/11/10/personal-mission-statement-of-14-ceos-and-lessons-you-need-to-learn.
3. Harry M. Jansen Kraemer Jr. *From Values to Action: The Four Principles of Values-Based Leadership.* San Francisco: Jossey-Bass, 2011, p. 13.

253

when you will encounter should-I-or-shouldn't-I moments. It is at those moments when the fortitude of your convictions and your values, and your self-awareness, will guide you to the right answer. Knowing what is really important to you and what your goals and priorities are will put you in good stead to assess each situation and chart the course of action that is right for you.

This is another reason why keeping score can be so helpful throughout the course of your career. When it comes time to assess (or reassess) your goals and priorities, what's important to you, your strengths and weaknesses, and so on, it's useful to look back at your performance. If you've been keeping score, you'll have a good record of your accomplishments (as well as your mistakes—both of which you can and should learn from). As I've mentioned, I've kept score throughout my career, and it is, indeed, really helpful to go back over those files to see where I've been—and to take stock of the path I'm on. Whenever I feel like I might be veering slightly off course, having a record to reflect on provides me with a strong dose of reality—and focus—so I can make sure I really am still following the route I truly want to be on.

START SEEING YOURSELF

Keeping score is a great way to collect the kind of information that can help you shape a personal values/mission/vision statement. Performance reviews, notes from colleagues and clients, any awards or certificates, and so on can do much to inform your personal statement as you get to know yourself.

It's not always easy to see our own strengths and weaknesses. It's not always simple to articulate the various values that are important to us. Doing so takes time and effort. Looking back over the performance reviews and records we've kept can help us see ourselves more objectively.

In addition to reviewing existing materials, it can be helpful to ponder some thought-provoking questions that are specifically designed to make us focus our thoughts. As you strive to become more self-aware, consider these questions:

- What position at what kind of organization do I hope to retire from?
- What are some of the major professional accomplishments I hope to achieve during the course of my career?
- What skills do I want to master? What skills do I need to work on?
- What interests me most? What disinterests me? What are my likes and dislikes?
- What do I feel my purpose is?
- What makes me happiest? What brings me down?
- What principles, values, and virtues mean the most to me?
- What do I want to be known for? What do I want my reputation to be?
- How do others see me? How do their perceptions differ from my own view of myself?
- Who do I want to be when I grow up?
- How do I define success?

These questions can help guide you as you get to know yourself, helping you define the values that are important to you. Think about these questions—and write down your answers. Put it on paper. Doing so will help you keep score as you progress through your career, and it will help guide you so you can be sure that you're honoring yourself and your values.

Respect What You Want—and Don't Want

I recently went to dinner with five executives, all of them women I've known almost my entire career. We've all achieved different titles and different levels of success. But, despite being bright, talented, and capable, none of my friends has risen to the very top of their industries. All of them were C Suite material, but none of them had made it to the corner office.

Why?

I couldn't help but wonder what it was that, in my mind, was holding these women back. What was it, I wondered, that kept these smart women from being successful? And so I asked them.

The answer surprised me.

Each and every one of them said that they had purposefully chosen not to pursue the top spots, largely because they didn't want positions that would shake up their lives and make them feel like their work–life balance was out of whack. They didn't want to have to relocate. They didn't want to jump from one company to the next in search of the next big promotion. They didn't want to sacrifice their lives even if it meant giving up great rewards in the form of generous salaries, lofty titles, or professional acclaim. They didn't want it. Any of it.

And, you know what? That's okay.

There's no doubt that making it to the C Suite—and staying there—usually requires no small measure of sacrifice. Those who make it to the top, whether junkyard dog or pedigree, male or female, often find they miss out on family functions, outings with friends, volunteer opportunities, and so on. I've known plenty of top-level executives who repeatedly missed their children's school concerts and plays. Countless executives have missed more than one soccer or hockey game that their children were competing in. Most of today's C Suite executives take working vacations during which they are rarely unplugged.

I myself am not immune to the tug-of-war that is the work–life balance (we'll talk more about this in Chapter 14, too). I've certainly made some sacrifices during the course of my career, but not unwillingly. Because I wanted it. I wanted the seat in the executive suite, and I was willing to do what it took to claim it.

But not everyone is willing to claim it. They don't want it. And that's okay.

Part of honoring yourself and your values is respecting what you want and don't want. Not everyone, for instance, is a born leader. Some of us are born followers—and that's a good thing, because the world needs followers. Not everyone is cut out to be or even wants to be, say, executive vice president of sales. Some of us would be perfectly happy to be national sales director or regional sales manager. Some of us prefer to be in the trenches getting our hands dirty rather than calling the shots and crunching the numbers. And that's perfectly fine. No organization could operate without good employees at every level.

The thing is that you have to know what level you want to be at. As we discussed in Chapter 3, if you want it, you have to claim it. Let's add to that: If you don't want it, you have to claim that, too. And, of course, you have to own your decisions.

Honoring yourself and your values means you have to know yourself well enough to know what you want—and don't want. It also means that you have to respect that in yourself. Although we tend to glamorize and glorify the C Suite, the truth of the matter is that not everyone wants to call the corner office home.

In fact, CareerBuilder has found that a lot of us don't want a seat in the C Suite at all. In a recent survey, the largest online job site in the United States found that "[m]ost American workers are not aiming for the corner office" and that "[a]pproximately one third (34 percent) of workers aspire to leadership positions, with only 7 percent aiming for senior or C-level management."[4] In another study, researchers found that only 31 percent of Millennials aspire to the C Suite.[5]

---

4. CareerBuilder. "Majority of Workers Don't Aspire to Leadership Roles, Finds New CareerBuilder Survey," *CareerBuilder.com*, September 10, 2014. Retrieved August 10, 2015, from http://www.careerbuilder.com/share/aboutus/pressreleasesdetail.aspx?sd=9/10/2014&siteid=cbpr&sc_cmp1=cb_pr841_&id=pr841&ed=12/31/2014.
5. Saba. "Looming Leadership Gap: One-Third of Global Companies Struggle to Find Senior Leaders and Only 12 Percent of Employees Aspire to the Corner Office," *Saba.com*, March 31, 2015. Retrieved August 10, 2015, from http://www.saba.com/us/press-releases/go/2015/looming-leadership-gap-one-third-of-global-companies-struggle-to-find-senior-leaders-and-only-12-percent-of-employees-aspire-to-the-corner-office-1.

Of course, any number of people also have found that, once they do get to the C Suite, they don't actually like it there. For example, Anna Kreamer writes in *Harvard Business Review* that as a "corporate executive I felt like I had to pretend to be something I wasn't—I didn't like being a manager, but I was a manager, so I had to appear to be interested in all the stuff that went along with being a manager."[6]

Being something you're not—or, rather, acting like you're someone you're not—can be exhausting. Living an inauthentic life, doing something you don't want to do (especially if you're doing it only because you think you ought to want to be doing it) can take a lot out of you. It makes you unhappy and, more often than not, hurts your performance as well. Claiming something you don't want is disheartening, demoralizing, and destructive.

Instead of following a path you think you should follow, focus instead on getting to know yourself and respecting what you want and don't want. Learn to recognize your strengths and weaknesses as well as your likes and dislikes. Think about what job you want to retire from. And then go for it. Want it, claim it, own it—and respect your decisions. Honoring yourself and your values means not beating yourself up for not wanting more. There's nothing wrong with being satisfied in the position you have—as long as you really, truly like it and give it your all.

DEFINE SUCCESS ON YOUR OWN TERMS

You go to school. You get good grades. You graduate. You go to grad school or night school. You earn all the appropriate certifica-

---

6. Anna Kreamer. "What If You Don't Want to Be a Manager?" *Harvard Business Review*, December 13, 2012. Retrieved August 10, 2015, from https://hbr.org/2012/12/what-if-you-dont-want-to-be-a.

tions and licenses. You get the right job and then you get promoted and promoted again. You invest in a growing 401(k). Somewhere in there you get married, buy a house in the suburbs, have 2.6 children, buy two cars (an SUV and a luxury sedan), and get a yellow lab named Max. You buy a summer home. You raise your children while excelling at work, eventually retiring from the C Suite or upper management.

To some of us, this sounds just about right, the very picture of success.

To others, it sounds like a complete nightmare.

There is, of course, no one picture of success. What sounds like the perfect career trajectory to one person sounds like a horror story to another. While one person might relish the idea of climbing the corporate ladder in, say, a top-five law firm and making partner by age 33, another might cringe at the prospect, preferring instead to learn the ropes at a small firm before branching out on her own in private practice.

Only you can decide what makes you successful. It might indeed be retiring from the C Suite, or it might not. It might mean winning a CLIO or a Pulitzer or the MM&M or the Brick. It could mean being named as a Top 50 Innovator or one of the 40 Under 40. Maybe to you success means earning a seven-figure salary. Or maybe it means catching every single one of your daughter's soccer games and all of your son's hockey games. It might mean dedicating a few hours every week volunteering for the Friends of the Library or Rotary Club or Historic Preservation Commission. It might mean hosting a dinner party once a month for your closest friends.

Maybe it's all of that. Or, maybe, success doesn't look anything like that to you. However you define success, only you can decide what will make you truly happy and fulfilled. So, as you get to know yourself, think about what success looks like to you. How would you finish each of these statements?

- I feel most fulfilled when _____.
- I feel happiest when _____.

- I feel satisfied when _____.
- I measure my success by _____.
- I believe my purpose in life to be _____
  _____.

Honoring yourself and your values means you have to define—and measure—success on your own terms. No matter how you do that, you have to want it, claim it, and own it. That means you have to get to know yourself, and you have to respect yourself, your desires, and your aspirations. And, of course, you have to be yourself.

Be Yourself

I've mentioned in these pages the notion of wearing a mask, of putting on that mask—call it a game face or suit of armor or thick skin if you like—and hunkering down to get something done, even if (perhaps especially if) it's not something to look forward to. We all, at one time or another, are required to do something for work that we might not necessarily like. As an HR exec, for instance, I've had to fire people, as I've mentioned before. There has never been a time when I had to terminate someone that I didn't feel horrible about it (unless it was because someone stole something). In most cases, people get fired because they're not in the right jobs at the right organization. It doesn't mean they're bad employees. But, oftentimes, it does mean that they have to be let go. At times like that, I've had to put on the mask and play the part that was expected of me. In situations like that, could I show as much empathy as I might have wanted to? No, because that could potentially be admitting liability for the company. So, I had to put on the mask, steeling myself against an uncomfortable situation.

But never did that mean I went against my values or disrespected my goals. I was always myself, even in tough situations.

You have to be yourself, or you will give yourself a world of grief. At no time should you sell your soul or compromise your values. You have to assess each situation and chart the course of action that is right for you.

At one point in my career, I was with an organization with which I felt a deep connection. I enjoyed the culture, my leadership team, and my colleagues. While the business was somewhat complex, I believed in our mission and felt my skills could make a difference.

During my tenure there, some negative articles about the business started circulating. Our company was under attack from all the major media outlets, and our industry was under siege for what was characterized as unsavory behavior and kickbacks. All of the so-called deals took place prior to my tenure and had long ago been approved by the Board of Directors. As executives, we knew the facts, but many of the characteristics highlighted by the media were not representative of the person I worked for or the company I was associated with. Even so, we were under investigation and would have to face hearings on Capitol Hill.

At that moment, I had to make a decision. Did I want to risk staying there if it meant my career would be forever linked to this organization? If I stayed, what could I do to become part of the solution for how we needed to address the issues? If I left, what message would that send?

After taking the time to research the facts and weigh the situation against my own moral compass, this junkyard dog made the decision to stay and to help rebuild the reputation of the company.

We started daily meetings and went on the offense. We hired a top-shelf PR firm and an ethicist. We addressed all the issues at hand and put together a plan to become one of the most ethical companies to do business with in the world.

261

This was a huge learning experience because we had to calm our employees, our clients, and our vendors. Our business model was under attack, and we had to prove the value of our business model and lobby for future sustainability.

We made it a point to reaffirm our core values with all of our employees. We used our annual Values Conference as a forum to solicit input on having a culture based upon integrity and servant leadership. It was a difficult period, but after we came out on the other side, the company was stronger and our business practices were stellar. This took leadership to a new level. The values of our company were not just words on a piece of paper; they were real, embodied in how we as an organization guided our decision making and treatment of others.

As an organization, we decided to lead with values, and I made it a point to honor my personal values as well. In doing so, I was able to help the organization I cared so much about, doing something that helped me grow professionally.

What does it mean to be yourself at work? It means to honor your values, respect your decisions, and behave authentically. That doesn't mean you won't ever have to put on a mask or steel yourself against tough times, however. Values-based behavior cannot be faked. So let's look more closely at what being yourself at work does and does not entail.

Being yourself means you are guided by your moral compass in everything you do at work, from how you treat your colleagues and customers to how you behave in meetings to how you go about doing your daily tasks. It means you remain true to your values, even during those times when you have to put on your mask. It means you're honest with yourself about your strengths and weaknesses.

Being yourself does not mean you should wear your favorite Dave Matthews Band T-shirt with the hole in the armpit to work on casual Friday. It doesn't mean you should decorate your cubicle with hundreds of Beanie Babies because you're not afraid to show your colleagues your softer side. It doesn't mean you should blurt out what you really think of a colleague's PowerPoint presentation in an attempt to be frank and honest. Nor does it mean you should wear a low-cut, clingy wrap dress to an interview because you believe it flatters your . . . assets. When a colleague asks how your weekend went, you need not go into how bombed you were or that you were so still hungover come Monday morning that you could barely drag yourself out of bed.

You should be yourself—but you still have to be a professional at work. You still have to maintain that line between professional and personal. Being yourself at work isn't a license to succumb to your basest instincts or to bare all.

It does mean that, because you know yourself and honor your values, you find, for instance, a way to decline or rework an assignment that makes you feel uncertain. If, say, you're tasked with preparing an in-depth, line-item budget for your department but preparing detailed Excel spreadsheets is not among your core skills, you might agree to do the assignment while mentioning that you'd like to collaborate with a colleague who has more expertise in using the software. Being honest about your abilities is much better than faking it and turning in a shoddy work product.

On the flip side, being yourself does not mean you get to turn down an assignment simply because you don't feel like doing it. It's one thing to say you could use some help; it's quite another to be a slacker.

If, however, you're asked to do something that goes directly against your values, is unethical, or is even illegal, you have a responsibility to speak up. This might require you to further discuss the request so that you can be sure you fully understand what's been asked of you. You might, for instance, ask what the company policy surrounding the task is. Only you can decide how far you want to take the issue. The bottom line is that you should never do anything that you truly believe violates your values. You have to be honest with yourself no matter what.

HONOR THOSE AROUND YOU

In a day and age when it seems that everyone is demanding authenticity and transparency, it can be easy to focus on what we expect from others, how we want to be treated, and what we want for and from ourselves. But we can't truly honor ourselves and our values unless we also honor those around us.

Honoring those around you means treating people with respect and dignity. It means following the Golden Rule and treating others as we ourselves want to be treated. This goes beyond being professional, friendly, and polite, although that's important, too, of course. It speaks also to respecting people's time, space, opinions, skills, and so on. The list includes:

- **Be on Time.** Showing respect for your colleagues means that you're punctual for meetings, come to them prepared, and follow up like you're supposed to. It means you get to work on time and don't leave before quitting time, even if a pressing deadline means you have to work late.
- **Avoid Gossiping and Chattering.** You should never gossip about your colleagues or speculate among others about what's going on in the department or in the organization as a whole. Nor should you spend too much time chattering away with colleagues, telling them in minute detail about, for example, everything you did over the weekend.
- **Respect Personal Space.** This goes beyond not getting physically too close to people. It also speaks to things like respecting closed doors, lowering your voice when working in or near cubicles, keeping bare or stocking feet off common chairs (and tables!), "borrowing" supplies from a colleague's desk, and keeping your eyes off a colleague's computer monitor unless you're invited to look.

We all could probably do more to make our office environments more pleasant for those around us. By remembering to honor those around us, the job is made simple: Treat others as you would like to be treated, no matter their title, tenure, gender, or pedigree.

Staying true to your values is a must-have on your career checklist. Honoring yourself and your values—and those around you—is crucial if you want to be happy in your work. Get to know yourself—your strengths and weaknesses, your likes and dislikes. Know what you want and what you don't want. Knowing yourself better will put you in good stead to stay focused on your goals, not the least of which because when you're true to your values and honest with yourself, you're better positioned to know what to say yes to and what to say no to.

Honoring yourself and your values allows you to live a more authentic life. That's no small task, and it can be a challenge for many of us to balance where we work and what we do and how we do it with what we want and what we like and who we really want to be. Attaining that balance can be really tough. We'll talk about that next, in Chapter 14, when we look at balancing work and life.

Tough-Love Lessons for Honoring Yourself and Your Values

- There is never a time when you shouldn't honor yourself and your values. But before you can hope to do that with any success, you have to get to know yourself. This means you have to become self-aware by undergoing some self-reflection—and you have to be honest with yourself while you're doing that.

- Knowing yourself isn't a one-and-done task you get to check off the to-do list. It's an ongoing, lifelong process. When you keep score of your accomplishments and mistakes, you are better positioned to be objective about your strengths and weaknesses.

- As they say, you can't get what you want if you don't know what you want. Part of honoring yourself means you have to know what it is that you really want—and what you don't want. Figuring that out is part of getting to know yourself, and it can require some serious introspection. But those who do it are much better positioned to achieve their goals.

- The most fulfilled among us are those of us who define success on our own terms. We know what we want and we go for it, all while being true to ourselves and our values. Remember the mantra: want it, claim it, own it.

- Honoring yourself means being yourself—but being yourself isn't carte blanche to do or say whatever you want or act however you like. Being yourself means you have to stay true to your values while still being professional at work and respecting those you work with.

= 14 =

Balancing Work and Life

From: "Jena Abernathy" <jabernathy@email.com>

To: "Megan Watson" <mwatson@email.com>

Subject: Work–Life Balance

Megan,

Work is a balancing act—in more ways than one. You have
to balance your junkyard dog and your pedigree. You have to
balance the professional and the personal. You have to balance
trust and intuition, hard skills and soft skills, what you value and
what is expected of you. And, of course, you have to balance
your life at the office with your life at home—that elusive work–
life balance that is so tough to achieve. I won't lie to you: It is
really difficult. But it's also crucial if you want to stay sane. The
good news is that there is a way to work your way toward the
C Suite without sacrificing everything else that's important to
you.

—Jena

If, as I reflect on my career, I were to rank my priorities over the years (and if I was really truthful about it), the order would be

1. Work
2. Work
3. Work

when, in reality, the order should have been

1. Family
2. Spirituality
3. Work

As much as I have loved (and still love) my work and am proud of what I've accomplished (so far) during the course of my career, I can't say with complete honesty that one of those accomplishments has been consistently achieving a healthy work–life balance. Work most often prevailed over other commitments, and I missed key moments in my daughter's life. I can recall each of those moments, but what I cannot recall are the urgent reasons I gave for missing them, other than that it was work related.

It can be a tough lesson to learn, that the office is merely your laboratory. It's where you come to do your work. The office is not where you live your life (even if you do spend half—or more—of your waking hours there). Your real life is outside those walls, beyond the bricks and mortar of the entity at which you have chosen to build your career.

Building your career is one thing, but when you dedicate your life to the place where you work, you likely will find that it will disappoint you. It will hurt you because it has many lovers (aka "stakeholders"). The organization for which you work is not beholden to you. You are replaceable. No one is indispensible. The reality is that the company you work for will survive without you.

Of course, just because organizations are fickle doesn't mean you shouldn't enjoy your work. If you want to build a fulfilling career, you must continually contribute to the success of the enterprise—and you should have fun doing so. But it's also important to find other, additional outlets that also can feed your needs and fill your soul.

I confess that I'm a workaholic, one who will always be in recovery mode. I've gotten better at balancing work and life, though, over the years, and so perhaps I can still help you in creating a balanced life. The good news is that it can be done. The bad news is that it can be really difficult. Perhaps the biggest challenge is in defining what "work–life balance" really means. So let's start with that.

GET CENTERED

Sometimes we fall into this trap that achieving a healthy work–life balance is about de-stressing or getting enough quiet time or sleeping longer. That's part of it, but there's more to it than that. Sometimes we just need to get centered again, giving ourselves time to collect our thoughts and get back to what matters.

How each of us can go about doing this is as varied as we are—what works for one person might not work for another. But over the years, I have found a few things that help me get centered again and feel more balanced:

- **Block Out Time for Lunch.** If I'm really overloaded, I'll actually schedule an appointment in my calendar, with myself, over lunch. I might go for a walk, or I might simply close the door and forward my calls into voice mail so I can get some quiet time. Sometimes I'll eat at my desk and tackle a project that I haven't been able to get to. But making time for myself always helps me get back to center.

- **Exercise Everywhere and Anywhere.** I've been known to put my gym shoes on and stride through airports just so I can get some exercise, walking from one terminal to the next in order to get those 10,000 steps in. I'll often put yoga sessions on my calendar so that I'm sure to block out the time to exercise. You have to be good to yourself—even if that means scheduling fitness appointments with yourself.
- **Focus on What Matters.** When stressful days turn into stressful weeks, it can be easy to lose focus. I keep pictures in my office to remind me of what's really important. Photos of my "happy place," inspirational quotes as screen savers, pictures that serve as symbols of my goals—all of those help remind me of my priorities and help me reconnect with what matters.
- **Make Time for Family and Friends.** During really busy times when I couldn't get away from work, my husband and daughter would come to my office so we could have dinner together. I've put dates with my daughter on my calendar so I would be sure to be home in time to tuck her in. Scheduling appointments with family and friends isn't about reminding yourself that they're there and need your attention, it's about blocking out the time so you can really be with them without being interrupted by colleagues or clients.
- **Close the Door.** Sometimes you just have to close your office door. If you need time to focus on an important project, mark your calendar as "busy," forward your calls into voice mail, turn off your e-mail reminder paper clip icon, and close your door. If you have to, leave the office and go work at the library or a coffee shop for an hour or two. Do what you can to avoid distractions so you can focus on important projects without feeling like you're being pulled in all directions.
- **Manage Clients and Colleagues.** Instead of sending out a report on Friday afternoon, send it out on Monday. That way, instead of fielding questions, requests for information,

or other feedback all weekend, you've got the entire workweek ahead of you to deal with it. Set boundaries with clients and colleagues about how late each night and how early each morning the texts, e-mails, and phone calls can begin. Don't let other people set your schedule or disrupt your balance.

Making time for yourself and treating yourself well means you have to find ways to get centered. Try different approaches to make sure you're being good to yourself—because if you aren't being good for yourself, you're probably not any good for anyone else, either.

Define What "Work–Life Balance" Means to You

Coined in 1986,[1] the notion of a work–life balance refers to the ability to manage our personal and professional lives so that neither one nor the other tips the stress scale completely out of whack. Since the 1980s, organizations have sought to implement work–life programs designed to help employees find some measure of balance between demands at work and demands at home.[2] And, yet, despite the plethora of corporate programs out there and regardless of all the self-help advice available in books, blogs, and posts, it seems we've made little progress in achieving work–life balance with any measure of success.

It is elusive. Some might even say mythical.

But why?

One of the challenges is that work–life balance is highly personal. What might seem a frenetic pace of life and work for one person might seem positively boring and routine for another.

1. Nancy R. Lockwood. "Work/Life Balance: Challenges and Solutions," *2003 SHRM Research Quarterly*, n.d. Retrieved August 12, 2015, from http://www.ispi .org/pdf/suggestedReading/11_Lockwood_WorkLifeBalance.pdf.
2. *Ibid.*

Another challenge is that we're constantly hearing about how impossible finding that work–life balance is. We're continually bombarded with messages that we need to strike that balance, that we need to better manage our personal and professional lives, and that we need to do more to better handle what's going on at the office and what's going on at home. We're urged to read the "5 Tips for Better Work–Life Balance" and to study the "8 Ways to Achieve Better Work–Life Balance." The implication is that each of us is failing miserably at achieving a healthy work–life balance, and so we start to feel bad when we realize we're not incorporating all or even any of those tips. The guilt we feel for not doing these things only adds to the stress, making us feel even more unbalanced.

So, first, let's stop beating ourselves up about not living balanced lives. Then, let's really think about what work–life balance means to us. Because it will mean something different to each of us. For some of us, work–life balance means prioritizing what, how much, and for how long we do what we do during office time, family time, volunteer time, and play time. For others, it might be balancing how much "on" time we have versus how much "off" time we have. For some, work–life balance might simply mean how much down time, quiet time, and sleep we get versus how many hours a day we're on the go, whether for work, family, or community. And for still others, work–life balance might simply mean feeling in control of how we spend our time, energy, and resources.

The notion of work–life balance is elusive, a gray area—perhaps that's why it feels so unattainable to so many of us. So many of us imagine work–life balance to be a black-and-white issue that should look something like the scales of justice, where the burdens of work and the burdens of life are equally weighted—and then we feel bad when the scales start to tip too much in one direction or the other.

If that's you, you need to get over it.

And the first step to getting over it is to define what "work–life balance" means to you.

272

This is where honoring your values comes in. This is where your personal values/mission/vision statement comes in. It's where wanting it, claiming it, and owning it—and respecting your choices and decisions—comes in. It's where defining your personal brand comes in. It's where knowing what you want and don't want comes in. It's where defining on your own terms what success means to you comes in.

See how all of this works together?

You'll never feel like you can attain a healthy work–life balance if you don't know what matters to you, if you don't know what you want, and if you don't know what your values are. If you have no idea of what success looks like to you, you'll constantly struggle to attain some abstract vision of success (likely defined by someone else) while flailing around trying to balance all the demands that you allow to be placed on yourself.

That's crazy.

Rather than subscribing to someone else's vision of work–life balance, think instead about what it really means to you. Think about what you feel like when you feel most balanced. Do you feel energized? At peace? Mindful? Well rested? How do you feel when your life is out of balance? Tired? Frazzled? Disorganized? Discouraged? Overburdened? Then ask yourself what it is that causes these swings. Does your work–life balance go out of whack when you've said "yes" to too many things when you should have said "no" instead? Is it when you've volunteered for one too many outside commitments? Or is it when you continue to check voice mail and e-mail even when you're supposed to be on vacation?

Much of this boils down to your values, your priorities, and your goals. When you honor your values, when you know what's most important to you, and when you know what your goals are, you're in much better stead to keep yourself in balance because you know what to agree to and what to decline, which can go a long way in helping you feel balanced.

273

DEALING WITH "MOMMY GUILT"

One of the biggest *aha!* moments in my life was when my daughter told me she didn't ever want my life. She didn't want a seat in the C Suite. She didn't want any of the perks or benefits that come along with having the corner office—and she didn't want any of the struggles or worries that come with an executive-level position, either. She told me that she loved me dearly but didn't want to go through anything I had gone through as I climbed my way up the corporate ladder.

When I heard that, I felt like I had failed—as a mother and as a role model for my daughter. I was hit with a nasty bout of Mommy Guilt.

Men don't struggle with guilt like women do. As women climb the corporate ladder, many of us struggle with balancing our careers and our families. Those of us who are mothers (or who hope to be mothers) often find ourselves juggling how we go about creating our brands as successful professionals while making the perfect home for our families: How can we climb the corporate ladder when we're also trying to raise children? It's not an easy balancing act—and it only seems to be getting tougher.

As authors Julie Bort, Aviva Pflock, and Devra Renner write in their book *Mommy Guilt,*

> [w]hile we are fairly certain that generations of moms have suffered from some form of Mommy Guilt, it appears that today's moms have been harder hit. Is it the supermom image, the feminist movement, technology, or geographically dispersed family units? It is a combination of these things and more. We cannot deny that we are expected to do it all. The question is, who has that expectation? The answer is us.[3]

Mommy Guilt is real, but how you handle that balancing act depends much on what your own goals, priorities, and values are. It

---

3. Julie Bort, Aviva Pflock, and Devra Renner. *Mommy Guilt: Learn to Worry Less, Focus on What Matters Most, and Raise Happier Kids.* New York: AMACOM, 2005, p. 6.

depends on how you define success and on how you define work–life balance—for yourself and for your family. No one else can define that for you, and you should never let society or friends or parents or anyone else dictate to you what your life should look like.

But defining work–life balance on your own terms doesn't mean you won't ever have to deal with feelings of guilt. Sometimes you'll feel guilty for dedicating yourself 110 percent to your career. Sometimes you'll feel guilty for giving everything you've got—and more—to your family. It's really difficult to erase those feelings of guilt. In fact, truth be told, I'm not sure you really can. But you can allow yourself to have those feelings and to stop fighting them.

When faced with Mommy Guilt (or Daddy Guilt—let's not forget all the fathers out there), revisit your personal statement. How does what you're doing affect your goals? Will doing or not doing something derail your path to success? What is that guilt trying to tell you?

Balancing Mommy Guilt with your professional aspirations might mean you have to hit the pause button or the reset button every now and then. I've taken myself off the career train several times. I've turned down jobs that were out of my comfort zone for whatever reason. Sometimes I've second-guessed those decisions. Sometimes I've felt guilty about passing on something, which has led to feelings of failure. But I've always been true to my own goals, priorities, and values—even when it's tough.

In fact, that's what it really boils down to: knowing what you want and what you're willing to do to get it. You can find all sorts of ways to manage the tasks that come with holding down a full-time job and being a full-time parent, which, of course, is a job that never really ends. You could consider nannies and flextime and shared shifts. You could hire housekeepers and landscapers to help you around the house and the yard. You could divvy up carpooling duties with the other soccer moms and hockey moms.

But all of those require choices as well: Is it worth the extra money to hire a nanny? Are you willing to share your job with someone with whom you'll also have to share accolades (and punishments)? Can you trust the landscapers to treat your prized rose bushes with the TLC you want to give them? Are you comfortable having someone else be responsible for making sure your child gets to the game on time and in one piece?

All of that is entirely up to you. There's no one answer—but there is a right answer. And that answer is that so long as you're doing your best, so long as you're honoring your values, and so long as you're sticking to your own definition of work–life balance, you're doing it right.

When to Say "Yes" and When to Say "No"

We've discussed in these pages (see Chapter 4) the importance of taking on extra assignments, volunteering for team projects, and doing whatever it takes to get noticed and get ahead. All of that is crucial if you covet a seat at the table. There's no doubt that, in addition to doing your best work every day, taking on additional, high-profile assignments, working on cross-departmental projects, and volunteering for the tough jobs are great ways to gain worthwhile experience that can help propel you up the corporate ladder. You should say "yes" to projects and assignments that will raise your profile, get you closer to the C Suite, and help you achieve your career goals.

The trick is to do as much as you can (and maybe even stretching a little to do a bit more) without jeopardizing the quality of your work, without driving yourself crazy, and without making everyone around you nuts, either.

This means that, sometimes, you'll have to say "no."

There are only so many hours in a day, only so many days in a week. There's only so much of you to go around. However much you might want to, you cannot do everything. If you want to have any hope of achieving something that even resembles work–life balance, you have to learn how to decline requests, whether from your office, your family, or your community.

For many of us, saying "no" is one of the hardest things to do. We feel guilty for declining a request, whether it's taking on an additional project at work, baking another batch of brownies for the bake sale, or being a chaperone on the field trip. When we decline projects at work, we worry about looking like a slacker, like we're afraid of something, or like we're incompetent. We don't like to say "no" because we're afraid it will make us look impolite, uncooperative, or unlikeable. For some reason, we can come up with a million reasons not to say "no"—even when we don't actually want to say "yes."

It's time to get over that. There's danger in agreeing to do everything: "By saying yes to too many things, we may be saying no to some very important things."[4] What's more is that when we say yes, we overburden ourselves, oftentimes with tasks or projects or chores that are not at all in keeping with our goals, priorities, and values. When we say "yes" when we really mean "I'd rather not," we are not honoring our values, nor are we focusing on what's really important to us.

Once you've defined what work–life balance means to you, it's important to consider every request in light of that definition, keeping in mind your goals, priorities, and values—at work and at home. Let's say, for instance, that your VP asks you to pull together a new strategy for design and innovation across your entire product line, and he wants it by a week from Tuesday, which is less than two weeks away. You recognize right away that this is a plum assignment. It's a high-profile project for a key executive in the organization, and it'll give you an opportunity to challenge your skills. But that deadline— yikes. There's no way you could make that deadline unless you work late every night for the week and a half or so before the due date. You'd be eating dinner at your desk, missing priceless family time. You'd have to bring work home over the weekend, which means you'd probably have to cancel that outing to the water park. Chances are you'd even have to miss your daugh-

277

4. Camille Preston. "Why Saying No Gets You Ahead," *Fortune Magazine*, August 19, 2014. Retrieved August 14, 2015, from http://fortune.com/2014/08/19/why-saying-no-gets-you-ahead.

ter's first-ever piano recital—something you'll never be able to see again in real life.

So, is it a "yes"? Or is it a "no"?

Or, is it a "yes, if" instead?

When it comes to saying "yes" or "no," too often we don't stop to think about another option, which is "maybe." If we continue with this example, for instance, when considering all the pros and cons, the answer might be neither "yes" nor "no" but something like "yes, if"—meaning that yes, you could do it (and would love to) if, for example, you could get a few extra days and extend that deadline, or if, say, you could add a colleague to help you complete the assignment, or if, perhaps, you could focus on one branch of the product line instead of the entire thing, or if, maybe, you could set aside another project you're already working on and tackle this one instead.

What does this do? It helps you avoid having to say "no" if the request is in line with your goals, priorities, and values. It allows you to be seen as a willing team player and even as a creative thinker who will do what it takes to get the job done.

Of course, that doesn't mean that your counter-request will be accepted. You might still end up having to say "no" in the end. But even if that becomes the case, you can feel comfortable in the knowledge that your decision was based on your goals, priorities, and values and was in keeping with your definition of work–life balance. It's a matter of which opportunities you choose to pursue and which you choose to take a pass on.

SAY YES *AND* NO: DELEGATE

Saying "no" can be especially hard for some people, particularly for those who fear being considered a slacker who isn't a team player and for "control freaks" who can't bear the thought of not being involved in projects, especially high-profile assignments. But there might be a way to have the proverbial cake and eat it, too: by delegating.

Delegating can help us say "yes" and "no" at the same time by taking on projects and then sharing responsibility or even assigning it wholesale to others who will help us get the work done. The trick is in knowing when and to whom and for which projects to delegate.

When delegating, think about who among your colleagues can best help you accomplish the task on deadline and within the parameters of the assignment. Think about who might work together on a team. Look closely at how much each person has on his or her plate so that you can avoid arguments over who's not carrying their load like they should be. No one wants to be assigned to a project with a colleague only to learn that colleague is going on vacation and leaving all the work to you, nor does anyone want to accept an assignment if they know they'll be working with the office rock star who all too often gets away without having to do any of the really hard work.

Delegating can be an effective way to say "yes" to a project without overburdening yourself, as long as you delegate the right tasks to the right people. Get a good team together, provide them with ample instruction, and check on progress as you work together to complete an assignment that you might otherwise have to say "no" to.

INEQUALITY EQUALIZER

Whether junkyard dog or pedigree, male or female, defining what work–life balance means to you, and defining what success means to you as well, will help you keep your ultimate goals in mind as you climb up the corporate ladder toward the C Suite. Those who take the time to define what is most important to them have a much better chance of—and a much easier path toward—attaining their goals and having it all.

Having It All—or Not

Work should be enjoyable. It should be meaningful. It should be challenging. But it shouldn't be everything.

We might say the same for all our pursuits. Remember that the key term here is "balance." We need to stop thinking in either–or terms. Our choice isn't work or life, it's how much work versus how much life. That means we have to prioritize opportunities, taking those that are in synch with our values and goals and taking a pass on those that aren't.

We discussed in Chapter 4 the importance of balancing opportunities and risks. We looked at how important it is not to let fear or hard work dissuade you from taking chances, because when you come out on the other side, it builds your confidence—and you'll know you can take on even more. But it's also crucial to weigh each opportunity against your goals, because it's very likely that you won't be able to—and might not want to—take every opportunity that knocks on your door.

It can be easy to jump at every opportunity, and we do this largely out of the fear that we'll never see such a great opportunity again. So we say yes to too many things—oftentimes without even thinking about whether we really want them—and end up overburdening ourselves. So overburdened are we that "one third of full-time workers say that managing work–life has become more difficult in the last five years."[5]

Why are we doing this to ourselves? Because we think we can—or should—have it all.

Whatever that means.

Just like your meaning of work–life balance is unique to you, so is the concept of having it all. To one person, having it all might mean working at a high-powered job at a Fortune 500

---

5. Ernst & Young. *One Third of Full-Time Workers Globally Say Managing Work–Life Has Become More Difficult—Younger Generations and Parents Hit Hardest*, News Release, May 5, 2015. Retrieved August 14, 2015, from http://www.ey.com/ US/en/Newsroom/News-releases/news-ey-one-third-of-full-time-workers-globally-say-managing-work-life-is-difficult.

company while raising a couple of children with a perfectly happy spouse, living in a five-bedroom center-entrance Colonial within walking distance of the office, and vacationing in the Outer Banks. To another it might mean a job in the C Suite, a life with no children, a penthouse with a view, nights at the opera, and weekends in Paris.

Can you have it all?

Who knows?

We could debate the notion ad nauseam and still not get anywhere.

It all depends on what you want. You'll never know if you're on the road to having it all—or if you've already gotten it all—unless you've defined for yourself what having it all means.

Look, some people might look at you and think you already have it all: a good job, a good partner, a good home. But if you're not fulfilled, what everyone else thinks doesn't really matter.

I think few of us are lucky enough to have it all, all at once, and in equal measure. One minute you might love your job, everyone you work with, and all the projects you work on. The next minute you might be looking for a new position because you feel your career isn't progressing the way you want it to. One minute you might love your house in the suburbs with its colorful flowerbeds and robust vegetable patch, and the next minute you might be longing for a condo in the city with just enough outdoor space for a gas grill and a bistro set. One minute you might love romping around with the kids, and the next you might wish for the relative peace and quiet of your office.

We have to learn that balance doesn't always (in fact, usually ever) mean that everything perfectly lines up in equal portions at all times. Things change—for any number of reasons—and sometimes the best we can do is to make sure we're pointed in the right direction, even if our path to "all" is a winding one.

That means we have to weigh each opportunity as it comes along, taking some and passing on others. And this doesn't refer only to career opportunities. Opportunities will come up in all parts of life, and you'll have to decide whether to take them or not.

CHOOSE TO DISCONNECT AND RECONNECT

I'm not sure when it happened, but our smartphones have become like appendages, extensions of ourselves that we just about literally can't live without. Many of us carry around with us multiple mobile devices, a smartphone for work and one for personal use, a tablet and a laptop. We receive e-mail all day every day. We check voice mail multiple times a day. We're never not at work.

This is one of the biggest affronts to work–life balance, and many of us are willing participants in the barrage of connectivity. We've programmed ourselves to respond instantly to every e-mail and text, whether work-related or otherwise. And so we're always on, no matter where we are and no matter what else we have going on in our lives.

Although some of us might argue that we have to be on for work, it's really a choice. As such, we can just as easily choose to set some parameters about how connected we are. In fact, there are all sorts of things we can do to disconnect from the office and all the other craziness in life.

- **Turn It Off.** Even if you really, truly feel like you absolutely cannot not have your smartphone with you everywhere you go every hour of every day, chances are you probably can set it aside for at least an hour or two without the world coming to an end. Set up parameters for yourself, such as not accessing mobile devices during mealtimes; keeping the smartphone, tablet, and laptop out of the bedroom; and restricting yourself from checking e-mail while on vacation to only one hour in the morning and one hour before bed. Nonstop usage of your mobile devices is a habit you created for yourself—and it's a habit you can break yourself of (and should break if you really do want some work–life balance in your world).

- **Calm Your Mind.** Mindfulness is something of a buzzword these days, but it has long been a useful tool for many people. Use mindfulness, meditation, yoga, and other relaxation techniques to reconnect with yourself. Focusing on your breathing for just a few minutes every day can do wonders to make you feel less stressful. Allow yourself time to breathe, time to relax (really relax, which doesn't mean flipping through a magazine while you're watching a movie), and time to think.

- **Write It Down.** Take an actual pen or pencil and some paper and, for a few minutes every day, just write. Write down whatever is on your mind. Journaling has been proven to help relieve stress, and the act of actually writing (as opposed to typing on a computer) can free your brain to be more creative, allowing you to reconnect with your inner thoughts and listen to yourself.

- **Get Organized.** You might not have it in you to organize every shelf in your closet, every cabinet in your kitchen, and every drawer in your desk at work, but even tidying up one area of your world can have a dramatic impact by making you feel less disorganized. Getting organized saves time and energy you might otherwise spend looking for "lost" items, making you feel less frazzled throughout your day. This can help you feel more connected to the things in your world that really matter.

Achieving some kind of work–life balance (whatever that means to you) can be helped by disconnecting (at least now and again) from the things that distract you from what matters so that you can reconnect with what is important to you. Taking time to calm your mind and free your thoughts can have a dramatically positive effect on reducing your stress levels, making you feel more balanced at the office and at home.

283

Respect Others' Choices About Work–Life Balance

Just as no one but you should be defining what the right work–life balance is for you (and your family), you shouldn't be deciding the issue for anyone else, either.

Studies have shown, for instance, that work–life priorities shift and change over the course of one's life, most notably when children come into the picture, but also when, for example, parents start aging and need additional care or our own health-related issues occur.

Studies also have shown differences in what "work–life balance" means among different generations. While I and many professionals from my generation have focused most of our lives on our careers, younger employees seem less willing to do so. A study conducted by PwC, the University of Southern California, and the London Business School, for instance, found that, among Millennials (the generation born in the 1980s and '90s), "work/life balance is one of the most significant drivers of employee retention and a primary reason this generation of employees may choose a non-traditional professional career track."[6]

Of course, differences among definitions of work–life balance arise not only among generations but among genders and cultures as well.[7] In a study conducted by Ernst & Young, researchers found that:

men across the board are more willing to make sacrifices to better manage work and family than women. Men are more likely to have changed jobs (67 percent) or careers (60 percent), or said they would be willing to do so, than

---

6. Dennis Finn and Anne Donovan. *PwC's Next Gen: A Global Generational Study—Evolving Talent Strategy to Match the Workforce Reality*. London: PwC, 2013. Retrieved August 17, 2015, from http://www.pwc.com/en_GX/gx/hr-management-services/pdf/pwc-nextgen-study-2013.pdf.

7. Henrik Bresman. "What Millennials Want from Work, Charted Across the World," *Harvard Business Review*, February 23, 2015. Retrieved August 17, 2015, from https://hbr.org/2015/02/what-millennials-want-from-work-charted-across-the-world.

women (57 percent and 52 percent, respectively). They are also more willing to give up a promotion (57 percent men, 49 percent women), move to another location (50 percent men, 46 percent women), move to be closer to family (46 percent men, 38 percent women), take a pay cut (36 percent men, 33 percent women) and move to another country with better parental leave benefits (26 percent men, 18 percent women).[8]

In the simplest terms, this means that different people have different goals, priorities, and values—and different ways of going about reaching goals and honoring values. This can be challenging in a workplace full of male and female Millennials, Gen Xers, and Boomers working in offices scattered around the globe, all of whom have to work together under a common set of guidelines. Some of us are lucky enough to work for organizations that offer flexibility in terms of work hours, location, and the like, but balancing everyone's needs against the needs of the organization as a whole can be challenging.

285

Key to maintaining this balance is to respect these differences. Understand that, for instance, your Millennial colleagues might not be willing to work eighty hours a week. Understand that those among your colleagues who are parents might actually need to leave right at five o'clock because they have to pick up the kids from day care. You might find that you need to cut people some slack every now and again because life does, indeed, get in the way.

Of course, that doesn't mean you should make excuses for people who simply don't feel like pitching in and carrying their fair share of the workload. Nor should you be the one who's

8. Ernst & Young. *Global Generations: A Global Study on Work–Life Challenges Across Generations*. London: Author, 2015. Retrieved August 17, 2015, from http://www.ey.com/Publication/vwLUAssets/EY-global-generations-a-global-study-on-work-life-challenges-across-generations/$FILE/EY-global-generations-a-global-study-on-work-life-challenges-across-generations.pdf.

constantly watching the clock and bolting out the door at five o'clock just because you want to go hang with your friends.

But it does mean that, for instance, when working on a new assignment with a new cross-departmental team, you work together to discuss parameters and guidelines, outlining not only who will do which tasks but also what the working hours and constructs will be in order to make deadlines—all while respecting that everyone on the team has to attend to their regular job duties as well as their responsibilities outside of the office.

Achieving work–life balance is tough. I'm not going to sugarcoat it for you. If it were easy, there wouldn't be 198,000,000 hits when you Google the term "work–life balance" and there wouldn't be 23,182 books available on Amazon that tackle the subject in one way or another. But maybe we could make it easier on ourselves—and on those around us—if we respect each other's needs and allow everyone to decide for themselves what work–life balance means to them. Perhaps if we stop making ourselves—and those around us—feel guilty for either working "too hard" or taking off "too much" time or staying home for "too long" to raise a family, we can all get a little closer to having it all—no matter what that means to each of us.

Tough-Love Lessons for Balancing Work and Life

- One of the first steps to achieving work–life balance is to recognize that the office is where you go to work, not where you go to live. Recognize also that, as harsh as it might sound, you are, indeed, dispensable, and that your organization is fickle. With that knowledge in mind, think hard about how much of yourself and your life you're willing to give to the office.
- You can't achieve work–life balance if you don't know what it means. No one can define that for you. You have to determine what your own unique work–life balance looks like to you, based on your goals, priorities, and values.
- Sometimes feeling balanced means saying "no" and not taking on more work or loading up with more responsibility. Sometimes, though, you simply do have to take on more work, suck it up, and realize that feeling unbalanced won't last forever.
- Achieving a work–life balance might mean taking on unexpected opportunities or passing on those opportunities. Each opportunity must be weighed against your own needs and values. Only you can decide whether an opportunity will keep you on your path to success or make you veer off course.
- Defining what work–life balance looks like to you goes hand in hand with respecting what work–life balance looks like to those around you. Chances are they won't look the same. Respect the differences and find ways to work within those differences while honoring your own values and plotting your own path as you climb the corporate ladder.

Conclusion

Fuel Your Career by Discovering Your Passion

The other day, I was in a meeting with a prospect for a C-level position at a major corporation based in the Midwest and known around the world. Also in the meeting was my partner, who is a fellow executive consultant. The candidate was a forty-five-year-old attorney with executive-level experience at a top-notch corporation. She was wearing a clingy, low-cut wrap dress with a blazer, and "the girls" were absolutely busting out. As we finished the meeting and parted ways, my partner, a long-time male colleague, said to me, "You need to fix that."

Do I have to say that we were both stunned at her appearance? Do I have to reiterate that she was forty-five years old? An attorney? With executive-level experience? Who, still, after a good two decades in business, had no idea how to present herself as a professional with C Suite ambitions?

Unbelievable.

This woman could have been the smartest woman who ever aspired to this particular C Suite role for this firm. She could have had the most impressive résumé of any of the prospects. She very likely could have been the best qualified of all the candidates, male or female, junkyard dog or pedigree.

But who knew?

Because the only thing anyone could think about was her cleavage.

Her cleavage—that's what took up all the space, all the air in the room. All the room in the room for anyone to hear what she was saying. Her cleavage was doing all the talking—and it was saying all the wrong things.

The sad thing is that this kind of stuff happens all the time. I was stunned.

"I was stunned." That's exactly how we began this journey together, way back in the Introduction to this book. And the thing is that I am repeatedly stunned, over and over, by aspiring professionals who seem hell bent on shooting themselves in the foot at just about every opportunity.

If we've learned one thing throughout this journey together, I hope it includes this: No matter how smart you are, how accomplished you are, how impressive your résumé, if you don't do well at representing your personal brand, at balancing the personal and the professional, and at honoring your values, you will have a devil of a time making it to the C Suite. You might get close. You might get really close. You might make assistant vice president somewhere.

But if your cleavage is doing all the talking, you will never make it to the C Suite.

Because even if you have the chops to get the job done, and even if you're the most passionate employee an organization could ever hope to have, it takes more than a wish to make it to the top of the corporate ladder.

It takes much more than wishing and dreaming to make it to the C Suite. You've got to know what you want. You've got to want it, claim it, and own it—and respect your decisions. You've got to have more than dreams; you've got to have goals.

We've talked a lot in these pages about what you need to do, what you should and shouldn't do. Having a successful career takes work. It's a balancing act on many levels: balancing your junkyard dog and your pedigree, balancing the personal and the professional, balancing hard skills and soft skills, balancing your goals and your values.

All of that is essential if you want to make it to the top of your profession.

But none of it matters if you're not doing what you love or loving what you do.

Find Your Passion

Some of us are lucky enough that what we love to do is also something we love doing. There's a difference there, albeit a subtle one. Some of us work in a job that we love. Some of us love what we do for a living. If we're lucky, our passions and our abilities collide.

Sometimes, though, we have to look outside the office to fulfill our dreams. What we're most passionate about might not be the industry we work in or even the organization we work for. Sometimes we have to look elsewhere to find something we're passionate about, something we're good at, something that matters, something that gets us fired up.

You can discover your passion through any number of routes—as long as you're open-minded. That's because passion is about doing the best you can at whatever it is you're doing. It means you channel all your passion in pursuit of a goal, whether it's to be the best accountant or the best lawyer or the best home health aide or the best event planner or the best software developer.

No matter what your goal, if you want to have a successful and rewarding career, you have to channel your emotions—your passion—toward reaching that goal. That goal has to be your reason for being. I find this to be a kind of virtuous circle: My goals guide my emotions, and my passions serve as the foundation for my goals.

This is another reason why it's so important to identify what you want and why you want it. You have to know what matters most to you. You have to know what your goals, priorities, and values are. You have to know what your own definition of success is.

When you're pursuing goals that matter to you—goals that you're passionate about—it's much easier to love what you do and do what you love. When you're doing what you love and loving what you do, you're in exactly the right place to excel. Your passion drives you to be the best you can be.

But if you're pursuing someone else's goal, if you're trying to achieve someone else's idea of success, chances are you're also trying to muster passion that you really don't feel. I know that if I'm trying to be passionate for a goal I really don't care all that much about, I end up just going through the motions, pursuing results like a zombie. That doesn't do anyone any good.

That's not to say that every day at work is all sunshine and flowers. Sometimes you—like everyone else—have to just suck it up and get the job done, whether you're in love with the notion or not. Some days you'll love your job. Some days you'll hate it. But as long as you know you're pursuing your goals and following your passion, you'll be able to love what you do.

Steve Jobs once commented that people who aren't passionate about what they do won't succeed. I completely agree. Passion can lead to greatness. Too much passion, though, can have an adverse effect, particularly if we don't know how to control our emotions. On the flip side, suppressed passion can be equally destructive, derailing our plans before we ever get a chance to pursue them.

Let's say, for example, that your parents lean on you to become an attorney. Maybe one or both of your parents practices law. Maybe your folks have been studying career trends and see that healthcare law is a growing field with a lot of potential. They encourage you (okay: push you) into pursuing a JD and taking the Bar. Not that there's anything wrong with that—it's a respectable, honorable profession, and we need good attorneys. But if your true passion is to, say, develop apps for mobile devices, chances are you will never be a great lawyer. In fact, it's quite likely that you may well end up hating law altogether and eventually change careers.

Sadly, this happens to a lot of people. Too many people toil away their entire careers in jobs they could take or leave. They're not passionate about what they do, they don't especially like what they do, and they're not exactly all that thrilled with the industry they're in. I see this all too often. I see people who have no idea what it's like to pursue their passion and fulfill their visions. They've let family, friends, culture, or circumstance dictate their life paths. Many struggle at their jobs, not because they're incompetent but because they have no passion for what they're doing. They're just earning a paycheck.

Work divorced of passion rarely leads to fulfillment or success.

That doesn't mean people who are disconnected from what fills them with passion can't be successful—I see plenty of people who somehow manage to climb their way up the corporate ladder on skills alone. But they usually only get so far before they burn out.

That's because living an inauthentic life is exhausting.

Junkyard dog or pedigree, male or female—whoever you are, whatever your background, know this: If you really want to be successful in life, you have to define success on your own terms.

For some of us, that means finding a career in an organization in an industry we love. For others, though, that means looking outside the office for a place where we can showcase our skills and talents and where we can pursue the interests about which we are most passionate. That might mean we have to paint a completely different picture of what "getting to the top" looks like.

293

That takes a little bit of moxie. "Moxie" is a slang expression my parents' generation used a lot. It actually comes from a unique New England soft drink whose name evolved into a colloquial term for perseverance, guts, courage, daring, and spirit. Many people with moxie are able to achieve enormous success. Whether educators or entrepreneurs or inventors or lawyers or writers or artists or athletes, the people with moxie are the ones who are rewarded with honor, recognition, respect, position, and all sorts of accolades and rewards, tangible and intangible.

The biggest of these rewards is personal fulfillment. It's knowing that you've achieved success on your own terms, doing what you love and pursuing your goals with passion.

How do you get to this point? By knowing what you want, knowing what matters most to you, and knowing what success means to you. How do you come to know all of that? Well, you have to think about it.

Revisit your childhood dreams. What dreams have you put on hold? What did you want to be when you grew up? Are you doing that? Or did you throw away those dreams because someone told you they were silly or impossible?

What are you really passionate about? Is there an area within your company that draws your interest? What gets you excited about showing up to work? What interests you so much that you'd do it for free if you could afford to? How connected do you feel to the company's mission? How strong is that connection to your own personal values?

What are you willing to invest in? What pursuit are you willing to invest your time, money, and effort into in order to succeed? What are you willing to put in extra hours for?

What do you really want out of life? Do you have the courage to say it out loud? Are you willing to claim what you want?

I mean it: You have to really think about these things. It's too easy to let life lead you off in any direction instead of directing your own life. So think about these things. Answer these questions for yourself. If you don't want to say the answers aloud, then write them down on a piece of paper. Tuck that piece of paper into your sock drawer. Every time you come across it, unfold that paper, read it, and recommit to reaching your goals and pursuing your passions, one step (or one sock) at a time. I don't care if this sounds silly—do it anyway. There is power in that piece of paper. It's harder to turn away from words when they're written down, staring back at you. It's harder to turn away from your dreams when they're calling out to you—even if they are calling to you from your sock drawer.

Use Your Passion

Once you've figured out what your sock drawer is saying to you, you need to find a way to heed that call. For some of us, our passion, or true calling, might lie outside of the office in volunteer work of some kind. For many of us, though, we channel our passion into our work—that is, to the work we do in our careers, our vocations as opposed to our avocations.

Either way, it's important to corral that passion and to use it wisely. Acting on your passions does not mean you get to let loose your emotions, saying whatever you want, doing whatever you want because you're so enthusiastic about your job. Remember our discussion about balancing assertiveness and aggression: People who come across as too passionate, people who lean in too far and too hard seem unprofessional, even if they actually do have a good head on their shoulders and know what they're doing.

There's a lot of talk these days about "leaning in," and we've talked a bit about that in these pages. Around that talk is much discussion about what it really means to lean in, when people (especially women) should or should not lean in, and how they should lean in.

The thing is that, just like with success and work–life balance and having it all and getting to the top, the notion of leaning in is, actually, a vague one, one that depends on any number of factors, including on-the-ground circumstances, the organization you work for, and the industry you're in. The extent to which you can assert your ambitions, claim a seat at the table, speak your truth, and demand to be heard depends on so many things.

We could debate endlessly the pros and cons or realities and myths that surround the lean-in concept. Much about the concept is valid: Everyone should be able to claim a seat at the table, regardless of gender or pedigree. We should all be working together to dismantle gender bias. All of us should be striving for equity, whether in pay, parental leave, assignments, benefits, or whatever. Each of us should be judged on our accomplishments, skills, and experience when it comes to our work—and neither gender nor pedigree should enter into the conversation.

That said, the reality is that not everyone should be leaning in every day and in every situation. Sometimes, you need to lean back. We discussed this a bit in Chapter 8, but it bears further examination.

I want you to be passionate about your work. I want you to be passionate about your goals. I also want you to know when and how to balance that passion with politics—that is, the politics of your department, your organization, and your industry.

It can be all too easy to let your passion get the best of you. You might well find yourself leaning in so far that you fall flat on your face. And, although there is absolutely nothing wrong with making mistakes—failure is a good teacher—there's no reason to set yourself up for failure.

Again we come back to balance. You have to balance your passion against the realities of your workplace. That means you might need to lean back at times, whether to listen and learn or to allow those around you to do the same. Sometimes it's simply not appropriate to claim a seat at the table, speak your truth, and demand to be heard. Sometimes it makes much more sense to be invited to the table, listen to what everyone else has to say, and ask to share your opinion and insight. Sometimes you might need to work the back channels before you can claim center stage.

The truth is that sometimes you have to play the game. In fact, you almost always have to play the game. As important as it is to be authentic and to honor your values, that doesn't mean that sometimes you don't have to put on the mask and steel yourself for the realities of your own workplace. Sometimes you have to be smart enough to know that right now is, in fact, not at all the right time to lean in.

Leaning back doesn't mean denying yourself or your passions. It means being smart enough to know what the appropriate behavior is. It means understanding what a given situation calls for. And, it means understanding that what might be appropriate behavior in one organization or one industry might be completely inappropriate in another.

I'll give you an example. My mother died unexpectedly, on the same day of my daughter's college graduation. She fell ill, went to the hospital, and died within just three days. I needed to handle my daughter's graduation and my mother's funeral at exactly the same time. Because I had taken a few days off to celebrate my daughter's graduation, I took only the allotted three days of bereavement leave to handle my mother's funeral and related affairs. I was emotionally empty and wished I could have communicated with my colleagues and clients to say, "I need to take some time off and away to absorb these two life-changing events." But I didn't feel like I had the luxury of e-mailing them to explain what was going on, how I was feeling, or that I wanted to take a few weeks off to get my life back together.

In some industries, I might have gotten away with being totally honest about my feelings, sharing them with my team, and admitting that I was an emotional wreck. Instead, the reality of my industry meant that I had to steel myself for being back in the office at a time when I was completely devastated. I had to put on that mask. Had I been my authentic self and leaned in by letting everyone see my authentic self—my sad, depressed, tearful self—I would have damaged my reputation at work and risked having my colleagues and clients see me as weak and emotional.

297

The fact is that sometimes you just have to silence part of yourself. That doesn't at all mean you dishonor your values or that you try to be someone or something you're not. It means that you protect and preserve part of yourself when you have to do something that might be unpleasant. That doesn't mean you should agree to do something unethical or unsavory or unlawful—not at all. It means that you have to be professional, it means you have to leave the personal side of you at home, it means you have to use your passion wisely.

Again this all boils down to balance. When you're using your passion wisely, you're balancing the professional and the personal, you're balancing your junkyard dog and your pedigree, you're balancing ambitions and politics, you're balancing your aspirations and reality. Remember that passion is powerful—and that with great power comes great responsibility. Use your passion wisely, and you'll find that it will help you attain success on your own terms.

Create Your Own Success Strategies

All the career guides and leadership books and management tomes in the world won't help you succeed in life and business if you're not passionate about what you're doing. Only you can decide what your passion is. Only you can decide what success looks like to you. I can give you some tips for making it to the corner office, and we've discussed some good ones in these pages:

- Balance Your Junkyard Dog and Your Pedigree
- Brand Yourself
- Want It, Claim It, Own It
- Make the Most of Opportunities and Risks
- Manage Up, Down, and Sideways
- Make the Most of Transformational Leadership
- Know the Business of Business

- Understand Business Etiquette and Cultural Competency
- Develop Trust and Intuition
- Network for Success
- Deal with Gender Issues
- Lend a Helping Hand
- Honor Yourself and Your Values
- Balance Work and Life

I can tell you to learn when to lean in and when to lean back. I can advise you to remember that when you make it to the C Suite, no one at the company is your BFF. I can suggest that you reconsider wearing a bikini to the company sales meeting.

But the truth is that much of what you'll learn throughout your career you'll learn from experience. Your situation will be different from everyone else's, just as your definition of success will be different and just as your concept of work–life balance will be different. There's no one-size-fits-all approach to business. So, you'll have to pick and choose the advice, tips, and strategies that feel right for you.

That doesn't mean that you should wing it, though. Once you've discovered your passion and figured out how to use it wisely so that you can excel at what you do, you should think about what you want to achieve and how you're going to do that. You should strategize your career.

We've discussed in these pages the benefits of crafting a vision/mission/values statement of your own to guide your career and your life. Writing this stuff down really helps. It's too much to just let it swirl around in your head, popping into your mind every now and again. If you really want to achieve your goals, it's really important to write it down. To make a plan.

Think about it: The best organizations create strategic plans that outline the goals and performance measures they want to meet. There's no reason you shouldn't do the same.

We talked about strategizing your career in Chapter 3. Strategizing your career begins with knowing what you want, claiming it, and owning it. Let's expand that a bit to get you thinking a little deeper. Think about the steps you'll take to get from one goal to the next. Think about how long you want to spend in each position. Think about what you want to accomplish at each stage of your career. Think about how your goals tie in to your values. Think about how everything ties in together with your vision of work–life balance and your definition of success.

Write down your professional strategic plan, which will guide you throughout your career. At the end of every year, take stock of your progress. Have you met your goals? Are you pleased with your accomplishments? Have you learned what you needed to learn so that you can move to the next step in your plan? Are you feeling balanced in your pursuits? Are you still comfortable pursuing the goals you originally outlined, or have your priorities shifted? Is your passion still your passion?

Think about these things. Give yourself a year-end performance review and assess where you are in your career. Write down your findings so that you can review them as you climb the corporate ladder. You can put that piece of paper in that same sock drawer that holds the sheet of paper with your goals written on it.

Follow Your Goals (Not Your Dreams)

Most of us are told to follow our dreams. I think that's really stupid advice.

You should follow your passion, and you should follow your goals.

What's the difference between goals and dreams?

A goal is something you want to achieve. It's something you can work toward and something you can measure. A dream is something you wish a fairy godmother or guardian angel would make come true without any serious effort on your own part, a la Cinderella.

I hate Cinderella.

We talked about Cinderella a bit in Chapter 3. She's a girl who's giving herself a pity party while she works like a slave to please people whom any fool can see will never be pleased. She toils away all day to fulfill someone else's goals, scrubbing floors and mending and waiting hand and foot on ungrateful people who don't care one wit about her. She doesn't try to get out of this situation, she just harbors a vague dream that, somehow, things will get better. Soon enough, luck intervenes and saves the day in the form of a fairy godmother who magically produces a couture gown and stylish glass slippers and sends Cinderella off to a ball. Once there, Cinderella waits around for some good-looking guy with a lot of money and a shoe fetish to ask her to dance. He appears on cue, but she runs away, ashamed he'll learn that she's a junkyard dog who could never stack up to his pedigree. He tracks her down (apparently he can't get his mind off those shoes!) and asks her to marry him, and, of course, she jumps at the offer and they live happily ever after.

301

What?

I think we should rewrite the Cinderella story. In my version, Cinderella networks with all the influential people she meets at the ball and expands her sphere of influence. She meets a woman in the restroom who asks her what she does, to which she responds by describing the organic cleaning solutions she has created. The woman hands her a business card and tells her to call her because she can help connect Cinderella to some angel investors who might be interested in helping her bring her products to market. Once the line is launched and a successful IPO follows, Cinderella establishes a foundation to help others pursue their education and accomplish their goals.

Cinderella stories aside, the truth is that in real life, you can forget about waiting for the good life to fall in your lap. No fairy godmother is going to help you land a good job or win you a promotion. Some good mentors and advocates might lend you a helping hand now and again, but you can't wait for someone to make you an offer so good it will completely change your life and make you successful. You have to go after the life you want. You have to show initiative. You have to have goals that you're willing to work for because you're passionate about them. Merely wanting is not getting. Success takes planning and effort. It takes time and energy to get the things in life that are most important to you.

So, instead of dreaming your life away, try planning for your life instead. Figure out what you want and then go for it. If you sit around and hope that luck intervenes to get you where you want to go, you'll be disappointed. But if you put your mind to it, if you find your passion, if you work toward your own definition of success, you'll find it—whether junkyard dog or pedigree, male or female, you'll find it.

Appendix

An A-to-Z List to Leveling the Playing Field

A—Act Like You Belong. No matter where you come from, junkyard or pedigree, put aside your internal fears and put on your mask. You have earned your position, now excel and go forward.

B—Be on the Cutting Edge. Think outside the box, understand technology and the applications to your work, and create efficiencies that will help you be more productive in your current role.

C—Claim It. Compete for the roles you want and claim your successes.

D—Define Success on Your Own Terms. Think about what "getting to the top" looks like for you, and focus on your goals, priorities, and values—and no one else's.

E—Engage with Your Team Members. Create solutions and find new ways to enhance the environment, build revenue, and improve performance while working across departments.

F—Figure Out How to Make Your Boss Look Good. Managing up, down, and sideways includes making your boss look good while building your own reputation as a formidable knowledge resource within the organization. When she looks good, you look good.

G—Gain Knowledge. Educate yourself by reading trade publications and industry journals as well as mainstream media such as *The New York Times*, *The Wall Street Journal*, and *The Economist*.

H—Host Meetings. Keep your colleagues and your boss updated by holding regular status meetings, in person or on video, so that you are visible and your message is heard. Prepare an agenda and never show up late, which gives the impression that you are more important than others.

I—I Will. Express yourself in the affirmative. Do not fall into the trap of "I might be able to" or start a sentence with "I know you may not like what I am going to say, but . . ." Be affirmative and firm, expressing yourself positively and confidently.

J—Join In. Sign up for Toastmasters, an improv class, and community service organizations to broaden your communication, public speaking, and leadership skills and to build your sphere of influence.

K—Keep the Faith. Do not lose sight of your goals as you progress throughout your career. You will hit speed bumps in your career and you might question your choices at times, but so long as you're staying true to your values, goals, and priorities, be sure to stick to it.

L—Leave the Girly Girl at Home. Leave the crumbs on the table, let someone else get the coffee, leave the pink pen at home, and leave the stilettos in the bedroom. No one expects the guys to order lunch, water the plants, or decorate the offices for everyone's birthdays. If you want to level the playing field, you have to put yourself on the same plane.

M—Make the Most of Meetings. Use meetings as a venue to show that you have done your homework, you know the topic, and that you are well versed in the business of the organization.

N—Never Lose It. Don't cry, lose your temper, curse at anyone, or otherwise lose your emotional balance. Try not to take things so personally that you negate your own power. That means no whining, no mention of hormones, no falling into stereotypical roles that could derail your course of action.

O—Open Yourself Up. Be open-minded when it comes to accepting constructive feedback. Make a point of becoming more self-aware. Embrace training and coaching. Do whatever it takes to improve yourself.

P—Promote Your Passion. Determine what it is that really motivates you to succeed, to excel, and to master your craft. Following your passion will carry you far even when things get tough.

Q—Quash Queen Bees. Avoid being stung by female colleagues who fear losing their power to those around them—and don't be one of those women. Whether you call it Queen Bee Syndrome or Feline Syndrome, find ways to work together with your female colleagues and help them ascend the corporate ladder with you.

R—Recognize Your Strengths. As you work to become self-aware, take stock of your strengths (and your weaknesses). Build upon those strengths as new opportunities present themselves.

S—Strengthen Your Network. Whether through social media, recruiters, industry peers, colleagues at conferences, or even neighborhood gatherings, do what you can to build your sphere of influence.

T—Take Calculated Risks. Make the most of opportunities that will enable you to broaden your skills, knowledge, and sphere of influence—and get you noticed for the right reasons.

U—Understand Corporate Culture. Study the political climate, culture, and expectations of the company you are working for. Avoid gossiping, but do understand who the players are and what games they are playing. You do not need to be a political animal, but you need to be politically aware.

V—Value Your Values. Values-based leadership is not a fad; it is a model for success and should be emulated. Lead yourself and your colleagues by minding your values.

W—Watch What You Wear. There is absolutely no reason to be the worst-dressed employee in your office. Even if others are dressing down to the extent that they might as well be wearing pajamas, make a point of dressing professionally whenever you're at work.

X—Xerophytes Unite! A xerophyte is a plant that adapts to harsh conditions. Do what you can to excel even under trying circumstances, and remember that you'll be the better for it when you come out the other side.

Y—Yes You Can. You will define success on your own terms. You will discover what work–life balance means to you. You will focus on your own goals, priorities, and values. You can and you will.

Z—Zigzag. Few of us are so lucky that our career trajectories follow a straight upward path. Most of us zigzag along, taking some promotions, taking some lateral moves, rejiggering as needed. Don't be afraid of detours so long as they're still headed in generally the right direction so that you can continue to pursue your passion.

Acknowledgments

Every successful woman recognizes that it takes a team to make anything happen, and writing this book was no exception. In the works over a span of decades, it long seemed to be a never-ending project. Perhaps I needed to experience one more role, one more candidate, one more search to finally make it happen. Despite all the starts and stops, the collaboration, and endless ideas, it is my hope that every reader will extract from these pages some nugget of knowledge that will serve them well in their career and, hopefully, help the next generation of great wannabe leaders face a world that welcomes success regardless of gender, race, or social bias.

I want to thank my great writing partner, Kelli Christiansen, for her wisdom, guidance, and collaborative spirit. Special thanks also go to my awesome editor, Jonathan Malysiak, and the entire team at Ankerwycke for their belief and unwavering support to share this knowledge with readers.

To the many women before me who opened the dialogue and blazed a new trail, thank you for your perseverance, tenacity, and courage. You gave hope and inspiration to a little girl with a drive to succeed and a mission to make a difference.

To Steve Nielsen, Rick Norling, and Ron Lambert—three great mentors—it was a privilege learning from you.

For all the great women I have worked with, met at conferences, and had the honor to mentor, thank you for your sharing your time, stories, and willingness to help close the gap. This is now your journey. Now it's your turn to want it, claim it, and own it.

About the Author

Jena E. Abernathy is managing partner/chair of Board Services, senior partner in Healthcare/Life Sciences, and member of the board of directors at a Top 10 executive search firm with offices across the country and around the world. Jena coaches candidates and assists clients in identifying board members, CEOs, and other C Suite leaders for hospitals, health systems, foundations, and academic medical centers as well as private equity, manufacturing, distribution, and healthcare corporations. Being fast-tracked early in her career, she served for more than twenty years in senior executive leadership positions with such companies as General Medical, McKesson, Fisher Scientific, and Premier, Inc. Known for her entrepreneurial and creative spirit, Jena is a nationally recognized leader in human capital management, succession planning, governance, performance excellence, and organizational development. Serving as the executive lead for Premier's successful Malcolm Baldrige National Quality Award, she brings forward a blend of strategic, operational, and practical insights. A frequent speaker and media contributor, Jena has written for and been featured in *Becker's Hospital Review*, CBS MoneyWatch, CNN, *Charlotte Business Journal*, *Financial Times*, FOX Business, *Health News Digest*, *The Journal of Healthcare Contracting*, *The Leader Board*, *TheStreet.com*, *Investor's Business Daily*, *Leadership Excellence*, *Miami Herald*, *Shape Magazine*, *Staffing Industry Daily News*, and *Trustee Magazine*. In addition, she has served on and in an advisory capacity for not-for-profit boards and has participated in many business and professional organizations. She earned a bachelor's degree in business administration from the University of Mary Washington in Fredericksburg, Virginia.

Index

Lifelong learning, 23–24, 99
Listening, 196, 296–297
Llopis, Glenn, 177
London Business School, 284
Long-term goals, 53–56, 104
Loyalty, 182, 184
Loyola Law School–Los Angeles, 36

M

Madison Dearborn Partners, 253
Malcolm Baldrige National
  Quality Award, 74
Management
  in all directions, 88–92, 106
  career, 102–105, 120
  relationship, 87
Managers
  communication with,
    139–140
  expectations of, 139–142
  as mentors, 239
Manners
  and business etiquette, 146,
    154–155
  good, 160–162
  in mentorships, 238
Margins, 129, 132
Mayer, Marissa, 229
McAfee, Andrew, 168, 169
McCafferty, Dennis, 148
McCleskey, Jim Allen, 112
McKinsey, 52
McKinsey Quarterly, 169
Meetings, 135, 304, 305
Men
  as CEOs of Fortune 500
    companies, 12, 19
  communication by women
    vs., 213, 217–221
  earnings of women vs., 34,
    211

leadership by women vs.,
    211
  leadership styles of,
    120–121
  work–life balance for
    women vs., 284–285
Mentees
  expectations of, 235–237
  finding, 238–241
  good, 236–238
Mentoring, 227–247
  benefits of, 247
  and career sabotage by
    women, 243–246
  and career success, 228–230
  finding mentors, 192,
    230–236
  and helping others' careers,
    241–243
  of others, 238–241
  reverse, 234
  traits of good mentees,
    236–238
Mentors
  benefits of mentoring for,
    230, 238–239
  defined, 230
  feedback from, 101
  finding, 192, 230–236
  in sphere of influence, 229
Mergers, corporate culture and,
    151–152
MicroMentor, 240
Mights, evaluating women based
    on, 21
Millennials
  business publications for, 97
  desire for C Suite of, 257
  game face for, 43–44
  work–life balance for, 284,
    285
Mindfulness, 174, 283

323